- ❏ Parka
- ❏ Pea coat
- ❏ Shearling
- ❏ Trench coat or Balmacaan
- ❏ Wool or cashmere muffler

FORMAL WEAR WARDROBE P. 178

- ❏ Black bow tie
- ❏ Cigarette lighter
- ❏ Coordinated cuff link and stud sets
- ❏ Dark Chesterfield coat
- ❏ Dinner jacket (tuxedo)
- ❏ Pleated formal shirt
- ❏ Patent leather evening shoes (or pumps)
- ❏ Waistcoat or cummerbund
- ❏ White silk scarf

BUSINESS TRIP WARDROBE P. 144

- ❏ Black and white T-shirts
- ❏ Black knit tie
- ❏ Black leather belt
- ❏ Black loafers
- ❏ Black socks
- ❏ Black V-neck cashmere sweater
- ❏ Dark, unstructured pants
- ❏ Dark wool crepe suit
- ❏ Nylon rain jacket
- ❏ Pajamas and robe
- ❏ Workout clothes

BASIC TRAVEL KIT

- ❏ Adapter kit
- ❏ Big Baggies for spillables
- ❏ Cleanser
- ❏ Cologne
- ❏ Condoms
- ❏ Contact lens cleaners
- ❏ Cotton balls/cotton sticks
- ❏ Deodorant
- ❏ Foot powder
- ❏ Hair care: comb, dryer, shampoo, conditioner
- ❏ Lip balm

- ❏ Mouthwash
- ❏ Sewing kit
- ❏ Shaving supplies: razor, blades, cream, brush, after-shave lotion
- ❏ Skin lotion
- ❏ Sleeping mask
- ❏ Soap (in soap box)
- ❏ Sunscreen
- ❏ Swiss army knife
- ❏ Tissues
- ❏ Tooth care: brush, toothpaste, dental floss, dentures, case, cleaner
- ❏ Tweezers, nail clippers

Medicine checklist
- ❏ Antiseptic lotion
- ❏ Aspirin
- ❏ Band-Aids
- ❏ Cold remedies
- ❏ Diarrhea medication
- ❏ Emergency contacts
- ❏ Eyedrops
- ❏ Identification bracelet
- ❏ Insect repellent
- ❏ Medical information—allergies, medications, blood type
- ❏ Moleskin for blisters
- ❏ Physician's name, address and telephone number
- ❏ Prescription medications
- ❏ Sunblock
- ❏ Thermometer
- ❏ Throat lozenges

BUSINESS TRIP CHECKLIST

- ❏ Address and appointment books
- ❏ Airline tickets
- ❏ Briefcase
- ❏ Business cards
- ❏ Calculator
- ❏ Computer
  - -accessories
  - -batteries
  - -power and modem cords
- ❏ Confirmations
  - -car
  - -hotel

- ❏ Correspondence
- ❏ Credit cards
- ❏ Expense forms
- ❏ Files
- ❏ Highlighters, markers, pencils, pens
- ❏ Letter(s) of credit
- ❏ Meeting material
- ❏ Money
- ❏ Notebooks
- ❏ Paper clips
- ❏ Passport
- ❏ Portfolio
- ❏ Price lists
- ❏ Presentation materials
- ❏ Proposals
- ❏ Publications
- ❏ Purchase order forms
- ❏ Reading material
- ❏ Reports
- ❏ Rubber bands
- ❏ Samples
- ❏ Stapler
- ❏ Stationery, envelopes, stamps
- ❏ Tape recorder and blank cassettes
- ❏ Time records
- ❏ Work pads

Before you leave home
- ❏ Arrange for your pets, plants, and lawn
- ❏ Arrange to have your mail and newspaper held at the post office or collected by a friend
- ❏ Empty refrigerator and turn it on low
- ❏ Leave a house key with a friend
- ❏ Lock all doors, windows, and car
- ❏ Notify your neighbors of your absence and how to reach you
- ❏ Reconfirm your airline ticket and other reservations
- ❏ Set timers or leave lights on
- ❏ Stop all deliveries to your home
- ❏ Turn off hot water
- ❏ Unplug all major appliances

SIZE CONVERSIONS

SHIRTS

American/English:						
14	14 ½	15	15 ½	16	16 ½	17
Continental:						
36	37	38	39	41	42	43

SWEATERS

	Small	Medium	Large	X-large
American:				
English:	34-36	38-40	42-44	46
Continental:	44-46	48-50	52-54	56

SUITS/COATS

American/English:					
36	38	40	42	44	46
Continental:					
46	48	50	52	54	56

SHOES

American/English:							
5	6	7	8	9	10	11	12
Continental:							
38	39	40	41	42	43	44	45

CARRY-ON

- ❏ Address book
- ❏ Aspirin
- ❏ Batteries
- ❏ Camera and film
- ❏ Confirmations
- ❏ Credit cards
- ❏ Electronic equipment
- ❏ Eyeglasses; prescription, sunglasses
- ❏ Foreign language dictionary
- ❏ Headphones
- ❏ Identification
- ❏ Keys
- ❏ Light sweater
- ❏ Medicine
- ❏ Mints/gum
- ❏ Money
- ❏ Outerwear
- ❏ Passport/Visa
- ❏ Portable stereo

D1355211

"Clothes make the man.
Naked people have little or no
influence in society." *Mark Twain*

CHIC
SIMPLE ®

MEN'S WARDROBE

THAMES AND HUDSON

First published in Great Britain in 1998
by Thames and Hudson Ltd., London

Grateful acknowledgment is made to the following for permission to reprint previously published material:

Richard Ford: Excerpt from "Hunting with My Wife" by Richard Ford (Esquire Sportsman magazine, Fall/Winter 1993). Reprinted by permission of the author.

Liveright Publishing Corporation: Excerpt from "A Poet's Advice to Students" from A Miscellany Revised by E. E. Cummings, edited by George J. Firmage, copyright © 1955, 1965 by the Trustees for the E. E. Cummings Trust, copyright © 1958, 1965 by George J. Firmage. Reprinted by permission of Liveright Publishing Corporation.

Twentieth Century Fox Film Corporation: Excerpt from an episode of The Simpsons by Matt Groening, ™ © 1998 by Twentieth Century Fox Film Corporation. All rights reserved. Reprinted by permission of Twentieth Century Fox Film Corporation.

KIM JOHNSON GROSS JEFF STONE
WRITTEN BY WOODY HOCHSWENDER
DESIGN BY WYNN DAN

PHOTOGRAPHS BY DAVID BASHAW
STYLING BY MARTHA BAKER
CARTOONS FROM THE CARTOON BANK
page 10: Don Reilly © 1997 from The New Yorker Collection. All Rights Reserved.
page 26: Mick Stevens © 1997 from The Cartoon Bank. All Rights Reserved.
page 106: Peter Steiner © 1998 from The Cartoon Bank. All Rights Reserved.
page 150: Leo Cullum © 1997 from The Cartoon Bank. All Rights Reserved.
page 170: Mary Lawton © 1998 from The Cartoon Bank. All Rights Reserved.
ICON ILLUSTRATIONS BY AMY JESSICA NEEDLE

British Library Cataloguing-in-Publication Data

A catalogue record for this book is available from the British Library

ISBN 0-500-01740-9

Printed and bound in Great Britain by
Butler & Tanner Ltd
Frome and London

"The more you know, the less you need." *Australian Aboriginal saying*

CHIC SIMPLE is a primer for living well but sensibly. It's for those who believe that quality of life comes not in accumulating things but in paring down to the essentials. Chic Simple enables readers to bring value and style into their lives with economy and simplicity.

How to use this book: Waking up to confront yourself and your wardrobe each morning brings about new challenges and questions. What you need is a system for understanding what's important to you. We try to help you ask the right questions and find the answers. To guide you quickly, we've developed the following icons to signal key information throughout our book. They highlight answers or add context to the information—remember, the more you know the less you need.

icons

 Basic. Essential clothing gear, perennially classic, and they'll stay with you for life. Building blocks that act as directional markers for the rest of your wardrobe.

Body. This outfit is flattering to a certain BODY type but perhaps not to others. As in all broad generalizations, there will be exceptions to the rule—and you also may not care—so read with one eye cocked at the mirror.

Color. Adding brights, pastels, earthen hues, and every shade in between can bring breadth to your wardrobe whether you're dressing up or down.

Dress Codes. With dress-down Friday becoming a weeklong phenomenon, DRESS CODES are now more about appropriateness. Life's not about dictation, but everyone can use a little guidance in this department.

 FAQ. Who? What? Why? When? Here are the answers to the most frequently asked questions (acronym courtesy of the Net).

First Aid. If you don't want something to happen, it will—it's Murphy's Law. That's why we created our FIRST AID section in the back of the book with preventive care tips and remedies for clothing mishaps.

How to. Where concept meets reality, this flags a moment of "Enough talk, how do I do it?"

On the Road. Traveling doesn't have to be exhaustively tedious. Just pare down to the essentials, think practical, drink lots of water, and relax.

 Pattern. Pattern is more than just plaid—a judicious use of classic PATTERN is another way of adding vitality to the basics.

 Profile. Throughout the long quest for style, there have been certain individuals, companies, and even products that stand out as important design milestones.

 Simple Truths. To paraphrase Occam's Razor, the simple answer is more likely to be the right answer. Wisdom and simple snippets of advice to help solve wardrobe crises.

 Texture. Material or surface can add to your clothes' visual and tactile impact. Different TEXTURES, especially when expertly countering each other, bring added dimension, not to mention extra versatility to your look.

 Value. Invest in VALUE. Which doesn't always mean buying what costs the least. Find out where you should invest and where you can skimp.

 Versatility. Crucial for casual Friday dressing. How easily can an item mix and match with a variety of wardrobe fundamentals? We'll show you how your basic wardrobe tools can take you from Friday's office party to the boardroom.

SIMPLE SOLUTIONS **Simple Solutions.** These are items or outfits that answer such a wide range of needs and are such a foundation to a wardrobe that we have flagged them as easy answers to most clothing problems.

contents

"*Your father's a suit, and when you grow up you'll be just a suit, too.*"

"He was usually seen walking or driving alone, dressed as if expecting to participate in some great event, though there was no function in the world for which he could be said to be properly garbed; wishing to be correct at any moment, he was tailored in part for the evening and in part for the day." *Djuna Barnes,* **Nightwood**

In order to move with confidence in the world, a man must have a wardrobe that suits him and his style of living. It is a task that requires a nuanced understanding of both fashion and oneself (two areas of inquiry many men are prone to ignore), as well as a firm grasp of the state of one's exchequer. Building a wardrobe is a lifetime pursuit, a journey rather than a destination. This book is intended to make the trip somewhat less hazardous and a bit more

fun

A.M.

Fashion begins on the inside. What sort of guy are you? Loose and easy, or uptight and out-of-sight? Most men are loath to admit to an interest in their own "intimate apparel," but images of men in their Skivvies, from *Risky Business* to the ubiquitous underwear billboards, are a fact of modern life. Before World War I, the majority of men wore bulky, full-length underwear, or union suits, under their clothes. But the returning doughboys were interested in comfort, and briefs were widely adopted in the 1920s. By the thirties, the shorts worn by prize-fighters became the prototype for a new cut of underwear that was both more forgiving and irreproachably masculine. Today's boxer shorts come in a vast array of colors and patterns (some of them terribly whimsical), usually in cotton broadcloth, with abbreviated legs and an elastic waistband. Women are said to find them sexy, and in the 1980s there was a vogue for boxers among the fair sex. Classic boxer shorts possess a kind of iconic value—a clean, unfussy sensuality—that teeny-weeny dark-colored bikini briefs do not. However, as jeans and slim-fitting trousers remain important in men's fashion, Jockey-style shorts never go out of style. As a practical matter, boxers go better with pleated trousers, Jockey briefs with plain-front pants and jeans. Most serious men's wardrobes have a generous supply of both. Always buy underwear made of 100 percent cotton and at least one size larger than your waist to allow for shrinkage.

So...you've finally gotten up, and it's closet-inspection time. Your clothes are your personal maintenance tools. At work, they are your means of individual expression and your business operations facilitators. At home, they are your way to unwind. Out on the town, they are your expression of style. Appropriateness and uncomplicated dressing are your keys to a manageable wardrobe. Be who you are, and nothing beyond—your clothes are there to follow your lead.

"This is your wake-up call, pal. Go to work." *Michael Douglas as Gordon Gekko, in* **Wall Street**

THE KINDEST CUT

The face looking back at you in the mirror—vulnerable, soft, hairy—deserves only the best, and this requires both traditional and modern tools.

A shaving brush with natural badger bristles, though pricey, is a stylish accoutrement as well as the best way to set up your beard for a perfect shave.

Double-track razors shave incredibly close with fewer nicks. The styptic pencil is incorporated into the design. Use smooth strokes with the grain of the beard.

When using a brush and shaving soap, you need only enough lather to create a lubricating film. Don't go for the whipped cream look.

"His skin was pale and he needed a shave. He would always need a shave." *Raymond Chandler,* **Farewell, My Lovely**

First, there is no substitute for the old-fashioned shaving brush and soap. The natural bristles of the brush set up the beard in a way no commercial shaving foam can ever duplicate. Plus, there's something enduringly stylish, not to mention environmentally sound, about using a brush and soap. But when it comes to the actual bloodletting, go with a modern double-track razor, rather swanlike with its fluted stem and flexible head. By comparison, other cutting devices seem clumsy, if not downright dangerous. Assuming you don't wish to face the 8:05 with a hemoglobin-splotched piece of tissue hanging from your face, there are several ways to minimize the carnage. To begin with, wash your face, even if it doesn't need it, since this helps to soften the beard. (Some guys even like to do it in a hot shower, for a maximum softening effect, but beware the foggy mirror.) Then wet the brush in scalding water and work up a lather in your shaving dish. Brush on, using a brisk, circular stroke to get those face bristles ready to die. (Drain the excess water from the soap dish each time you shave, so your soap doesn't turn to mush.) Now shave with the grain of your beard, which will minimize nicks as long as your blade is reasonably sharp. There are certain areas—like around the chin and below your nose—that will always seem to have a shadow; in those places you can shave against the grain, usually on the second pass. Give special attention to the chin, especially to that funny little nook between it and your lower lip. Go slowly here and also at the Adam's apple, since these areas tend to cut easily.

Now look in the mirror. You've got that clean, fresh look of a seeker of wisdom and truth. You believe in you. Even if no one else does. Go out and get 'em.

Soap and Water. Before you expose your face to cold steel, wash it with hot water and soap. This has less to do with cleanliness than with softening the beard and opening the pores. After washing, rinse again with hot water, but don't towel off. Now your face is ready for shaving cream.

Aftershave. Shaving scrapes away part of the epidermis and leaves the skin exposed, raw, and extremely sensitive. After you've shaved, do a final rinse with cold water to close the pores, and apply an aftershave cream with sunscreen to retain moisture and protect your skin from the sun's rays.

"It was a rich com-
pound of whiskey,
after-shave lotion,
shoe polish,
woolens, and the
rankness of a
mature male."
*John Cheever,
"Reunion"*

smell essentials

Old Spice, introduced in
1957, is sure to appear one
day in the Periodic Table of
Elements as the base of all
men's memories of fragrance.
A primal influence on many
modern Oriental-style fragrances, it's a comforting
smell, one of trust and confidence. Excellent for attracting
women, since you smell like
their dad. Father knows best.

Scents and Sensibility. That there has been a major change in attitude toward masculine grooming and fragrance in the latter half of the twentieth century is undeniable. Although the use of men's cologne is ancient (the word originated in the 1600s from the citrus-scented fragrant waters of the German city of Cologne), the explosion in male fragrances has been fairly recent. In the 1950s, the sudden popularity of Canoë among college men ushered in a new era of mass-market scents. However, Guerlain's Eau Impériale and Vétiver have long been classics. Today, Anick Goutal's unisex Eau de Hadrien continues the citrus tradition. How to choose one over another? Comparative sniffing is the only way. Fresh, pungent citrus is the oldest male scent, and probably the least intrusive. Long-lasting florals should be used judiciously. Wood, spice, and tobacco are typically combined with other essences as a minor note, since they can be aggressively masculine. In these days of car pools, crowded subway trains, and elevators, it is best to err on the side of lightness. A stylish man will want to build a small wardrobe of fragrances for various occasions. Aftershaves close the pores, soothe nicks, and smooth the skin. Colognes and toilet waters have more perfume than aftershaves and therefore last longer. Never splash on fragrance. Do dab a bit on your pocket square, especially if you expect to go dancing. Remember, you're making the entrance, not your cologne.

"I love the smell of napalm in the morning, it smells like victory." *Robert Duvall, in* **Apocalypse Now**

Manly Smells. When you get right down to it, there are only six basic aromas from which the various aftershaves and colognes are derived. CITRUS: Added to colognes, neroli oil (the essence of oranges) and petitgrain oil (extracted from orange tree leaves and twigs) are therapeutic to the senses. WOOD: Freshly fallen pine needles blanketing a forest floor have inspired religious figures and perfumers alike, emitting deep, musky, and, indeed, spiritual qualities. FLORAL: The claim is that floral scents elicit the strongest emotional responses. The fragrance of white flowers may be the most tantalizing and seductive of all. LEATHER: A baseball mitt, a weathered saddle add a superb richness to an otherwise delicate concoction of fragrance. SPICE: The sharp, exotic overtones of cinnamon and allspice can create a mysterious presence, a transporting signature. TOBACCO: Not the stench of three a.m. but the earthy flavor of an extra-fine cigar or pipe. The complex aromas of tobacco are a cologne unto themselves.

what are

my clothes

Meeting. Some people view business meetings as a form of psychodrama, but in terms of style, they are really more like performance art. You, of course, are the performance here, and it's smart to start with a reassuring business suit, a garment that's actually designed to allow the real person to emerge. But it doesn't hurt to include a stylish idea in your ensemble, whether it be a beautiful dress shirt, a luxurious briefcase, or a striking bow tie. You want to be known as a man of ideas, after all. Limit yourself, however, to one brilliant idea per outfit.

Golf with a Client. Now that egregious pink-and-plaid golf clothes are largely a thing of the past, it is safe to venture up to the first tee at even the most exclusive clubs in the kind of clothes most guys love to wear: piqué cotton polo shirts, khakis (substitute linen on torrid days, gray flannel on cold ones), and a proper golf hat to shield you from the sun. Jeans are too casual, and beware of crewnecks, since some clubs specify shirts with a collar. It is also a good idea to equip your golf shoes with soft spikes—many clubs now require them. And then it's "fore" time.

saying

today?

The uptown financier has a different set of clothing priorities than the downtown artist or the Silicon Alley pioneer, just as the art director of an advertising agency dresses differently than an account executive at the same firm. And each day has its unique sartorial demands. Are you meeting with clients or working from home? Lunching with an important account or buried in budget meetings with your senior staff? Entertaining clients at night or racing home to coach Little League? The clothes you should invest in are the ones that suit your life style and carry you through the myriad demands of your workday—and do not seem out of date within a year or two or even three of making a purchase. Whatever you do, there are certain wardrobe basics that form a foundation upon which to build. Once you have a solid collection of such timeless essentials, you can begin to experiment in the wider world of personal style.

 One Suit, Many Voices. These days, acquiring clothes is about shopping for versatility. Maintaining a flexible wardrobe means staying attuned to what and where an outfit works. We've just shown you how the same poplin suit can be worn on three different occasions—as a matching suit, as separates for a golf outing or a casual day at the office.

Casual Friday. If it's Friday these days, you've got more freedom, and with freedom comes the agony of choice. Obviously, you want to stay within the range of acceptable attire at your office. Also, for travel, dress comfortably and wear your jacket instead of packing it. Take your cues from the higher-ups. A sport jacket is good. Anything ratty is bad. If the boss lopes around in Nikes, you probably can, too—if not, go brown leather. If you're the boss, wear what you damn well please.

Why build a wardrobe anyway? Investing in a wardrobe is not all that different from investing in the stock market: You try always to invest in what's solid and long-range; you hold on to your winners through thick and thin; and you carefully weed out your losers, the items that no longer earn their space in your portfolio or fit into your life. (You even get tax breaks for discarding both at the end of the year: for selling off stocks that have depreciated and donating old clothes to charity.) Once you have a well-rounded portfolio of everyday clothes, you can begin to take a flier—to experiment a bit in fashion. After you've established a nice wardrobe of business suits and some coordinated accessories, you may be ready for that Armani jacket or those Gucci boots or the alligator belt that seem to have your name on them.

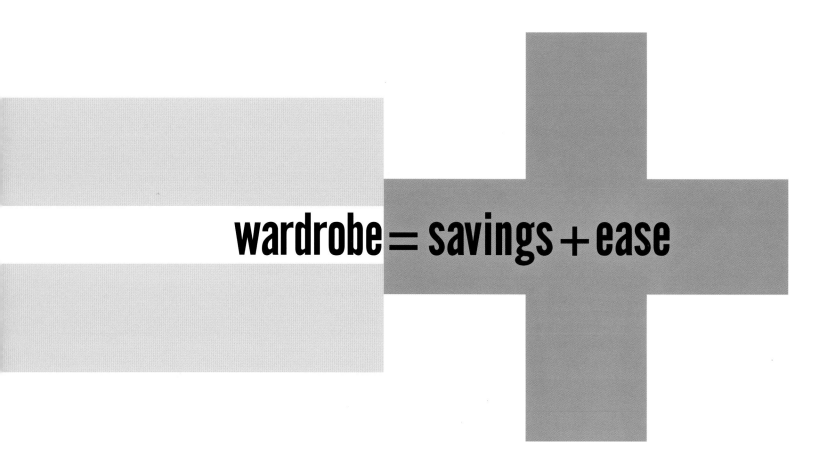

wardrobe = savings + ease

"Probably every new and eagerly expected garment ever put on since clothes came in, fell a trifle short of the wearer's expectations." *Charles Dickens,* **Great Expectations**

Wardrobe Budget

ASSETS:	LIABILITIES:
gray flannels	snakeskin vinyl jeans
navy blazer	collarless suit jacket
toe-cap dress shoes	square-toed, chunky loafers
lamb's-wool V-neck	geometric-patterned sweater
chesterfield coat	logo varsity or leather jacket
tweed hacking jacket	amusing necktie
patent-leather evening shoes	size XXXL carpenter's jeans
cashmere T	crepe-soled wing tips

How do I save money by spending more money on clothes?

Always buy quality. Developing a taste and eye for fine fabrics and construction will eventually lead unerringly to garments that last longer, both physically and stylistically. There will be fewer mistakes in your closet, and the minor errors you do make can often be corrected by a few relatively inexpensive alterations. Well-made suits, for example, have considerably more latitude built into them for letting out the seams in key places. Really good clothes stay in style.

what makes a classic a classic?

While fashion endlessly generates trends that are "hot," classics always stay cool. Porsche 911s. Chet Baker. Cast-iron skillets. Schott motorcycle jackets. Zoris. Swiss Army knives. Levi's 501s. Harley-Davidsons. Ray•Ban sunglasses. No. 2 pencils. Bandannas. Adjustable wrenches. Jack Purcell tennis shoes. Cabernet sauvignon. Classics are adaptable and ageless.

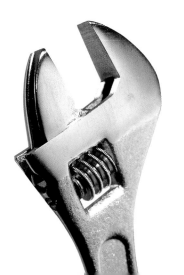

The Classic Navy Suit. Fashion and fads come and go, but the heart of a man's wardrobe (and, increasingly, a woman's) remains the suit. Even if you don't wear suits to work every day, you need to own a tailored ensemble for special occasions—weddings, funerals, appointments with the IRS. Your first suit should be as timeless and classic and perfectly fitted as your wallet will allow. And it should probably be blue, although gray is okay, too. (Black has become a voguish color in tailored clothing for men, but if you are particularly fair of hair and complexion, this is probably not right for you.) Start with the rich, deep, dark blue of success—a blue that is both slimming and serene, businesslike and chic. In short, navy blue. The navy suit is the cornerstone of a man's wardrobe. Successful men often own several, and some go as far as to have entire wardrobes made of outfits in this color. If you own only one and don't live in Anchorage, the suit should be of tropical-weight wool, so that it can be serviceable throughout the seasons. To go with this dark blue suit, you need only a starched white dress shirt, a black knit tie, and black leather shoes to attain a very high level of masculine style. (This was, incidentally, the exact daily costume favored for nearly every situation by the original James Bond character in the Ian Fleming novels. Note also that he used a regular four-in-hand knot for the tie. Windsor knots were characteristic of SMERSH.)

HOW TO Good woolen suits should not be stuffed into the closet but aired for twenty-four hours after each wearing. Hang separately, preferably on a wooden dumbvalet, before returning the suit to the closet. If this routine is followed, suits will require very few dry cleanings—about once a season.

faQ

How many suits should you own? Enough so that they can be effectively rotated. That is, you should have enough tailored outfits so that you never have to wear any one of them twice in one week—and never two days in a row. So, for some men three is enough. Others will own more than a dozen. How ever many, go with quality over quantity.

"I started out in the mailroom in 1962 and
my wardrobe has pretty much stayed there."

"And we dress, sir—?" he murmured, feeling Osnard's gaze burning the nape of his neck. "Most of my gentlemen seem to favour left these days. I don't *think* it's political."

This was his standard joke, calculated to raise a laugh even with the most sedate of his customers. Not with Osnard apparently.

"Never know where the bloody thing is. Bobs about like a windsock," he replied dismissively.

John Le Carré, **The Tailor of Panama**

Whether one toils in a corporate office or sits behind a computer at home, dressing for work is a highly individual act. How best to express yourself with clothes that suit your profession, physique, and personal sense of style? Your look also depends on what the day will bring. Will you be meeting with the boss? Lunching with important clients? Attending an industry function after work? In nearly all professional contexts, presentation counts—usually for more than you think. The focus is on what kind of wardrobe you need to succeed and be comfortable in every **SITUATION**

THE BULLETPROOF CLOSET

SIMPLE SOLUTIONS

The modern man's wardrobe has more demands than ever before—despite the relaxation of formal rules and the long-term trend toward casual attire. Business clothes now encompass myriad interactions, from meetings and luncheons to social gatherings after work. Weekend wear has taken on new significance. The sports we play all seem to have their own high-performance gear. So you want, first and foremost, to have a bulletproof set of clothes, irreproachable basics that meet your needs, as well as the coordinated furnishings and accessories to pull your various looks together.

Unless you are an artist or a prophet, most of your fashion choices are going to be shaped by your professional life. Most men dress to emulate the successful men of the group in which they work. You want to belong to the group and look like its leaders. But you also want to be up to date. A hidebound Ivy League look can sometimes seem as eccentric as Jean Paul Gaultier. Dress for the times. Wear good clothes. Don't wear flashy or inappropriate neckwear. Keep your clothes clean and well pressed. Avoid novelty fashions. In recent years, tailored clothing has slimmed down, a result of fabric innovations, construction techniques, and the winds of fashion. Linebacker shoulders are out, narrow lapels are in. Ties have become more classic, too. Your choices in neckwear should be related to the color and pattern of your suits. A strongly patterned suit calls for plainer neckties, and vice versa.

If there is one thing you should take away from these pages, it is that investing in classics will pay off in the long run. The list at the right is a great place to begin.

In fashion "simple" solutions last the longest and cost the least.

Simple Business Wardrobe
- navy blue suit, p. 25
- black leather belt, p. 93
- black leather shoes, p. 95
- white shirt, p. 64
- blue blazer, p. 50
- gray flannel slacks, p. 58
- khakis, p. 59
- black socks, p. 92
- solid tie, p. 77
- linen pocket handkerchief, p. 81
- overcoat, p. 99
- briefcase, p. 101

 What should I do with clothes that don't work or just don't fit?
Dejunk your closet—take a couple of hours and a beer (maybe a couple of those too) and deal with your mistakes in the wardrobe department. Have a large empty box for the discards, including ties from old girlfriends or ex-wives, pants that can't be let out, and jackets with lapels best used for hang gliding. Recycle them to a thrift store. Repeat twice a year. Make a list of your needs.

The black
leather belt
goes with
just about
everything.

The white oxford-
cloth cotton shirt is
suitable for almost all
occasions.

A dark jacket is the
most versatile
piece in a man's
wardrobe.

Dark flannel trousers make the
transition from business to
casual. Own several pairs.

A solid dark tie is a
wardrobe essential.

Black leather cap-toed
lace-ups are suitable for
business and even for-
mal affairs. Wear with
dark dress socks.

Socks can be a fashion
statement or misstate-
ment, but black is
always safe. Just be
sure they're long
enough.

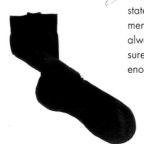

CHOOSING A CUT

There are three traditional suit silhouettes for a man to choose from:

1. THE AMERICAN, or natural-shoulder suit, the most conservative of which is known as the sack suit, and which was popularized by Brooks Brothers. **2.** THE BRITISH, which has lightly padded shoulders, follows the lines of the body, and is typically side-vented. **3.** THE ITALIAN, which has a slightly higher shoulder, clings more tightly to the body, and is usually unvented. Within these schools there are sub-divisions and refinements, but for the man starting a wardrobe, the logical choice is a path between the extremes. This is usually a sort of Anglo-American compromise, a cocktail of British and American style. Such a suit will have some padding and some waist suppression to give the wearer a bit of a v-shape, but nothing of aircraft-carrier proportions. The lapels on a single-breasted jacket should not be too wide and not too thin, extending just a bit less than halfway between the collar and the shoulder of the jacket. The goal is a suit that will stand the test of time.

> "I love meetings with suits. I live for meetings with suits. I love them because I know they had a really boring week and I walk in there with my orange velvet leggings and drop popcorn in my cleavage and then fish it out and eat it. I like that. I know I'm entertaining them and I know they know." *Madonna*

SILHOUETTE OF A SUIT

A navy, one-button soft suit. Tailored but with a comfortable look. Easy to pair with different slacks or jackets.

A straight-point collar with French cuffs dresses up the casualness of the suit.

A true white collar with matching cuffs and contrasting blue body— high business formal.

Black wing tips are very appropriate for business wear.

The classic British cut, whose stripes, according to legend, are a nod to the "ledger books" of London stockbrokers.

Double-buckle black shoes add a contemporary edge yet are suitable for almost any business occasion. The silver buckles complement the belt and watch metals.

soft

traditional

Today there are two major choices in suit construction: the traditional "constructed" look, which is what has been the norm for several generations, and the newer "soft" style. This new "soft" approach usually features a relaxed, year-round fabric, and also has the normal padding in the chest and shoulders. But it lacks a stiff inner facing of canvas, thus allowing more freedom while still retaining a tailored appearance and affording more latitude for wearing pants and jacket as separate components. This allows more versatility, great when you're on the road.

SUIT ARCHITECTURE
elegant staples

The softer shoulder of a sack suit gives a natural and pleasing contour, but posture is important.

If you are tall and thin, buttoning the top two of a high-buttoning three-button jacket can lead to an Ichabod Crane effect.

Under a suit, the band-collar shirt manages to convey a look that is serious and creative without a tie.

Two-button. Ever since JFK wore them in his campaign against Nixon, the two-button single-breasted has been the best-selling suit in America. It works for most figures and tends to lengthen the body, since its elongated frontal V shows more shirt. With a blue oxford shirt, red silk tie, and black brogues, it's a fail-safe look that anyone can wear—and look good in.

Three-button. Prior to the sixties, three-button suits were the norm. Now they are considered "fashionable." Designers tend to make them so that the top two are buttoned. Some men prefer the classic three, in which the lapel rolls to the second button and the top button remains unbuttoned, hidden behind the lapel. Try it both ways and go with what works for your body type.

Good wardrobes tend to contain a variety of suit styles, some dressier than others. Some have two buttons, some three. Some are single-breasted, some not. Taken together, these suits fill the gaps in a gentleman's closet. Building around these basics, he adds the personal touches that mark him as a man of style.

Since the double-breasted jacket places two layers of fabric across the chest, it is marginally warmer than the single-breasted—something to keep in mind on hot days.

A vest, when properly tailored, helps to slim and define the physique.

Vested suits also give your wardrobe greater flexibility, since subtracting the vest on certain days gives the suit a new look.

Double-breasted. A bit flashier than the single-breasted, the double-breasted suit, with its double row of buttons and upward-slashing lapels, is a good choice for somewhat dressier occasions. It also works in business situations where looking imposing counts (let's hope, for your sake, this isn't every day), especially if complemented by a striped Sea Island cotton shirt with a contrasting spread collar and French cuffs, and a rich foulard tie.

Three-piece. For reasons of cost, the vested suit has become somewhat of a rarity. The three-piece suit, so redolent of maturity, stability, and steadfastness, also seems a victim of the relentless trend toward increasing casualness of the masculine wardrobe. The extra layer is, however, a nice touch, and a man who removes his jacket at work (as most of us do) will still feel somewhat dressed in a vest. Great for wearing a pocket watch.

What looks good on ME?

The first rule of fashion: Suit yourself. The key to building a solid, enduring wardrobe is to purchase clothing that suits you particularly well—that complements your figure and face. Nobody's perfect, but since we don't have to walk around naked, the right clothes can mask our physical flaws and accentuate the positive. The short, thin man can make himself look taller and heavier. The fat man can tip the scales in the opposite direction. While there are exceptions to every rule, dressing for your body type remains the most important strategy in fashion.

Tall. Stress horizontal lines. Stay away from pinstripes; they only emphasize your narrowness. Jackets should accentuate width: shoulders sloped, waist loose, pockets flapped (a ticket pocket helps). Double-breasteds are ideal. Wear patterns—Glen Urquhart or windowpane plaid, checks—and tweed. Avoid fabrics that cling. Three-button jackets, though fashionable, tend to lengthen the body. Similarly, shirts with long-pointed collars and narrow ties make the face look leaner and longer. Try spread collars. Eschew dainty pointed shoes.

Short. Pinstripes and chalk stripes (though not too widely spaced) and dark solid colors flatter the short man. Jackets should be single-breasted, square-shouldered, two-or three-buttoned, preferably with long lapels and unflapped pockets. Avoid long jackets; a shorter jacket gives the appearance of longer legs. Choose shirts with vertical stripes and long-pointed collars. Tie knots should be smallish (no Windsors). Trousers should be slim in line (you're the one guy who can safely go without cuffs). Stand straight.

Heavyset. Suiting fabrics should be smooth, not bulky (avoid tweed and seersucker). Double-breasteds are a hazard, but the peaked lapels do carry the eye upward away from the waist. Plaid is your enemy, pinstripes your friend. Medium and dark colors are becoming. (Late in life, Orson Welles wore only black.) Watch out for spread and button-down collars—your face usually needs the long-pointed type. Wear bold ties—tied long, so that they reach the waistband of your trousers. Suspenders instead of a belt. Narrow-toed shoes and small-sized jewelry. Chin up.

Buffed. Athletic men can be a tough fit, since the difference between chest size and waistline (in tailoring jargon, the "drop") can be extreme. If your drop is more than eight inches, look for "athletic suits" that take this into account. If you've got a ten-inch or greater drop, you may need custom or made-to-measure tailoring (ditto for shirts). In general, modestly padded or natural-shouldered single-breasted suits in dark colors (to minimize bulk) are the ticket. Jackets with a low-button stance are desirable. When it comes to sports clothes, wear what you want. You got it, flaunt it!

"Muscles are great. Everybody should have at least one that they can show off." *Andy Warhol*

When you buy a workout bench, spend the extra money to get a dual adjustable bench—besides the normal routines, it allows for both incline and decline exercises.

Simple Home Gym

Clothes can never completely mask the physique underneath. Working out regularly not only makes you look good in your clothes, but also helps arrest the physical drift, particularly around the waist and thighs, that over the years necessitates costly alterations and, eventually, a new (bigger) wardrobe. Even if you have a gym membership, there are always times when you work late or can't squeeze in a workout. A home gym makes it a lot easier to stay in shape, especially on weekends or when your job is taking over your life. To keep your home gym from becoming another dumbvalet or tie rack, here are a few suggestions:

1. Join a gym for only a couple of months at first.
2. Get a personal trainer to teach you the basics.
3. Take the next six months of gym costs and buy a good adjustable weight lifter's bench and a set of free weights, including dumbbells.
4. Keep a log of your progress.
5. When you realize you haven't made an entry for a few weeks, take the clothes off the bench and start again.
6. It's one day at a time. A few simple exercises. Like brushing your teeth. Forever.

After you own a good navy suit, your next choice might be a gray nailhead in worsted wool.

A navy blue chalk stripe is an excellent option for meetings and important business engagements.

Now you're ready to loosen up a bit and introduce a little color and pattern, like a mini-houndstooth check in soft brown.

(faQ)

What's the difference between a pinstripe and a chalk stripe?
A pinstripe is a fine or broken (beaded) thin line with a spacing of $1/16$ th to $1 1/2$ inch; a chalk stripe is wider, resembling—you got it—a chalked stripe, and often set $1 1/2$ inches apart.

BUILDING A SUIT WARDROBE

Not everyone needs a dozen suits in all the classic patterns and styles. Maybe it's only one great navy blue and a serviceable gray that you carefully rotate. The question is: What sequence should you buy in? The important thing is to start with the basics, a simple foundation on which to build. The navy suit comes first. A well-dressed man typically owns several in various shades, cuts, and fabrics. The next step would be a muted gray worsted wool, perhaps in a bird's-eye or nailhead pattern. Right behind that is a patterned suit, in either pinstripes or a muted windowpane plaid. Now you're ready to loosen up, perhaps with a mini-check or a Glen plaid. With these regulars stored away neatly in your closet, you can begin to fill in the fashion gaps. Five or six suits will get you through the cold months and the sweltering ones.

A good pinstripe suit makes a graphic, self-assured statement and is something you can always take to the bank.

The black-and-white Glen plaid wool suit is a classic pattern, at once forceful and restrained.

Finally, you can begin to experiment, with a rich brown herringbone wool-and-mohair three-button model.

FABRICS & PATTERNS

General Guidelines. **Fabric.** After silhouette and color, the most important decision in choosing tailored clothing is the type of fabric. Today's fabrics are lighter than ever before, reflecting both technological innovations in spinning and weaving and the quest of designers to make the modern suit more comfortable and flexible. Wool remains the heart of a man's tailored wardrobe, and worsted wools—smooth, closely woven fabrics named for the place where they were first produced in England—are the fabric of choice for most suits. Worsteds hold their crease very well, and the new Super 100 worsteds are thin enough to wear on a New York City subway in July. Crepe-textured wools have also come into their own, especially for so-called fashion suits by Italian designers. And everything from Lycra spandex to rayon is now added to wool to make it more forgiving. When selecting a suit, rub the fabric between your fingers. Does it spring back into shape? Check the label. Is the suit 100 percent wool or mostly wool? Does it have a nice feel, or "hand," to it? A suit is only as good as its fabric.

Patterns and Mixes. Without patterns and textures fashion would be a bore, but the use of too many patterns can make the eyes swim and ruin the effect of an ensemble. Dressing should not be an op art adventure. Limit yourself to two patterns in any outfit (three is possible if you have impeccable taste)—for example, a nailhead gray suit, striped tie, and solid colored shirt. The suit and tie supply the pattern; the shirt is neutral. In general, try to avoid wearing two patterns that are very similar. When mixing patterns, there should be a change in scale. If you are wearing a pinstriped suit and a striped tie, the stripes on the tie should be wide, so that they don't conflict with the suit. If you're suspicious, start over with a solid tie.

GLOSSARY OF TAILORED FABRICS

Crepe: a worsted fabric with a pebbly or crinkly surface.
Flannel: a tightly woven fabric (usually wool) with a napped surface that conceals the weave.
Sharkskin: sleek twill weave worsted in two tones of yarn.
Tweed: a general term for wool fabrics with a rough surface and firm texture.
Twill: a weave with a distinct diagonal rib on the fabric; gabardine is a closely woven twill.

GLOSSARY OF TAILORED PATTERNS

Bird's-eye: a weave pattern producing a diamond-shaped design.
Chalk stripe: a stripe resembling a chalked line.
Glen (Glen Urquhart) plaid: a boxlike pattern plus an overplaid, named for a valley in Scotland.
Herringbone: twill fabric in which equal numbers of threads slant right and left to form a chevron pattern.
Nailhead: a design of small dots suggesting nails.
Windowpane: large box plaid formed by vertical and horizontal stripes.

SEASONLESS FABRICS—THE TRAVELER'S FRIEND

A dark wool crepe suit is great for travel. The soft cut is comfortable and doesn't wrinkle, and the color helps hide stains.

A black knit tie could be the only tie you take: it goes with everything and doesn't wrinkle or show stains.

To help avoid creasing, always wrap your jackets and suits in plastic or acid-free tissue.

The unconstructed pants in a dark color can serve as stand-alone slacks or as a pair of "odd" trousers with a sport jacket.

Black shoes go with everything. Slip-ons like these can work as casual or business wear, depending on what you pair them with.

Zegna Super 100

No name stands for innovative modern fabric tailoring more than that of Ermenegildo Zegna, the Italian manufacturer who uses traditional tailoring silhouettes but employs advanced construction wool-processing methods. The company created its famous Super 100 wool—a tightly woven fine merino that bounces back from all kinds of routine abuse—in the 1960s to reflect changes in the modern office, when central heating had rendered heavier wools unnecessary. The secret is in the twists of the yarn, which are spun to make the fabric more resilient, according to Djordje Stefanovic, the fashion director at Zegna. Its breathability also makes it comfortable in nearly all climates and conditions. Zegna suits with their aversion to wrinkles are great for travel.

What fabrics travel best? New lightweight worsted and crepe wools are comfortable in most climates eight months a year, and they travel extremely well. Wear cashmere on the plane (it wrinkles in luggage). Pack tailored items last in plastic bags to minimize creasing, and hang them in a steamy bathroom when you arrive to take out any wrinkles.

WINTER SUIT FABRICS

Even in the era of the all-season suit, certain fabrics have cold-weather properties that specifically qualify them for space in your closet. These are usually clothes with a rugged character and construction—and sturdy traditions to match.

English country dress, including hacking clothes, were the forerunners of much of modern tailored clothing. And the fabrics they were made in remain staples for contemporary cuts. Thick, nubby tweeds. Rich barley-corn wools. Durable cavalry twills and covert cloths. Canvas, duck, corduroy, and leather. With the advent of central heating and the decline of the great country houses, such fabrics passed out of fashion for everyday business (although they have periodically staged revivals). So the average guy's closet will consist mostly of lightweight, all-weather suits. However, as you build your wardrobe, there will be room for venerable specialty pieces that reveal the depths of your style. The hacking jacket or hacking suit coat is slightly longer than an ordinary jacket, shaped at the waist and flared at the hips, with deep side vents, angled pockets, and a ticket or change pocket on the right-hand side. These are typically made in tough, thorn-proof tweeds. Norfolk jackets have box pleats at each side, front and back, and an all-around belt, which is usually bound with leather-covered buttons. Herringbone wool and cavalry twill are common fabrics for this classic. Not everything in your closet needs to be high-tech.

Glossary of Winter Wardrobe Fabrics
BARLEYCORN: small tweed or woolen pattern used in suits and sport coats. CHEVIOT: originally a coarse wool from a breed of sheep in Scotland, now a rough wool in herringbone or twill weave used for suits and sport coats. CORDUROY: fabric with a cut-pile surface of wide or narrow wales, from the French for "cord of the king." DONEGAL TWEED: tweed named for the north-ernmost county in Ireland, characterized by thick twists of multicolored yarns. HARRIS TWEED: trade name for an imported tweed hand-woven by islanders on Harris and other Outer Hebrides islands. MOLESKIN: rugged satin-weave cotton with a soft napped surface. SUEDE: leather whose flesh side is buffed to a velvet finish; the name is derived from the French word for Sweden, where the process originated.

"...someone has to give you your first gun or the opportunity to get it and use it, and you have to live where there is game or fish if you are to learn about them, and now, at thirty-eight, he loved to fish and to shoot exactly as much as when he first had gone with his father. It was a passion that had never slackened and he was very grate-ful to his father for bringing him to know it."
Ernest Hemingway, "Father and Sons"

Outdoor motifs inspire many men's classics, from the thorn-proof twill jacket to the hunting-icon tie.

Sometimes high-tech clothing doesn't hack it: here, a sueded moleskin hacking suit.

Traditionally, the earthen tones of English country wear were accented with strong, bright colors—from red ties to bright striped shirts to yellow waistcoats.

THE BLACK SUIT

Black is a seasonless color, looking appropriate in summer as well as winter—the key is the fabric.

Don't be afraid to mix black and navy, as in this tie, as long as one color is dominant.

The black suit is a nice statement of evening formalness—a step above the traditional business suit.

The elastic vamp adds a contemporary edge but is still appropriate in a variety of situations.

Instant Modern. The black suit, originally a symbol of propriety and masculine power, has re-emerged as a hip mainstream element in the modern wardrobe. One of its leading proponents is Donna Karan, a designer who uses black as a base color in her women's collections, which are known for their urban sophistication and their subtle masking of figure flaws. The suits travel well and make a smooth transition from day into evening. In general black has a slimming effect, and it works the same magic on the heavyset man as on the full-figured woman. However, very fair men should tread carefully here, since black can make them look pallid. Also, black has strong connotations of hipness, so it is probably not the best choice for serious corporate business meetings. Wear black to art openings, cool parties, and, in a pinch, to black-tie affairs, where it can pass as a tuxedo.

Mr. Pink:

Why can't we pick out our own color?

Joe:

I tried that once, it don't work. You get four guys fighting over who's gonna be Mr. Black.

Lawrence Tierney and Harvey Keitel in

Reservoir Dogs

Black History: The color worn by clerics and mourners, black's journey to hip fashionability is an intriguing one. As John Harvey points out in his book *Men in Black*, it was in the nineteenth century that men of wealth and power began to dress as if going to a funeral. This was partly to distinguish themselves from women, who wore more vibrant colors. But black also was a reaction against the colorful foppishness of dying monarchies and thus symbolic of the bourgeois democracy. In the twentieth century, black eventually took on sinister connotations. In postwar America, with the advent of the "beats," black has been a badge of rebellion in the form of black leather and turtlenecks. In a sense, the modern black suit for men, like the "little black dress" for women, has come to represent a fashion statement by subtraction, a compass point of minimalist chic that ensures safe passage through the shoals of style. Solid though cool.

SUMMER SUIT FABRICS

Tropical-weight wools have taken some of the sweat out of summer business attire. A nine-month superlight worsted wool suit, then, is a wardrobe must. But on really torrid days, linen, seersucker, and cotton suits will keep you from turning into a puddle on the sidewalk. A tan or olive cotton gabardine or poplin suit is a versatile addition to the businessman's spring–summer wardrobe, as is a patterned sport jacket, whether in cotton madras, striped seersucker, or a silk blend. A summer-weight blue blazer is a good idea, too.

Glossary of Summer Wardrobe Fabrics

LINEN: probably the oldest fabric (used to wrap Egyptian mummies), it is made from flax; its tendency to wrinkle is part of its charm. POPLIN: a sturdy ribbed fabric, usually of cotton, silk, or rayon, used in suits and raincoats. RAYON: a manufactured textile produced from regenerated cellulose (plant) fiber. SEERSUCKER: from the Persian shir-o-shakar (literally means "milk and sugar"), a fabric with crinkled stripes used in suits, shirts, and pajamas. TROPICAL WORSTED: suiting weighing eleven ounces or less per yard.

The seersucker suit, a summertime classic from the South, was Damon Runyon's trademark.

Suede and buck shoes are a spiffy way to step out between Memorial Day and Labor Day.

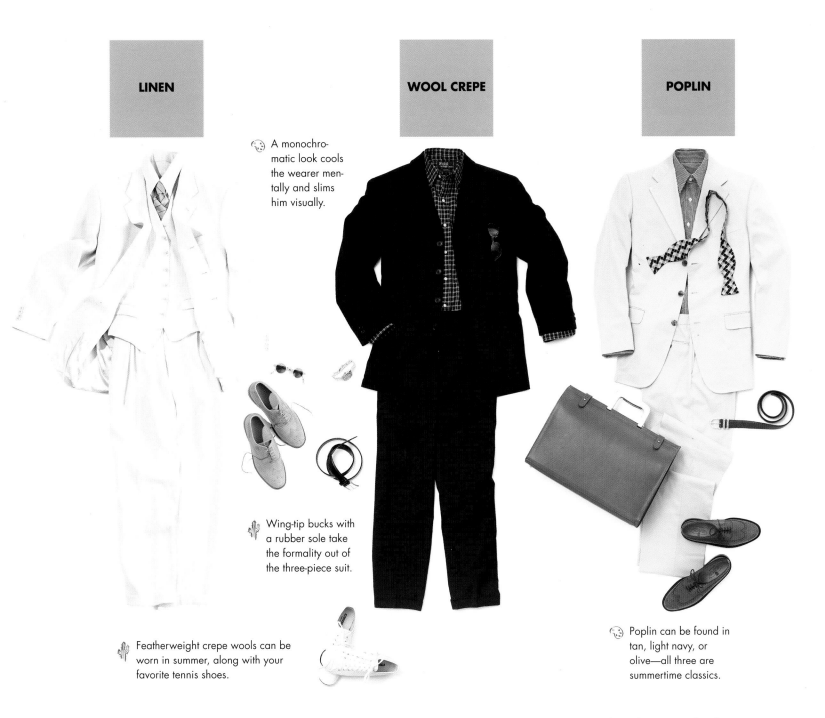

LINEN

WOOL CREPE

POPLIN

A monochromatic look cools the wearer mentally and slims him visually.

Wing-tip bucks with a rubber sole take the formality out of the three-piece suit.

Featherweight crepe wools can be worn in summer, along with your favorite tennis shoes.

Poplin can be found in tan, light navy, or olive—all three are summertime classics.

"Stingo, you're all dressed up, where are you going, you're wearing your cocksucker, you look so nice," she said all in a tumbling rush, blushing crimson and correcting herself with a wonderful giggle even as I, too, formed the word *seersucker*! *William Styron*, **Sophie's Choice**

multiple personality:
the gray flannel suit

Revisionist View. Immortalized as a symbol of drab corporate conformity with the publication of Sloan Wilson's 1955 novel, *The Man in the Gray Flannel Suit*, the suit itself is extraordinarily adaptable and belongs in any modern wardrobe. (In the book, it actually functions as a metaphor for insecurity, as opposed to the relative security of the military olive drab that the protagonist, Thomas Rath, and others like him, wore in the war.) A gray flannel suit can be dressy or sporty, depending on how it is turned out. In the 1950s, the prototypical man in the gray flannel suit satisfied his longing for color with sport clothes, many of them egregiously vibrant. Nowadays, the gray-flannel guy simply dresses the suit with more imagination—foulard silk pocket squares, bright-toned shirts—or he deconstructs the concept entirely. On the streets of Paris, a common sight is a gray flannel jacket worn with jeans. A dark gray flannel double-breasted suit can easily be worn on somewhat formal occasions with a white shirt and dotted tie. The same suit with a black turtleneck gives a more relaxed impression. The smooth texture and neutral tone of the gray flannel provide an excellent ground for experimentation. In the end, the important question remains: Who is the guy inside?

A classic watch with a classic look—the Timex Mercury—it keeps on ticking.

Gray Flannel Classic. The stereotype of safe corporate fashion: a single-breasted gray flannel suit combined with a pink oxford cloth dress shirt, black knit tie, and black leather cap-toe shoes. Note the plain white square-fold pocket square. Worn daily, this outfit would put one to sleep. Wear it in a corporate casual culture and it rebels.

Taking the mono-chromatic as far as it will go can add formality and rein-force the "down-town" feel.

A turtleneck works only if the fabric is as rich as the suiting fabric. Choose a merino wool or cashmere, never just cotton.

French cuffs help dress up the infor-mality of the "uni-form" jacket.

Gray Flannel Cheek. Nowhere is it written in stone that gray flannel cannot be cut in more interesting shapes, like the charcoal wool military-style jacket above. Paired with black stretch khakis, cor-dovan shoes, and a tone-on-tone shirt and tie, gray flannel cries hip.

Gray Flannel Chic. The double-breasted gray flannel, with the substitu-tion of a black cashmere turtleneck for a shirt and tie, can make the transition from day to evening. Add a pair of leather half boots, and the ensemble moves from corporate to cool. Its all in personal style.

the blazer

Blue blazers go with almost anything: striped shirts and solid shirts; solid knit ties, wild patterned ties, and no tie; khakis, flannels, and jeans; loafers, wing tips, and duck-hunting shoes. Some well-dressed men practically live in them. A classic blazer can even be worn to the office, although at most companies this is a Friday phenomenon. It's the one indispensable item to travel with, both for wearing on the plane and for informal business and social situations. With a dark shirt or black crewneck, it can even take you through a night at a disco or club. It's the first sport jacket you should own. Get a good one.

Do blazers have to be navy blue?
Blazers can come in a number of colors, but navy is the most traditional. However, in the last few years black has become extremely popular, and there is camel hair, too. If you win at Augusta, green is appropriate.

No piece in the masculine wardrobe is more versatile than the blazer, especially in navy blue wool or cashmere. The name is said to derive from a nineteenth-century warship, *HMS Blazer*, whose commander transformed his scroungy crew by insisting that they all wear jackets with blue-and-white vertical stripes. Since then, jackets worn on sporting occasions, particularly yachting, have been called blazers. Like regimental ties, blazers are part of the dress code at many traditional sporting clubs. Members of the Royal Yacht Squadron of Cowes, in England, for example, are required to wear white trousers and brown shoes with their blazers at all times. Despite its elite origins, the blue blazer is actually one of the most democratic of garments, fitting in with almost every item in your wardrobe. A blazer can be either single- or double-breasted. You would do well to own more than one.

Here is David Niven-like aplomb in the simplicity of a well-cut blazer, flannels, and pale shirt. It can take you around the world or at least to your in-laws.

What buttons are appropriate with a blazer? The tradition of wearing brass buttons on a blazer derives from the custom of navy officers stitching gilded uniform buttons to their sport jackets. If you are not an ex-officer or yacht-club member, it stands to reason that such naval motifs would be meaningless. Indeed, double rows of chunky gold buttons with kedge anchors may be a bit Gilbert & Sullivan for most men, especially at the office, where the blazer tends to be somewhat overused, anyway. However, polished brass buttons, particularly plain ones, have become so much a part of the iconography of these jackets that it is now safe for anyone to wear them. Of course, plain black or blue buttons work just fine. When it comes to heraldic crests, which are sometimes affixed to the breast pockets of blazers, wear them only if they mean something to you. The power of a blazer should be in its fit, not in its ornaments.

You can't have too many of them, and each has its special role to play. One may be for informal cocktails, another for sleeping with the dogs.

sport jacket

Well-bred men of a certain disposition are often loath to part with any old sport jacket, precisely because it is comfortably broken in. "Trust not," warned Thomas Carlyle, "the heart of that man for whom old clothes are not venerable." Within a gentleman's wardrobe, the sport jackets multiply the separate pants-and-jacket combinations that can be made, thus giving new life to other garments and vastly increasing his overall stock. They also suit a variety of different moods, from debonair (checked cashmere with dark flannel trousers) to ruddy and muddy (brown Harris tweed with covert-cloth pants). Sport jackets tend to be more visually striking than suits—consider the graphic snap of a vibrant houndstooth check or a wide-wale corduroy jacket—and to have more detail—for example, patch or hacking pockets, suede collars, leather buttons, or a half belt in the rear. It is not uncommon for sport jackets to have three working buttons, or even more. Since sport jackets have personality, they give your wardrobe flair. Combining sport jackets with the rest of the wardrobe takes a bit of skill and trial and error. In general, if the sport jacket has a pattern, choose solid color pants. If the jacket is solid, you can be more imaginative in your choice of trousers. It also makes sense to pair light jackets with dark trousers and vice versa. Almost any sport jacket will work with khakis or jeans. Many designers now make oversized sport jackets that they call "coat jacks," a cross between a coat and a jacket, and these facilitate layering. Tweed is probably the most common winter sport-jacket fabric. It tends to be remarkably sturdy, as befitting garments that were developed for rugged country wear. Tweed jackets can last for generations, like a fine wine, aging only improves them.

It is smart to buy some sport jackets on the large side, so they can be worn with sweaters or even Polartec vests and pullovers.

faQ

Is Harris the only tweed? There is herringbone tweed, Donegal tweed, saxony tweed; or—the finest tweed of all—Harris tweed, a hand-woven fabric from the islands of Lewis and Harris in the Outer Hebrides, for which local artisans color the fibers with naturally produced dyes. Cashmere is one of the most sumptuous jacket fibers and a very good choice for a blazer or other type of sport jacket (or even a coat). Made from the hair on the underbelly of goats in the Kashmir region of the Himalayas, where the supply is almost entirely controlled by China, cashmere is a precious fiber. One pays accordingly. (While pure cashmere clothing is quite expensive, cashmere-wool blends are easier on the wallet.) Cashmere provides great insulation for its weight and thus makes for excellent transition clothes. In most American cities, right through November, you can usually get away with no coat and just a cashmere jacket during the day. And it always looks and feels great.

Suede and leather jackets. A suede or leather blazer adds a rugged component to the tailored wardrobe and can be worn as a suit coat or as an outer coat on fall and spring days. They function as either knockabout weekend wear or dressy casual clothes in town. Wear with a cashmere turtleneck, plaid suit pants, and polished black loafers for that Madison Avenue look, or with jeans and a sweater for a kicked-back downtown feel. They are not really meant to be worn to work with a dress shirt and tie, but plenty of guys do.

High-buttoning soft jackets. A vogue for sport jackets with more than the standard two or three buttons has characterized the final decade of the twentieth century, just as the original high-buttoning frock coats set the course of men's tailored clothing at the end of the nineteenth. There is a bit of Edwardian elegance in some of these modern jackets, which often have four or five buttons. In others there is a distinctly French artisan spirit in the shirtlike collars and patch pockets. No accent needed.

trousers

"I grow old . . . I grow old . . . I shall wear the bottoms of my trousers rolled.

Shall I part my hair behind? Do I dare to eat a peach? I shall wear white flannel trousers, and walk upon the beach."

T. S. Eliot, **The Love Song of J. Alfred Prufrock**

Break the monotony. Give your suit pants a day off. Since jackets outlast pants, every man needs an array of "odd," or mismatched, trousers to supplement his suit wardrobe. These can be in corduroy, cavalry twill, moleskin, tweed, khaki, or flannel—fabrics that pair up nicely with your various jackets. As casual Friday begins to exert its influence beyond just one day of the week, the mix-and-match aspect of tailored clothing will come more and more into play. Indeed, many fashion designers nowadays prefer to show their tailored collections using mismatched suits, deconstructing the traditional masculine ensemble. This is a reflection of fashion on the street, where stylish men might wear, say, blue pinstripe trousers with a rugged shirt and boots, or a bankerish pinstripe jacket with a T-shirt and jeans. In addition to the contrast in color, odd trousers give the wearer an opportunity to juxtapose contrasting textures—for example, the smooth symmetry of cavalry twill pants against the nubbiness of a Donegal tweed, or wide-wale corduroy trousers against a soft cashmere blazer.

SLACKS

If you were trying to pare down your wardrobe to the absolute minimum, the two essential trousers would be gray flannels and khakis.

A good pair of gray wool flannel pants can carry a man through many semi-formal and business situations but can also be dressed down with a kind of casual elegance, as Fred Astaire did so memorably, threading a silk tie through the belt loops. You can wear them with almost any shade or style of jacket, and they have a feeling of luxury about them. Logically, a man's wardrobe will need more trousers than jackets, because trousers tend to wear out faster. Not only are their seats and knees vulnerable, but they visit the laundry and dry cleaner more frequently, thus accelerating wear. There is also the abiding fact of the mutability of waistlines, especially male waistlines, which necessitates trouser alteration and wardrobe updates throughout a man's life.

SIMPLE SOLUTIONS

Pleated versus Plain Front. The pleating of trouser fronts is a twentieth-century innovation. As trousers began to be cut wider, the front pleats allowed for a more orderly presentation. Comfort was also a consideration. Pleats afford additional roominess when a man is sitting down or placing his hands in his pockets. Pants generally have a single or double pleat, the double kind being slightly more dressy. The English drape style of the 1930s—full-cut, double-pleated trousers with an extension waistband and side-tab adjusters—set a swank standard that is still imitated today. Slacks—or trousers that are not part of a suit—generally do not have pleats at all (although there are plenty of exceptions). As a rule, pleated trousers, which sit high on the waist, assist in camouflaging one's paunch. They should never be purchased so tight across the midsection that the pleats pull open. Because of their clear advantages, they have become, since perhaps 1980 or so, the dominant dress trousers in the United States. However, plain-front pants do cycle in and out of the culture, and they staged a comeback in the 1990s. The clean, unbroken line in the overall tailored silhouette slims the wearer. It is not an either - or situation. Most men have both pleated and plain-front trousers in their closet.

PANTS

Khakis, or chinos, came into fashion after 1945, when college men who returned from the war began wearing olive-drab slacks to classes. Chino, the military cotton twill fabric, was carried over into civilian life, and the style has never left us. Today we wear khakis almost everywhere (including places where they rightfully wear out their welcome, like church and the theater). They are democratic garments, as ubiquitous among women as men, as preppy as they are proletarian, both hip and square, and so, endlessly, on. Purists consider the button-fly version to be the Real Thing. Not only is this how the military made them, but a button fly stretches better than a zippered fly when one sits. In moments of extreme passion, of course, the zippered kind suddenly seems superior.

Suspenders. An important change in the evolution of trousers style has been the disappearance of suspenders. Before mid-century, nearly all trousers were high-waisted and held up by suspenders. The ubiquity of jeans, which fit on the hips, has helped to accelerate the practice of wearing trousers lower down, below the natural waistline. However, most men look better with trousers worn higher, at the natural waist, since the paunch is covered entirely by fabric. If you have a widening waist, suspenders help to hide it and allow pants to hang more gracefully. Well-made suit trousers have six suspender buttons sewn into the inside waistband. (Without them, the would-be wearer of suspenders is out of luck, since the clip-on type is really for casual use or construction work.)

How long should my pants be? The proper length of trousers is a matter of some debate. The term for the proper length is referred to as the break. Generally, pants should be long enough to cause a slight break over the instep of the shoes. Too much break looks sloppy. In nearly all cases, suit trousers should be cuffed (short men sometimes opt for cuffless pants to increase the unbroken vertical line of the ensemble). The cuffs themselves should be from $1\frac{5}{8}$ to $1\frac{3}{4}$ inches.

Do you jingle while you walk? Are balled-up bills, taxi receipts, and phone numbers from chance occurrences spilling out of your pockets wherever you go? No matter how affluent and well-turned-out you are, you won't look good if your pockets bulge with junk.

wallets & pockets

Wallets made of leather are a basic necessity for the well-dressed man, assuming you have any cash left over after your many assignations with your tailor. The old-fashioned center-folded man's wallet filled with photos and Celtics ticket stubs, stowed fatly in your back pocket, is a thing of the past. Slim, adaptable wallets are the way to go. Many men now have a large billfold that they use for carrying money, traveler's checks, letters of credit, and their passport while on the road, and a smaller wallet for carrying credit cards, business cards, and other small documents while in town. When packed tightly, the smaller card wallet holds your credit cards in place even better and still fits neatly in the inside pocket of a suit jacket. By the way, not all leathers are created equal. Cowhide is stout and practical. Pigskin is in the upper class. Alligator and ostrich are among the choicest. Whatever the wallet style, you should bring it along whenever you are buying a suit, so you can ensure that the suit fits smoothly with all your normal accessories in the pockets. **Agendas.** Those massive agendas that became ubiquitous in the 1980s have given way to more manageable leather books, and even electronic memo pads. If you are a gentleman with many engagements, from breakfast through dinner, you may want to have a large agenda for the office and a slim leather agenda with a single page devoted to each day of the week to carry along with you. **Penknives.** A small penknife is a handy thing to have, even if you would prefer a buck knife to protect yourself from ferocious colleagues. The smallest Swiss Army version has two blades, including one with a file surface for nail care, and a tiny pair of scissors, which is indispensable for trimming frayed ties and loose threads on clothing. Or shop in antique and second-hand stores for a penknife with patina, a simple instant heirloom. Some old ones were intended to be used with a watch chain.

Pocket Science. These days, leaving cash in a wallet greatly reduces the chances of getting the wallet returned when it is misplaced—which, inevitably, happens. So you will want to keep your wad in your pocket. (Leave a fiver in your wallet with a note suggesting the bearer use it for return postage. And place all the cards and licenses on a copy machine and make a copy.) To keep your cash well organized, invest in a nice money clip, preferably silver or gold, with enough flex to accommodate plenty of bills—and to bounce back when you're tapped down to just a few. Keep keys and coins to a minimum. Leave your comb in your jacket. Stop fiddling around in there.

building a shirt wardrobe

Since most of us dump our jackets within minutes of arriving at work, the shirt has become, along with the necktie, a principal means of fashion expression for men.

Wardrobe. To meet the exigencies of life, a man needs a carefully maintained group of dress shirts in various colors, including several in white, neatly ironed and stacked in the wardrobe for quick selection. As the designer John Weitz is fond of saying, "Nine-tenths of our days are spent sitting at desks in offices, and we might as well be bare-assed below table level." A clean, crisp dress shirt makes an impression, whether overt or subliminal, so you will want to wear each only once before laundering. Because at some point the laundry will rip and shred your dress shirt, it makes sense to have a generous supply of them, particularly the basic straight-point-collared dress shirt with two-button barrel cuffs. A dozen or more are mandatory for most office workers, to allow for daily rotation and a reasonable lag between launderings.

Fit. Shirts are generally purchased without being tried on, which creates obvious problems. Know your neck size and sleeve length to the half-inch, and have yourself remeasured if you've gained or lost a lot of weight. When purchasing an all-cotton shirt, buy it one-half inch larger than your size in both the neck and the sleeve to allow for shrinkage. Never compromise, even if the store has your favorite stripe only in your exact size. Buy big. If the collar fits perfectly when you take it out of the package, take it back. There's nothing you can do about a tight collar once the shirt has been washed.

Collar Shape. Shirt collars are like an extension of your face, which is in turn the focal point of your entire fashion presentation. The collars you choose can either enhance or detract from the image. If you have a full or round face, long-pointed collars—$3\frac{1}{2}$ to $3\frac{3}{4}$ inches in length—create a lengthening effect that offsets the fullness of the face. Conversely, button-down collars are to be avoided by heavyset, full-faced men (precisely the sort of guys, the designer Alan Flusser often points out, who usually wear them). The spread collar is ideal for men with medium to long and narrow faces, since it imparts an illusion of width. Rounded collars, needless to say, only accentuate a round face. Men with long, thin necks should consider high-banded shirt collars or tab collars. The medium, oval-faced man can wear what he wants, but medium-size collars suit him best.

Band Collars. In the 1980s, men's wear manufacturers created a vogue for the so-called band-collar shirt, actually a facsimile of the nineteenth-century dress shirt, which was made with a detachable shirt collar to make it easier to wash. Today, the band-collar shirt does not come with a detachable collar and is meant to be worn casually.

Collar Bars. Another collar expression from the turn of the century that makes periodic returns. It is either a simple pin or a clip to gather the collar ends beneath the knot of the tie. A variation of the tab-collar look.

Collar Gallery *(counterclockwise from bottom left, then center).* **1.** THE LONG, STRAIGHT-POINT COLLAR flatters a variety of facial types and can be worn with any style of suit. **2.** THE CUTAWAY, OR SPREAD, COLLAR, popularized in the 1930s by the Duke of Windsor, is usually worn by thin-faced men with a predilection for dressiness. **3.** THE BUTTON-DOWN COLLAR was copied by Brooks Brothers from an English polo shirt that had collar points buttoned to keep them from flapping. It is the quintessential Ivy League style. **4.** THE TAB COLLAR, with snap button, keeps the tie in place, with a nice forward tilt, throughout the day, also first worn by the Duke of Windsor. **5.** THE ETON COLLAR, so named for Eton schoolboys, requires a collar pin.

Procol Harum, "A Whiter Shade of Pale"

Fabrics. If quality is your aim (and it should be), 100 percent cotton will be the fabric for your dress shirts. Cotton breathes and absorbs perspiration, which adds up to comfort. It also holds colors well and stands up to repeated washings. Pima cotton, a designation found on better dress shirts, is named for Pima County, Arizona, and represents a fine-quality long-staple cotton that was developed for American cultivation from Egyptian cottons. Sea Island cotton refers to an excellent cotton with a silky hand, originally raised in the West Indies and later grown on islands off the coast of the south-eastern United States.

Shirt Simple. Historically, the white shirt evolved as the standard of business appropriateness because it requires laundering after each wearing, thus distinguishing its wearers in the work force from less impeccable "blue-collar" types. It serves as a perfect neutral ground on which to play the various patterns and colors of one's suits and neckties. A white open-neck shirt with Levi's is a great casual look that is timeless. Yet, buttoned or tied, it provides the option of instant formality—a clean, starched one should be kept in an office drawer for evening or special events. Not all white shirts are created equal, of course. Egyptian and Sea Island cottons, with their satiny texture, stand at the top of the pyramid. Poplin and broadcloth are next, followed by the rougher weave of oxford cloth, the fabric of the basic Brooks Brothers button-down. For hot weather, linen and silk offer both luxury and comfort. Look for single-needle stitching, a more costly method of sewing that results in consistent, careful seams—and gauntlet buttons on the sleeve opening above the cuff.

CASUAL WORK SHIRTS

Friday Shirt. Expanding the vocabulary of dress shirts, men are wearing more rugged shirts with or without their neckties. Denim and chambray shirts are at the forefront of this movement, worn affectionately by baby boomers who perhaps wish to bring the talismans of their rebellious youth into the corporate environments they had vowed to change. Madras plaids, tattersalls, khakis, and figured shirts increasingly are being worn to the office. Some are made of conventional dress-shirt fabrics but have a casual-shirt configuration—for example, a white cotton broadcloth camp shirt with flap pockets. In most cases you need a thinner-tying tie to fit under the collars of such shirts. Remember, the collar points should rest on the body of the shirt when the tie is knotted. When they don't, you look stuffed.

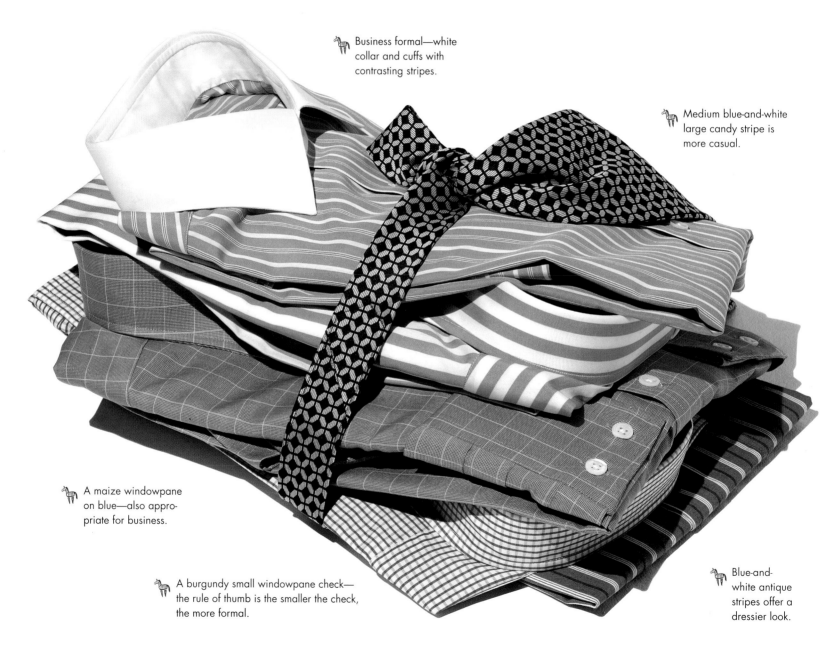

Business formal—white collar and cuffs with contrasting stripes.

Medium blue-and-white large candy stripe is more casual.

A maize windowpane on blue—also appropriate for business.

A burgundy small windowpane check— the rule of thumb is the smaller the check, the more formal.

Blue-and-white antique stripes offer a dressier look.

Men's shirtings come in a wide array of patterns, colors, and fabrics. Candy-stripe oxford. Pencil-stripe broadcloth. Blue pima oxford. Pink end-on-end. And so on. The play of patterns and textures can rev up a wardrobe—or make your eyes swim.

Mixing. A man should not be afraid to experiment a little with shirt and tie patterns. In some ensembles, the dress shirt serves as a neutral backdrop; in others, the shirt becomes the star. One should always exercise restraint when mixing a patterned shirt with other garments. Shirt, tie, and suit must all be compatible; one false move can make you look as if you were pulsating. As a general rule, limit yourself to two patterns per outfit. For example, if the shirt is striped, then either the suit or the tie should be solid. It is also best to avoid combining patterns that are too similar in motif or that have no change in scale.

Stripes on Stripes. Stripes can get along together as long as they are of sufficiently varying gauges. A widely spaced, bold-striped tie will pair well with a narrow-spaced, hairline-striped shirt. Indeed, any fine-line striped dress shirt works with virtually any boldly patterned tie, whether it be paisley, foulard, medallion, or an all-over print. The colors, however, must balance well. On occasion, you can get away with an outfit of three patterns—for instance, a pinstripe suit, a very narrowly striped shirt, and a thick-striped tie. But be careful: you don't want to look like a schematic diagram for a Pentium processor.

Checks. It is usually difficult to wear checks with other checks, unless there is a sharp differentiation in scale. A bird's-eye suit should not be worn with a diminutive-check shirt. A Prince of Wales–check suit would certainly clash with a tattersall shirt. However, a muted Glen plaid suit worn with a striped shirt and a figured tie makes perfect visual sense. And a tattersall-check shirt works with a tweed suit, like herringbone, since it expresses the country flavor of the suit while counterposing a very different pattern. A rep tie in related colors would finish the picture.

Tattersall is a checked pattern of two or more contrasting colors on a light background—the name comes from the eighteenth-century horse-auction house of the same name in London and the common pattern of their horse blankets.

Reality Checks. Combining checks with other checks is risky business. However, checked shirts pair especially well with thick-striped ties, figured ties, and solid knit ties. Other good combinations: striped shirts and dotted ties; hairline-striped shirts and rep ties; contrast-collar shirts and dotted or figured ties.

COLOR

The colors of fashion are personally evocative, and the subtlety and skill with which a man uses them have a great effect on his everyday image.

In recent years, the word "suit" has come to denote not just a tailored ensemble but the boring, predictable company man within it, his personality as dour and regimented as his uniform. But business dressing does not have to be a dull, monochromatic exercise. Even a plain gray or blue business suit can be enlivened with well-matched, colorful accessories. **What colors are best for you?** While there are few ironclad rules, certain color guidelines make good sense. Redheads, for example, should avoid brilliant colors, especially red, in favor of browns, medium grays, and greens. Fair people should avoid lighter shades of gray, tan, and yellow. Dark-haired men have the most latitude; they look terrific in dark gray and can safely wear bright ties. Brown-haired men look good in blue but should probably avoid dark brown suits. Men with gray or white hair look best in dark blue and should be leery of pale tones, which tend to render them inconspicuous. The next question is: **How does one mix colors effectively?** Two principles serve as guidelines in matching suits, shirts, and accessories: color *harmony* and color *contrast*. Color harmony involves combining different shades of the same color: navy suit, light blue shirt, dark blue–figured tie, and black shoes. The harmonizing impulse is very strong, and most men tend to dress in this manner. Choosing hues that contrast can also make for effective combinations. With a blue suit, a red-and-white striped shirt, a maroon and gold tie, and brown shoes are reasonable options. The choices are limitless, but a degree of sophistication is required. In general, choose shirt colors that are lighter than the suit. Close matching of shirt color to suit evokes a Cosa Nostra underling and should be reserved for off hours.

A Bit of T&A. Since most successful, well-dressed men lean toward the classic in tailoring, a certain genre of bold, colorful dress shirt has arisen as a means of relieving the solemnity of it all. The best known of these are made by Turnbull & Asser of Jermyn Street, London. Shirts by T&A, as it is known among acolytes, typically combine the flamboyance of strong patterns and colors with the formality of high, generous collars and French cuffs. The rich, jewel-toned shirts of Charvet of Paris and the striking shades of Thomas Pink of London also belong to this movement, which makes the shirt the player rather than just a backdrop in the ensemble.

"I can't wear a pink shirt to work. Everybody wears white shirts. I'm not popular enough to be different."
Homer Simpson

THE BLUES

Blue Wardrobe *(from left to right)*
• Blue gingham check
• French blue polished cotton
• Blue double-track-stripe broadcloth
• Mini-herringbone denim

Next to white, blue is the most versatile color in the masculine shirt wardrobe. Indeed, after a long day of meetings, lunch, more meetings, and a business dinner, a blue shirt looks a lot neater than white. Blue also goes with just about everything and suits all complexions and hair shades. Not surprisingly, it's the favorite clothing color in both the United States and England. While a light blue oxford-cloth dress shirt has long been a conservative business staple, the deeper cornflower and French blues are becoming more fashionable, paired with a dark tie. And, of course, the casual Friday phenomenon has made even the rich indigo of denim shirts acceptable in some offices.

Striped shirts pair well with bright-figured ties.

The dark monochromatic color coupled with strong vertical stripes creates a thinning effect.

Blue is a harmonizing color that can quietly coordinate the rest of an ensemble.

The square toe, though considered a contemporary look, was popular with men in the Edwardian era.

Striped shirts, originally called "regatta shirts" and deemed unsuitable for business wear, are now conservative staples. In general, the narrower the stripe, the more conservative the shirt.

The three-button wool crepe suit can be made formal with a tie or casual with a cashmere T-shirt.

"Blue is the color worn by all Britons of good standing. In war we stain our bodies blue; so that though our enemies may strip us of our clothes and our lives, they cannot strip us of our respectability." *George Bernard Shaw*, **Caesar and Cleopatra**

ON THE CUFF

In an era of nose rings and studded tongues, the well-dressed wrist is a frequently overlooked element in men's fashion. Don't let it be. When wearing a suit, a man should always show one-half inch of shirt cuff—the same as at the collar. This involves two preliminary steps: first, having the jacket tailored properly, and second, buying shirts with sleeves long enough to allow for shrinkage. If the shirt has French cuffs, it will require suitable cuff links, usually in silver or gold. The fabric-knot style, quite popular among eighties power dressers, is acceptable for day wear. The little bicolored balls evoke the two-tone old-boy masculinity of rep ties and contrast-collar shirts. Double-sided links connected by a chain are more difficult to put on than the retractable-bar type, but they fit more evenly and offer an esthetic touch to both sides of the shirt cuff. A resurgence of interest in French-cuff shirts has led to a revival of antique cuff links, which are now carried not only at vintage jewelers but at fine men's wear stores too. There's nothing wrong with theme and novelty cuff links, which often add a touch of whimsy to your look. Not too cute or flashy, though—you don't want the boss or clients to think you're a lightweight (unless that helps in your line of work). Jeweled cuff links are usually reserved for evening, when they add sparkle and individuality to the black tuxedo and white shirt. Generally speaking, masculine jewelry should be small, unobtrusive, and well matched to the outfit and situation. So save your emerald links set in 18-karat gold for black-tie affairs or visits to the Liberace Museum.

Wrist Shots. A double cuff that turns back and is usually fastened with a cuff link, the French cuff makes an elegant statement at the wrist. Again, if you purchase a shirt with a contrasting collar and cuffs, the cuffs should always be French cuffs.

Cuffed (opposite page, clockwise from top left) 1. Typewriter keys, subdued enough for daytime but also perfect for the color scheme of black tie. 2. Fabric-knot cuff links place an understated dot of color and texture at the sleeve. 3. Simple angled metal links sit better on the cuff and bind the two sides more smoothly; jeweled cuff links should be worn after dark, either with a dressy suit or with black tie. One set of silver and one set of gold bars or ovals can last a lifetime. 4. Novelty links, particularly elegant vintage ones, are conversation pieces and a great way to dress up a suit.

Vintage Rolex with rose-gold face is classy, individualistic, and appropriate on all occasions.

The stainless-steel dive watch, fine for work and the weekend and perfect for casual Fridays.

"I love watches. I own many. Not for the time, but for the way

TIME MACHINES

White-gold-and-silver wristwatch can go from work to evening—the Roman numerals make a more formal statement.

Steel wristwatch with lighted dial. Its simplicity and practicality can take you anywhere.

The wrist is an area for chic understatement. So why overwhelm it with a giant chunky watch or one of those plastic jobs that beep uncontrollably at the worst possible moment? Just as large finger rings on a man suggest other vulgarian tendencies, an overly aggressive watch hints at the grasping intensity of a David Mamet character. Similarly, a thin, skimpy watch pegs you as effete, a pushover. Instead, go for the classic. Rugged construction. Refined shapes. Stainless steel. Sweep hands. Numerals. Flexible band for comfort. The kind of wristwatch Gary Cooper might have worn in *The Fountainhead*. A good everyday business watch, whether it be a Rolex or a Timex, is one that tells you at an instant whether you're late or not—and, with careful observation of the sweep hand, how long your rival has been droning on in a meeting. You will own a different watch for sports, especially if you are involved in lap-timed ones. And for black tie, it makes sense to have a special watch, perhaps a vintage piece or a swank tank—the thinness, rectangular shape, Roman numerals, and leather strap reinforce the dressed-up mood. Indeed, it makes very good sense to build a watch collection that mixes and matches effectively with the rest of your wardrobe.

they look. Why do I need to know the right time?" *Issey Miyake*

BUILDING A TIE WARDROBE

A man collects and receives (and refuses to wear) countless neckties throughout his life. How many should you own? Five seems like enough (one for each workday). But to some men, fifty is not enough.

Fashion and Ties. Ties are the simplest, least expensive way to update and invigorate your wardrobe, and acquiring them is an ongoing process. If a man wears a jacket and tie to work, he needs a generous supply—at least a dozen—both to relieve the monotony of daily dressing and to keep pace with changing fashions. For example, heavily figured ties were all the rage in the 1980s, but the end of the century has brought a reaction against such busy patterns. Stripes and solids, simple and direct, have made a comeback. Without altering the relatively changeless aspects of your wardrobe—suit silhouette, shoe shape—you can stay in the swing by updating your ties. The style of tie you buy and wear is a highly subjective matter, but following a few basic guidelines can help in building a wearable collection.

Quality. As in all things sartorial, start with quality. High-quality ties are woven of 100 percent silk, lined with silk, and inter-lined with muslin. Hold the tie at either end and gently pull. A good tie will spring back into shape. Better ties use the same silk facing fabric to make the self loop at the back, which on the finest ties is stitched into the center seam. Inexpensive ties simply sew a label across the folded blade. Examine the silk. Is it rich and lustrous? In the end, you have to judge by the tie's feel, or "hand."

Universal Tie. If you were tired of constant decisions, you could live with only one tie. The black knit tie, in wool or silk, is perhaps the most versatile necktie a man can own. It's appropriate in any context (including funerals), goes with everything (from patterned shirts to denim), and can be easily rolled for packing on trips.

"The man who walks alone is soon trailed by the F.B.I." *Wright Morris*

Typology. DIAGONALLY STRIPED ties belong in almost every man's wardrobe, regardless of whether you went to prep school or fought in a regiment. The downward knifing of the stripes tends to alleviate the fullness of one's face and give graphic punch to the outfit. Most men own several such REP (or repp) ties, made of corded silk with a crosswise weave and diagonal stripes. REGIMENTAL ties look just like rep ties, but the colors and widths of the stripes pertain to a particular British regiment (all of whose members may have perished long, long ago). Few Americans can tell the difference. CLUB ties are of two basic types: a solid silk background with small insignia repeated in rows, or solid regimental stripes. Again, the designs have become so popular that few people know what they mean anymore. FOULARD ties are made of a lightweight silk twill and often have printed figures; they go well with striped shirts. CHALLIS, a lightweight worsted fabric used in both solid and printed tie designs, works well with nubbier shirts and tweedy suits. MACCLESFIELD ties (the term is used interchangeably with SPITALFIELDS, districts in England where they were originally woven) have rough, open silk weaves with small, compact, allover patterns—like the beautiful silver-and-black check of the wedding tie. POLKA-DOT ties are worth mentioning for their overall elegance and simplicity, as well as for their great utility when combined with pinstriped suits. GRENADINE SILK ties are loosely woven with an irregular surface.

Friday Whimsy. The bow tie in daytime suggests a thoughtful, even professorial type, not to mention an individualist. It has practically become an idiosyncratic look, except for formal evening wear. But it is an option that's nice to have around on occasion. On a hot day, for instance, a madras bow tie goes especially well with a seersucker suit. A brocade bow tie with a dark suit is a nice change of pace for the theater. If you choose to wear bow ties, they must be hand-tied (see tying instructions, page 183). A pre-tied or, worse, clip-on bow marks you as an outsider.

ties take you all the way to casual Friday

4

"Give me a sincere tie—I'm on my way to a very important meeting in my life."
Clark Gable, in **The Hucksters**

This chic quartet is all you need. No matter how many ties you have, you probably wear only a few regularly. These are your favorites, the ones that you dig and that work with your other stuff. In fact, four good ones can carry you through the week: 1. A brightly patterned silk tie that looks good with both solids and stripes, like an Hermès, which also looks the money. 2. A classy small- or medium-dot silk tie, the perfect foil for pinstripes and other dressy suits (large dots are less formal). 3. A woven silk Macclesfield tie, both elegant and masculine with its intricate, smallish patterns. 4. A striped silk rep tie, which exerts a salutary effect on the male countenance, its downward diagonals cutting away from the fullness of a fleshy face.

Woven tie

Striped rep tie

Medium-dotted tie

Hermès abstract-pattern tie

GETTING IT RIGHT

Unforgettable. When you experience a great style epiphany, a moment of blinding insight that transforms your entire Weltanschauung regarding, say, suits and striped ties, you want to lock it away in your fashion memory forever. And then you forget. It may be a tie and shirt combination that you liked a lot but decided not to wear that day. You could wear that second choice next week with the same suit—if you remember. It makes good sense to do what fashion professionals have long done: Polaroid the look, then tack to the back of your closet door. As any stylist will tell you, when you've put together an outfit with just the right clothes and accessories, make an image of it. With today's digital cameras, you can easily download these certified good looks into a computer for easy access. It's not for posterity, of course, but it may come in handy during a momentary style crisis. Snap on.

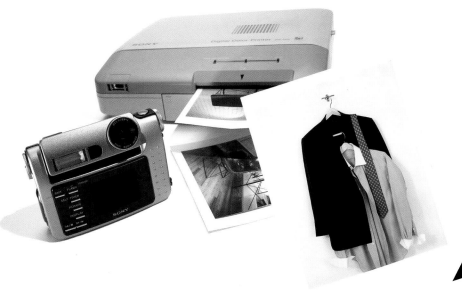

Sometimes standing before the mirror in the morning a man manages a magical combination, an exceptionally satisfying congregation of shirt, tie, and jacket. It may not be a mix that follows all the rules, but the little bit of heresy involved makes it even better. Take the outfit opposite: a windowpane (large check) charcoal-gray suit worn with a fine-line windowpane tie and a large-check pocket square—all similar patterns, in similar scale. Very risky, no? Yet the overall look works on a couple of levels. There is a mix of strong counterpoints—the pinned, rounded (club) collar against the sharp single-breasted peaked lapels; the crisp pink and white of the shirt against the soft, dark charcoal of the suit—as well as close harmonies, in this case not of color but of pattern: the windowpane theme carried through the suit, tie, and pocket square. Rules are made to be broken, but you've got to be sophisticated enough to know that you are breaking them. This is what transforms dressing into an act of personal style.

Pocket Square Do's and Don'ts. A plain, inexpensive white cotton handkerchief is perfectly acceptable as a pocket square with any suit.
• Colored pocket squares should complement or coordinate with (never match precisely) the color or pattern of the tie.
• Opposing textures of pocket square and necktie are a nice touch: for a silk tie use a linen square; for a wool tie, use a silk square.
• Never blow your nose with a pocket square. Carry a separate handkerchief for that (as the saying goes, "one for show and one for blow").
• Don't show too much linen—an inch to an inch and half above the suit's breast pocket is plenty. If your handkerchiefs have monograms, don't let them show outside the breast pocket.

"To be nobody-but-yourself—in a world which is doing its best, night and day, to make you everybody else—means to fight the hardest battle which any human being can fight; and never stop fighting." *e. e. cummings*

Eyeglasses were originally symbols of wealth and privilege, dating from a time (the late Middle Ages) when few people could read, let alone gain access to a book. Nowadays glasses are, variously, signs of intelligence, advancing age, or willful nerdiness. In an age of soft contact lenses, spectacles might even seem somewhat obsolete. But glasses are also accoutrements of style and can become a person's signature look. Think Buddy Holly, Groucho Marx, Spike Lee, Yves Saint Laurent, Clark Kent. Who would they be without their glasses? Choosing your glasses is a little bit like choosing your identity.

GLASSES

Case Study. Eyeglasses need to be stored in a hard case or else they will get scratched or eventually crushed. Most opticians now carry hard cases. Designer glasses usually come in chic designer cases, but not everyone wants to spend the extra money. Men who need to take their glasses off and put them on again often during the day should invest in a nice structured case, either metal or leather. It will protect the eyewear and also make a subtle fashion statement of its own.

Wire Rim. Lightweight and durable, they have a professorial, contemplative look that was very popular in the sixties, and is again in the nineties. Gold and bronze are best for light-haired men; chrome and black for brown- and gray-haired men.

Horn Rim. The quintessential nerd glasses, most horn rims are not made of animal horn at all but of plastic. Horn rims make you look smart, if somewhat unglamorous. Computer geeks and rocket scientists wear them. So do architects. Heavyset men can use rectangular-shaped frames to offset a chubby face.

Tortoiseshell. The favorite of preppies every-where, tortoiseshell frames are no longer made of tortoiseshell but of plastic. The distinctive speckled effect, resembling an animal print, is fashionable and flattering to most complexions.

Reading Glasses. When you find yourself squinting mightily at the phone book or NASDAQ listings, you are about to confront the dimming of life in general—or another style opportunity. Reading glasses confer instant wisdom and maturity. Half lenses, perched precariously on the end of one's nose, enable the farsighted to look out over the glasses at other extraneous objects. Folding glasses have a special kind of elegance.

City & Country. Some men wear their clothes in a way that suggests urban sophistication, with carefully contrived elegant touches, like contrast-collar dress shirts and puffed silk pocket squares. Others choose to convey a more down-to-earth persona, using soft wool fabrics, plaid shirts, and friendly ties. This clash between the sophisticated and the bucolic reflects the history of men's fashions, which owe their conventions to both city life and the more Arcadian existence of the English country gentleman. As the writer Alison Lurie has pointed out, urban and rural British dress was based on the principle of harmonizing with one's environment.

mixed messages

In the country, browns, tans, blues, and greens, especially in the muted tones associated with damp weather, were favored. Soft, fuzzy textures like tweed corresponded to the textures of bark and leaf. Corduroy mimicked the look of a plowed field. Urban clothes tended to be hard-surfaced, like the gray stonework of the office buildings. How you wear your wardrobe is a very individual thing, but be aware that the dialectic between city and country has resulted in a new synthesis in which a more casual and rustic style has successfully blended into the modern workplace.

The casualness of the plaid is balanced by the straight point collar, the antique cuff links, and the wing-tip shoes.

The button-down collar "relaxes" the look, yet remains businesslike.

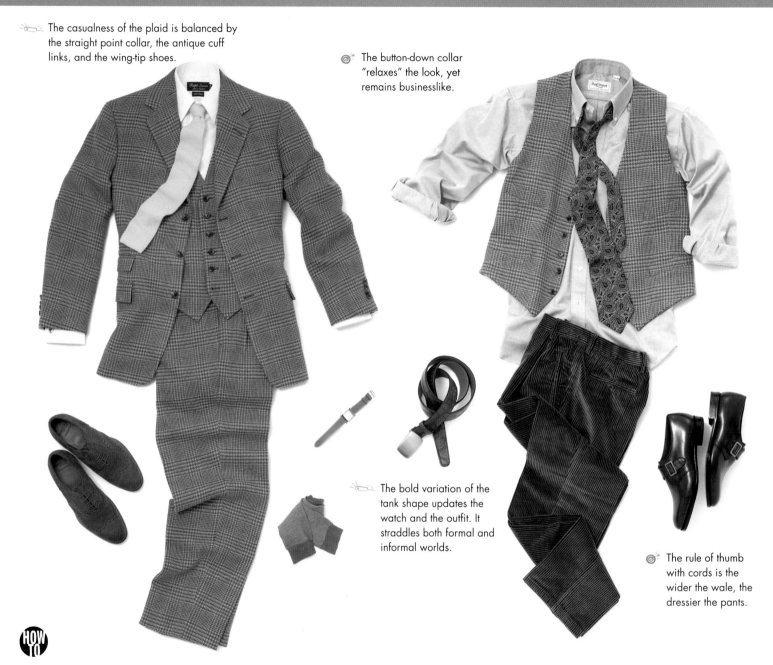

The bold variation of the tank shape updates the watch and the outfit. It straddles both formal and informal worlds.

The rule of thumb with cords is the wider the wale, the dressier the pants.

4 in 1. The three-piece suit multiplies the options you have. First and foremost, it gives you a strong and authoritative tailored look when worn as intended, with all three pieces coordinated with, say, a white cotton dress shirt, cashmere tie, and brown suede wing-tip shoes. Such a suit in Glen plaid, both sporty and formal, will be appropriate anywhere, except at some financial institutions. Remove the jacket and wear the vest with a pair of corduroys, a button-down shirt, and a paisley tie, and the look becomes more relaxed. You are now one of the "creatives" instead

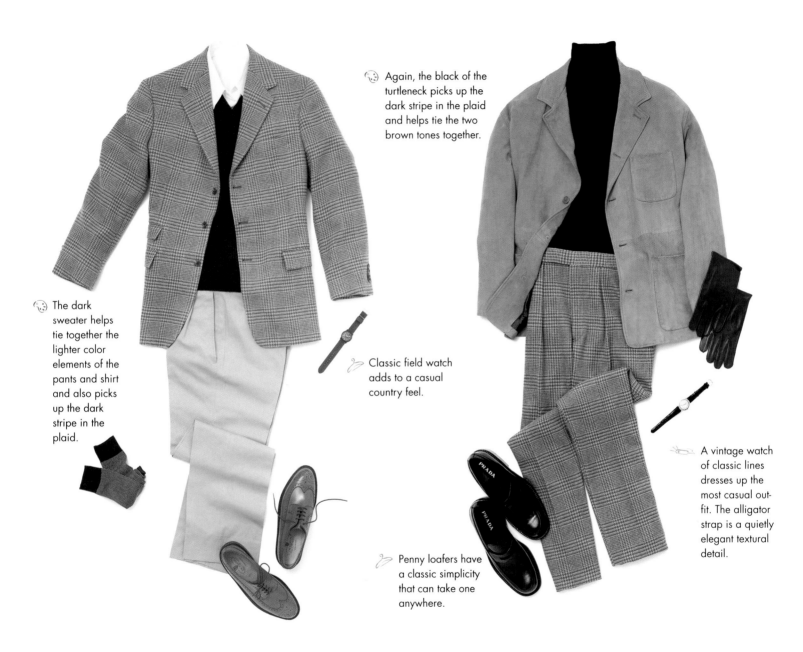

Again, the black of the turtleneck picks up the dark stripe in the plaid and helps tie the two brown tones together.

The dark sweater helps tie together the lighter color elements of the pants and shirt and also picks up the dark stripe in the plaid.

Classic field watch adds to a casual country feel.

A vintage watch of classic lines dresses up the most casual outfit. The alligator strap is a quietly elegant textural detail.

Penny loafers have a classic simplicity that can take one anywhere.

of one of the "suits." Your wool Glen plaid jacket has definite country roots (it was named for the Glen Urquhart valley in Scotland). The jacket worn with a V-neck sweater and tan slacks seems perfect for a woodsy walk on a fall day, or perhaps some casual urban strolling.

Lastly, the pleated, self-belting trousers can be a standout addition to a casual outfit, dressing up a suede blazer and cashmere turtleneck for those times when you need to be well turned out but a jacket and tie will not do. It's all about understanding what you have and how to use it.

sleeveless cardigan

wool vest

vested interest

lapel vest

Polartec vest

tweed vest

leather vest

The vest dresses up or down, depending on how it is worn. The vest adds interest to a suit, where it can be either a matching piece of the tailored ensemble or a contrasting layer. Now the vest has resurfaced as a stand-alone accessory, and many men wear vests casually, with a sport jacket, a band-collar shirt, or even jeans and a T-shirt. A vest should fit snugly but not be skintight, and the penultimate button should cover the waistline, the cutaway points extending just below the waist. Vests and belts do not go together unless you are not going to wear the vest closed.

suede vest

ribbed sleeveless cardigan

Do you button all the buttons?
Because of the royal girth of Edward VII, who had to leave his bottom vest button unfastened, tradition has dictated that one doesn't button the bottom.

work
sweaters

Cardigan. Worn with a shirt and tie to the office, the cardigan, a sweater that buttons like a jacket, conveys a gentle, forbearing image. Named for the seventh Earl of Cardigan, who led the charge of the Light Brigade during the Crimean War, it was popularized by the singer Andy Williams on television in the 1960s. Sweaters were originally developed for workingmen and athletes, and the cardigan, particularly when made of alpaca, came to be associated with golf. A black or charcoal-gray cardigan in cashmere or merino wool goes well under a variety of suits and leaves the wearer feeling somewhat dressed after the suit jacket has been doffed.

V-neck. This versatile style permits a triangle of dress shirt and tie to show, thus making it office ready. In plain colors like gray and blue, or in a sleeveless argyle pattern, it is an attractive alternative to a waistcoat under suits. It's flattering, since the V shape draws the eye downward to a point and offsets the fullness of the face. Cashmere V-necks have the advantage of being very lightweight and soft, so one can remain cool and comfortable in a heated office. In more artistic work environments, the cashmere V-neck can be worn with a T-shirt—or just against bare skin.

Mr. Rogers goes downtown, with his usual cashmere cardigan, but in a totally black-and-white palette it becomes a powerful, casual business look that is suitable for evening entertaining.

The polo sweater, like its brother the polo shirt, has moved from sportswear to street wear, and offers a relaxed but dressy look beneath a suit jacket. It has become a versatile component of the new casual dressing in the office. Worn with a shirt and tie quietly revealed beneath its buttons, or over a dark T-shirt, or even alone, it looks good in a wide range of business situations.

SOCK 'EM

One of the great unchallenged laws of masculine attire is that a glimpse of hairy leg above the stocking is shocking. So for business wear, you want an ample supply of dark, calf-length socks. The idea is to maintain a fairly monochromatic line all the way down from pant leg to shoe, without any star-tling interruptions. Sophisticated dressers eventually create interest with their hosiery. Wool argyles and figured socks introduce some color and pattern at the ankle. In general, hosiery color should echo the colors of the suit or tie without exactly matching either. Black is safe and they always match.

BELT 'EM

Good leather belts are a sound investment. They should match or be related in color to your shoes. While belts and buckles have gotten larger over the years, garrison-width belts and bulky novelty buckles are not a terrific idea for most offices. Braided leather and leather-covered metal buckles, once found only on casual belts, have become fashionable for business wear. For heirloom elegance it's hard to beat a plain silver buckle with an alligator belt. But save your chain belt or saddle belt with double-pronged buckle for weekends unless you work at a biker bar.

Casual Work Shoes. The new, more relaxed spirit of business dressing is symbolized by loafers. They can be found in all styles and shapes; the skimpy, low-vamp models popular during the 1980s are no longer de rigueur. Dress shoes with ridged or rubber lug soles—reflecting the pervasive rugged, outdoorsy trend in fashion—are now worn with suits in many offices. Monk-strap shoes, with a side buckle instead of laces, can be worn as either dress or casual shoes. The half-boot or Chelsea boot, originally worn by manual laborers, is now seen with everything from casual trousers to pinstriped suits. Suede shoes, which came into vogue in the 1930s thanks to the Duke of Windsor's sense of style, can either be quite elegant, like the lace-ups made by Church's of London, or more knockabout, like various rubber-soled wing-tip models.

SOLE SEARCHING

Shoe Simple. The cap-toed black leather brogue is perhaps the dressiest and most adaptable business shoe. It gets along well with your navy suit and is also on speaking terms with your tuxedo (be sure to polish highly before wearing to a black-tie event). You can wear it to a wedding or a funeral, a nightclub or a board meeting. While the lawyerish plain cap toe is a bit stark, there are versions with a band of perforations at the toe and heel. In any case, buy a pair. Make sure the shoe's last, or shape, follows the line of your foot as closely as possible. Shoes should feel comfortable the first time you put them on. When you get them home, polish them (new shoes are most vulnerable to scuffs and scratches), and take good care of them. Leather shoes should not be worn on consecutive days, since the shoes need time to dry between wearings. They need a day to breathe. Always store them with a pair of shoe trees. The cedar type is best, but the less expensive plastic ones work just fine. Remove the shoe trees after they have been in for a day to avoid overstretching the shoes.

WHERE THE LEATHER MEETS THE ROAD. Clothes do not make the man, but his shoes are a telltale indicator of something. Style? Breeding? Reliability? A guy wearing a beautiful new suit with a pair of worn-down, salt-stained, crepe-soled black lace-ups is clearly someone whose act is not completely together. The issue of comfort notwithstanding, most men need more than a couple of pairs of Air Jordans to meet the challenges of life. Since shoes, like suits, should not be worn two days in a row, a man should own enough pairs so that they can be rotated. Fred Astaire, whose shoes performed dazzling feats, kept trunks full of fine bench-made English shoes and insisted that he wore all of them regularly. As with anything in fashion, begin with high-quality basics, establishing a foundation on which to build.

IT'S A SHOE-IN

(faQ)

Can you wear brown shoes with dark suits?
Ask any Englishman—or Murray Pearlstein of Louis, Boston—and the only question will be, Why do you ask? Dark brown, well-cared for, and burnished with age looks perfectly respectable with most business suits. The older the leather, the more elegant the presentation.

"He's a gentleman: Look at his boots." *George Bernard Shaw,* **Pygmalion**

A logical place to start is with a sturdy pair of black leather lace-ups, either plain cap-toed or with perforations on the saddle or the tip. (Big black 1950s-style wing tips, oil tankers for the feet, no longer suit the more fitted look of contemporary tailored clothing.) On the principle that one's shoes should be at least as dark as one's suit, black goes with everything, especially gray and blue suits. Next would be a pair of brown wing tips or other type of plain or perforated saddle-brown shoe. These can be paired with tweed, gabardine, or brown suits. Then you are ready for a slip-on, perhaps a classic tasseled loafer in cordovan or chocolate suede, or a horsebit-buckle Gucci-style shoe.

WET &

A Classic Raincoat is indispensable for everyday business wear, even if you own a closetful of Gore-Tex jackets. It can be either a trench coat or a balmacaan (single-breasted with raglan sleeves), usually in cotton or wool gabardine, a fabric developed by Thomas Burberry in 1856 as a less stifling alternative to the rubber-lined macintosh. A good raincoat will be long enough to cover your suit jacket, which many sport rain jackets are not. It will also serve you on crisp, dry days when it is not cold enough for an overcoat. Reversible raincoats, like the one shown at left, are somewhat scarcer than they were a few decades ago. Some have a water-shedding fabric on one side and a wool topcoat fabric on the other. They give the wearer a second look and make an important wardrobe point: Good raincoats can be worn interchangeably with a regular topcoat in chilly weather.

A Dressy Overcoat belongs in every wardrobe, unless you live in the Sunbelt. The coat should be classically cut so that it can carry you through any occasion. It can be single-breasted—like a dark herringbone chesterfield with a fly front (a placket covers the buttonholes) or double-breasted—like a camel's hair or cashmere polo coat with patch pockets, cuffed sleeves, and half belt in back. The ideal coat length is just below the knee. Anything shorter cuts you visually in two and makes you look boyish. Anything too much longer engulfs the wearer and tends to drag on steps. When purchasing an overcoat, make sure you are wearing a suit jacket underneath to ensure that the sleeves are long enough and that you can put it on without the shoulders bunching.

COLD

There will never be a bag big enough for all of the paper in your life. Think in terms of hours of work, not stacks of files. Pack only as much as you can work on. Carrying work around may help your guilt but it doesn't help the job.

LEATHER BOXES

Hard Cases. Briefcases, attachés, or whatever else you use to lug around your paperwork and personal effects are also part of what you wear. The end of the twentieth century has been a time of casual elegance in men's wear, so lightweight, stylish briefcases have become the order of the day. While canvas and nylon bags have made major inroads in the market, leather continues to have great masculine appeal owing to its innate beauty and durability. These days, soft leather briefcases, often with a shoulder strap (a vestige of the "peacock revolution" of the 1960s), have somewhat replaced traditional hard, rectangular attachés. A variation on them is the expanded laptop briefcase, which has a separate, cushioned compartment for carrying your computer. But the traditional tan leather hard case, like the one made by Peal & Co. for Brooks Brothers (left), remains a classic. It has room for whatever you need, including your PowerBook, and its hard structure provides you with a table on the train and some legroom on the subway. Leather boxes are also traditional for men's furnishings. A leather tie case enables the traveler to keep his ties unwrinkled. Handkerchief cases segregate your linen from your underwear. Jewelry boxes with a fabric lining are essential for storing studs, cuff links, and tie bars. Leather manicure sets and shoe polish kits eventually find their way onto the top of your dresser. A leather toiletry case or Dopp kit with a waterproof lining is a must for overnight travel. (Cigarette cases and other stash boxes are probably too politically incorrect to mention.) The more complete one's wardrobe, the greater the need for handsome leather boxes to keep things organized.

Reality Trek. Even when John F. Kennedy Jr., a glamorous paragon of modern-day publishing, wears a pinstripe suit, he carries his stuff in a knapsack. While tough black nylon has made significant inroads, with manufacturers as diverse as Prada and Jansport capturing large parts of the market, leather remains a popular choice. Aside from its orthopedic advantages, a knapsack leaves your hands free to read the newspaper or fight your way through the commuting throngs. One caveat: quite unexpectedly you end up back-bumping lots of people and things, like Fritos displays in tight little bodegas.

MONDAY

Formal. Certain items in your wardrobe have great flexibility, taking on different personalities depending on the clothes with which they are combined. Take the classic camel cashmere polo coat, a big, roomy plush coat, with patch pockets in front and a half belt in back, which fairly exudes money and good breeding. The expense of the cashmere alone marks it as a luxurious garment. When worn with a dark business suit, the polo coat identifies its wearer as a briefcase-carrying member of the corporate elite. A bold statement of style and power.

FRIDAY

Informal. But the polo coat can also be a casual, sporty coat. It came to this country in the 1920s via members of English polo clubs, who wore them over their shoulders between chukkers on the verdant meadows of Nassau County, Long Island. The style was picked up by American college students, especially Ivy League types on the Eastern seaboard, and thus worked its way into the classic repertoire of well-heeled establishment folk. With a wool polo sweater and wool gabardine pants, it presents a picture of casual elegance, from the city to the country.

The tennis hat, a flat-crowned, soft-brimmed hat similar to a fisherman's hat, keeps the sun out of your eyes. Also worn by Woody Allen to keep the world out of his face.

The traditional tweed driving cap, with snap-down visor, once adorned only sporty nobs in two-seater cars and was accompanied by words like "Righto!" Plenty of regular sports wear them now, but they are not flattering to all face shapes.

Genuine Panama hats, made of the fine straw of the *jipijapa* plant and handwoven in Ecuador, supply summer elegance to one's upper story. The name has been extended to refer to almost any men's straw boater or brimmed straw hat with a ribbon band.

Logoed caps, especially vintage baseball caps, offer sun protection in an age of ozone-layer trepidations—as well as group identification in an era of anomie. Some people, curiously, even wish to be identified with their local discount retailer. The classiest are "gimme" hats, which by definition are free.

A vintage cowboy hat by Stetson, a manufacturer of all types of headgear. Western hats have long been worn by urban cowboys. Unless you're a ten-gallon type of guy, skip 'em. In some contexts they stick out like a mortarboard.

The fur trapper's hat has become fashionable in frigid climes, crowning the domes of both men and women. It provides excellent warmth using nature's insulator, usually rabbit or raccoon fur—and a bit of heat among the animal-rights crowd.

HAT TRICK

The look of the masculine noggin has changed radically from the 1950s, when all gentlemen wore hats and office buildings had separate entrances for the hatless. Automobile tops got lower, JFK went bareheaded to his inauguration, and prevailing casual winds have knocked the fedora off American men's heads. Today's hats are rugged, sporty, and inspired by function, not formality.

The Polartec fleece cap, with excellent insulating and water-shedding capabilities, has challenged the traditional knit watch cap for cranial eminence. Soft, durable, and washable.

"Have a nice weekend."

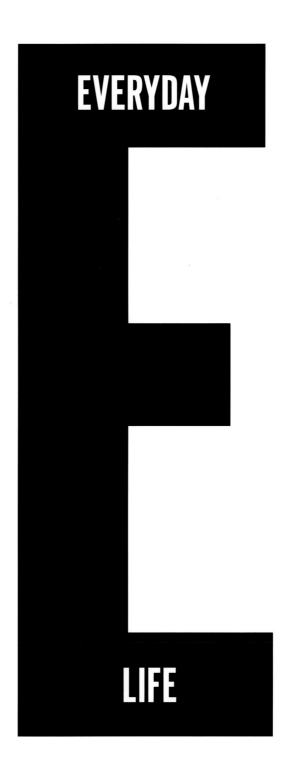

"Breakfast was Bond's favorite meal of the day. When he was stationed in London it was always the same. It consisted of very strong coffee, from De Bry in New Oxford Street, brewed in an American Chemex, of which he drank two large cups, black and without sugar. The single egg, in the dark blue egg cup with a gold ring around the top, was boiled for three and a third minutes. . . . Then there were two thick slices of whole wheat toast, a large pat of deep yellow Jersey butter and three squat glass jars containing Tiptree 'Little Scarlet' strawberry jam, Cooper's Vintage Oxford marmalade and Norwegian Heather Honey from Fortnum's. The coffee pot and the silver on the tray were Queen Anne, and the china was Minton, of the same dark blue and gold and white as the egg cup."

Ian Fleming, **From Russia with Love**

everyday clothes

Most of our sartorial existence revolves around work, but there is also the downtime, whether vacation, weekends, or even the twilight time between leaving work and going out. In an age when the line between work clothes and casual clothes has become blurred, there is now a great profusion of off-hours styles—sportswear, leisure clothes, club clothes—all blended with varying degrees of style and skill for the tailored wardrobe. Clothes to pack for a weekend getaway or a jaunt to Patagonia, with side trips to the tango bars of Buenos Aires. Clothes to wear to the COMDEX conference or to meet your wife's boss at the club. Clothes that you rely on, live in. Our favorite clothes. Clothes that make you feel good.

Saturday morning

Okay. So you sleep naked. But robes and pajamas are not just for sleeping. They are also lounging attire, clothes to eat breakfast in, and clothes to go out on the porch and get the morning paper in. Even if there is no one around to see you in them, they should at least be comfortable and attractive. Cotton oxford, chambray, and silk are fabrics to look for in pajamas. Seersucker is good for hot weather. In winter, flannel is the obvious choice. Before central heating, robes were an important part of men's wardrobes. A gentleman might have owned, among others, a silk foulard robe in a paisley pattern for lounging around the house, a solid-color velveteen jacket for entertaining, a terry-cloth robe for the beach or after a workout, a plaid or tan flannel robe with brown trim to wear on winter nights before retiring. Even if you think pajamas are square, you could still use a good robe or two. There is something a trifle corny about donning pajamas after a romantic liaison and something sexy about putting on a beautiful robe.

"Do I wear the top or bottoms tonight?"
Nancy Kwan, in **The World of Suzie Wong**

comfort clothes

Dressing for Your Computer.
A new fashion dynamic is sweeping the land, and it has nothing to do with status and seduction. With so many people working at home, the concept of public appearances recedes into the background and pure comfort comes to the fore. For some, the social demands of working require at most a single consulting meeting at lunch or after work. Style is reduced to the bare minimum. You really are dressing for you.

It's what we really wear, what we put on when we don't need to impress anybody, be anybody. When we just want to be. No thought. No edges. No styling. No statement. The sweatshirt you grab first thing on a Saturday morning. The leather moccasins you slip on to get the morning paper. Real comfort is not just the way they feel against your skin but the way they relax your head. This is a highly sub-jective, sometimes unfathomable realm. Richard Nixon wore dark busi-ness suits and lace-up shoes to walk on the beach. Scotsmen wear kilts. Everyone has his idiosyncrasies. The idea is to make you feel functional, unaffected, protected, cool.

denim

Denim sounds like an advertisement for the ideal man: Sexy. Rugged. Utilitarian. Gets better with age. Denim is the one fashion item that spans all generations, cultures, and political persuasions (Reagan wore them, and so does Clinton). Nearly everyone wears jeans (an anglicization of the French *Gênes*, for the Genoese sailors who wore a type of sturdy cotton pants made in Italy) or some other clothing made of the twill weave called denim (from the French *serge de Nîmes*, an early indigo denim fabric produced in the city of Nîmes). With the increasing informality of modern life, jeans are now the great staple of American costume, worn in all realms of life from the suburban mall to the wild West, from the office to the theater (alas). Creative types wear jeans with blazers or a crewneck sweater even to important business meetings. Unless you are a partner in Dreamworks, however, you probably should not.

The classic indigo-blue color, from the fermented leaves of plants of the genus *Indigofera* found in India and China, was not applied to the original jeans made by Levi Strauss in 1853. Those were an adaptation of a brown canvas fabric Strauss had been selling to miners for tents and wagons. In the 1860s, he switched to an indigo-dyed denim from a mill in New Hampshire. Denim is now dyed all kinds of colors, and distressed with many types of stone-washing and chemical processes. Elvis Presley wore black denim in the 1957 film *Jailhouse Rock*, and black has become denim's second color. Black jeans worn with a dark jacket have become almost a uniform among downtown types. White jeans, with their summery, resort look, cycle in and out of popularity.

Buying a pair of denim jeans used to be a snap; if you knew your waist and inseam, you just plunked down your money and gathered up a few pairs. But now there are so many cuts that selection can be a challenge. There are the traditional or classic cut (lean and straight throughout); the easy or relaxed fit (fuller in the seat and thigh); loose fit; and baggy (strictly for the homeboy at heart). Rappers like Naughty by Nature popularized oversized jeans, a look inspired by prison garb (where belts and shoelaces are forbidden), and taken to almost absurd extremes. A search for authenticity has inspired the jeans market in recent times. In 1993, Levi's introduced its Capital E 501s (a lot number assigned in the 1890s), which are cut to pre-1967 specifications, hand sewn, unwashed, and made at the company's original factory in San Francisco. Since the whole idea of jeans is their sexy, comfortable fit, some trial and error is advisable. You'll end up having some jeans you wear for fixing your motorcycle and some you wear on a date.

Pre-1967 Levi's 501 jeans, with the button fly, have become collectibles. (Fly-front jeans called Lee Riders were introduced in 1926 by H. D. Lee.) Levi's 501s became part of the permanent collection of the Smithsonian Institution in 1964. One 501 detail, the crotch rivet, was discontinued because of its heat-conducting properties. On a camping trip in 1941, the president of Levi Strauss, Walter Haas Sr., ventured too close to the fire and an executive decision was made.

DENIM SOLUTIONS

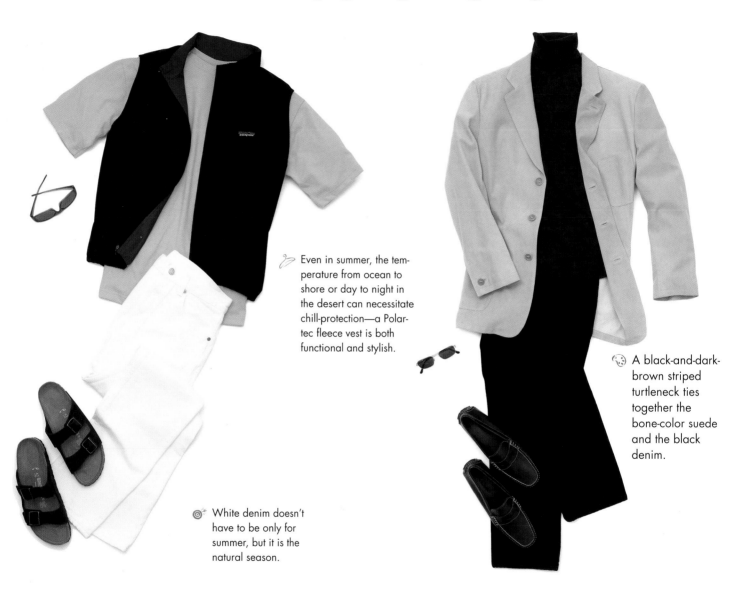

Even in summer, the temperature from ocean to shore or day to night in the desert can necessitate chill-protection—a Polartec fleece vest is both functional and stylish.

White denim doesn't have to be only for summer, but it is the natural season.

A black-and-dark-brown striped turtleneck ties together the bone-color suede and the black denim.

Denim Active. The most common way to wear denim is casually—so people tend to associate them with T-shirts and athletic shoes—the all-purpose, no-sweat American uniform. Denim is durable and comfortable, but it doesn't have to be sloppy. In fact, it can give a crisp edge to a look. It also doesn't always have to be blue.

Denim Nighttime. Black jeans have become the chic, don't-have-to-think-about-it choice for adventures after dark. Black has always been associated with bohemianism in fashion, and denim has long been mixed with more dressy pieces by sophisticated dressers. Yves Saint Laurent put denim in his Rive Gauche collection as far back as 1969.

Designer jeans, all the rage in the seventies, have made a comeback, as the trend toward office casual has led to jeans being worn in a more tailored manner.

Alternate work look for a summer casual Friday. For the office, a brown pair of loafers. Leave the more casual shoes in the car.

White dresses up with a blazer and fine cotton polo.

Button braces on denim is either an affectation or is stylish, depending on the individual.

The juxtaposition of all the elements, from the "fancy" blazer to the "utilitarian" jeans, adds drama to the outfit.

Denim Versatile. While denim was originally work clothing, one should be careful about wearing it to work. Unless you're part of a rock act, don't wear grungy, torn denims in a professional environment. Keep them clean, but not dry cleaned and creased. Denim can be perfect for informal conferences and business retreats at resorts.

Denim Formal. Some people are so wedded to the ease and symbolism of their jeans that they wear them everywhere, in all situations. This includes the independently wealthy, aging hipsters, and Frenchmen. Jeans can supply a touch of anarchy to an otherwise dressed-up ensemble. Ralph Lauren has worn denim with a tuxedo.

SIMPLE SOLUTIONS

T-SHIRT

The simple T-shirt began its fashion life covertly, as a garment to be hidden under other garments. It has emerged as an overt expression of personal style, carrying both printed messages and also the more subtle, sensual message of one's body. Nothing is more anonymous yet more declarative of the self than a white cotton T-shirt. The sleeveless athletic shirt of the 1930s was adapted from the top half of the tank swimsuit worn by American men in the early years of the twentieth century. It was supplanted in the 1940s by the T-shirt with short sleeves worn by the servicemen of World War II. By the fifties, the T-shirt had become sportswear, as young men took their style cues from movie idols like James Dean and Marlon Brando, who wore them with jeans. Today it is a wardrobe staple, woven in fabrics ranging from piqué cotton to Lycra stretch mixes to cashmere. It is sleeveless, long sleeved, and three button in its Henley incarnation. Pack two brand-new cotton ones on a vacation, one black, one white, and they will take you from the pool to a casual dinner out.

T-shirts come in all fabrics, weights, and textures. Silk, cashmere, cashmere-linen blends, viscose, spandex-cotton blends, and rayon make the simple undershirt a unique creature. Ribbing, popular in the sixties, adds body.

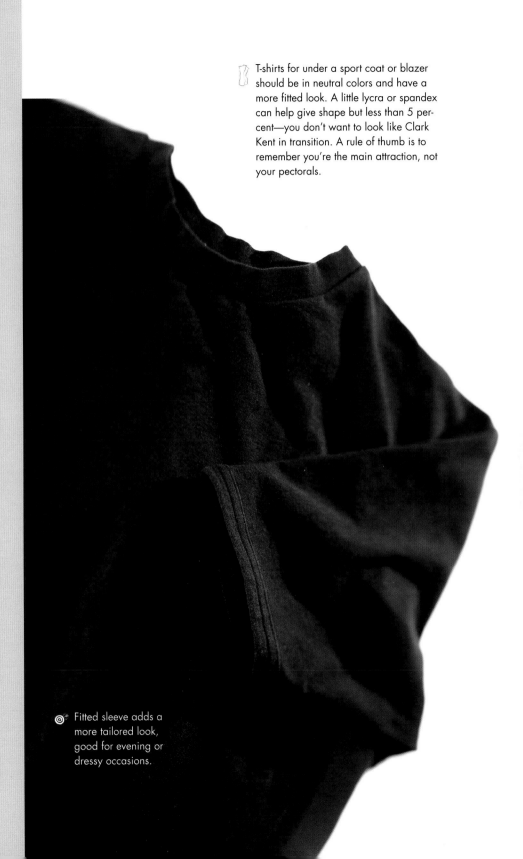

T-shirts for under a sport coat or blazer should be in neutral colors and have a more fitted look. A little lycra or spandex can help give shape but less than 5 percent—you don't want to look like Clark Kent in transition. A rule of thumb is to remember you're the main attraction, not your pectorals.

Fitted sleeve adds a more tailored look, good for evening or dressy occasions.

SUMMER ESSENTIALS

When the living is easy, clothes should have a sense of ease. And cool.

Fabric. Just as the tailored wardrobe shifts in summer from heavy woolens to tropical-weight wools, one's casual, everyday wardrobe lightens up, too. Thin, smooth fabrics are the ticket. Cotton, with its ability to absorb perspiration, becomes a man's closest friend. There are all kinds of cotton, though, each with its own advantages. Take, for example, the classic polo shirt. You can get it in the waffle-knit piqué, made famous by Lacoste, or in petite piqué, which has a finer nub to it. Then there is mercerized lisle cotton, which has a silky finish and is very popular on the golf course. Even dress shirts can take a warm-weather tack. Heavy broadcloth cottons should be put away in favor of more open weaves. For ties, stick with silk foulards and lightweight wools. Summer sweaters should be made of cotton, although cotton-and-silk or cotton-and-rayon blends are common. Linen should also be high on your list of summer fabrics. A featherweight linen blazer can make the thought of wearing a jacket somewhat bearable.

Color. Summer colors are lighter, brighter, and more whimsical. It is a time for lightness and warm hues—red, orange, green, green-yellow, and yellow—in bolder intensity than they would be in fall or winter. Bright yellow or orange, for example, are difficult to wear in winter (except for skiing or search and rescue), but they make sense in summer. Since the chroma, or intensity, of your summer wardrobe colors is so much brighter, you will also need a good complement of warm-weather neutrals—khakis and whites, primarily—to tone things down.

What kind of shoes can one wear with shorts? Like follows like; casual or athletic shorts go with a casual shoe, athletic sneakers, or sport sandal. As shorts become more formal, don a driving shoe, polished loafer, or a nice leather sandal. Boat shoes, like Topsiders, straddle both worlds no matter what their condition. Just be sure to avoid black socks.

Sandals. Long a symbol of spiritual humility and rustic simplicity, sandals have enjoyed a major revival in men's fashion. In the 1990s, designers began showing them in their collections, often with business suits, perhaps as a way of renouncing the materialistic 1980s.

Leather. Although rubber drugstore zoris may be all you need, genuine mystics and artistic types stick with traditional leather sandals. The most common style is the fisherman sandal, a heeled sandal with cross straps and one buckled strap encircling the ankle. But suede Birkenstocks remain popular too.

Sport. Activewear manufacturers like Nike, Reebok, Teva, and Timberland have created a whole new category called sport sandals. These comfortable, durable shoes usually are made with molded composite soles, similar to a sneaker, with adjustable Velcro straps.

"A colour-sense is more important, in the development of the individual, than a sense of right or wrong." *Oscar Wilde*

SHADES

Sunglasses Have Attitude. Besides being great to hide behind, they also make a statement about you. They can connote outrageous cool (Tom Cruise's Ray•Bans in *Risky Business*), imperious authority (General Douglas MacArthur in aviators), coquettish mystery (Audrey Hepburn in cat's-eye shades in *Breakfast at Tiffany's*), or supreme arrogance (Halston in head-to-toe black cashmere and big mirrored shades at his Olympic Tower offices). There are now sunglasses to suit every possible activity in life, including skiing, mountaineering, and volleyball. But for a man's wardrobe, as usual, we begin with the classics, the sunglasses that flatter the face and contribute to an overall masculine style. WAYFARERS by Ray•Ban, introduced in the 1950s, were popular with the Rat Pack and their White House pal, John F. Kennedy. But they reached new heights in *Risky Business*. They are classic and flattering to most facial types. Tortoiseshell with green lenses is very preppy; black on black is ultracool. AVIATOR frames have a military heritage and were probably popularized by wartime images of MacArthur. Peter Fonda's *Easy Rider* brought them back into vogue again in the sixties. They do very little for the overweight or full-faced man. MILITARY-style wire-rim sunglasses are a little more rectangular than aviators, but give off those same in-control vibes. WRAPAROUNDS are all the rage again. They stand for Extra Cool. Of course, when everybody else is wearing them, how cool can they be? You need a certain kind of face for wraparounds (thin and smallish), so they are not for everybody. In general, the most important thing in choosing shades, like anything else in your wardrobe, is how well they suit your physiognomy. Round-faced men should go for rectangular-shaped sunglasses. Large faces need large lenses. And so on.

WEEKEND: SUMMER

The sixty-hour respite from work calls for a change of pace in clothing. The keynotes of summer weekend style are color, casual styling, and comfort. Perhaps the most important item in this category is the sport shirt, from dressier types with collars that can take a tie to open-collar and crewneck shirts. Allover prints, cross and vertical stripes, checks and plaids are some of the patterns. The body-fitting seventies-style sport shirt has come back into fashion. These are often striped, V-neck, and made with Lycra spandex to mold to your muscles. You've got to be buff to look good in them. Every man is a country gentleman on weekends, so denim and chambray (lighter than denim) shirts are good to have. A summer-weight blazer in either gabardine or linen is a must. Navy is fine, and so is ivory. It will take you through cocktails or an evening out. Some patterned sport jackets, in madras or stripes, lend sophistication to the weekend wardrobe. A good supply of slip-on shoes and khaki trousers is mandatory. Shorts come in a great variety of styles and fabrics, and you will collect and wear them to your taste. Gurkha shorts, the kind with a double self-belted waistline, in olive khaki or white, are a handsome, roomy option. But most guys have a whole drawerful of shorts—plaid, khaki, cargo-pocketed, nylon racers, sweats, jams, swimming trunks—to throw on as needed. However, even if you've got stems like Baryshnikov's, it's probably not wise to wear shorts to the office on Friday.

Hawaiian Shirt. Splashy print shirts made in Honolulu started a trend in Hawaiian shirts in the late 1930s. Originally produced by native craftsmen, the shirts featured floral motifs printed on cotton, rayon, or silk that can be either chic or touristy. Worn with creased white cotton or linen trousers and deck shoes, these sport shirts have the air of old-time resort sportswear. With jeans and dirty sneakers and hard by a keg of beer, they are somewhat less swank. Look for them at vintage clothing stores. The really bold, fantastic ones sell for hundreds of dollars.

"Summer is when we believe, all of a sudden, that if we just walked out the back door and kept on going long enough and far enough we would reach the Rocky Mountains."
Edward Hoagland, **The Tugman's Passage**

Beige Power. For summertime wear, it makes sense to juxtapose a warm neutral against brighter colors and patterns. While blue and gray are the background colors for fall and winter, beige is an all-purpose summer neutral. For one thing, it doesn't absorb the sun and cause you to swelter in the heat. It also goes well with most colors and complexions. A pair of relaxed-fit beige khaki shorts matches up with almost any color sport shirt. A tan or off-white linen suit is another excellent choice—it can make you feel elegantly dressed or supremely casual, depending on how it is accessorized. Even the wrinkles the suit collects over the course of the day are part of its rumpled, casual charm. Paired with an aqua-blue cotton piqué polo shirt, it is a picture of tropical sang-froid. Tan khakis or tan cotton gabardine slacks are about the most versatile trousers in your warm-weather closet. They can be worn more formally, with a shirt and jacket, or dressed down and dirty for partying.

Jams. Surfer jams with Hawaiian or tropical prints, drawstring waist, and loose legs probably get their name from a shortening of "pajamas." There are numerous variations, some of which resemble the look of hip-hop clothing. Wear them one or two sizes bigger if you want them to hang from your hips.

Zoris. Drugstore sandals, also known as zoris, from the Japanese word for flat sandals with a thong, are the apotheosis of a fast fashion that works. Cheap. Functional. Hip. Nonchalant. Some guys even have the audacity to wear them with black tie. In Japan, zoris come in all styles, including formal (made of bamboo and velvet), which are worn with traditional kimonos.

River Guide Shorts. A hybrid of walking shorts and swimsuit, river shorts were created as tough-wearing utilitarian gear for rafters with deep pockets complete with drain holes, so during the more aquatic moments of a river trip the shorts are self-bailing, like the rafts. They make a great travel take-along with their double-duty role.

swimsuits

The swimsuit is certainly one item of apparel that is far less important than the body within it. Curiously, the degree to which a man has lost his figure seems inversely proportional to the size of the swimwear he chooses to put on. Men of sagging avoirdupois seem invariably to go for the spandex-brief style of bathing costume, which exposes yards and yards of unruly flesh and specifically encourages the belly to droop massively over the bikini waistline. Twenty-year-old oarsmen and body-builder studs, on the other hand, typically wear baggy, discolored, throwaway shorts—the kind borrowed from some other endeavor or sport, often with an obscure college's athletic department logo—just to show everyone else on the beach that they are nonchalant. And they look better than you will ever look in your Gucci thong. This is just another example of the callousness of nature, the cruelty of genetics, etc., and one must carry on, with dignity. Good old-fashioned men's swim trunks—the type with an elastic waistband, a buttoned key pocket, and a mesh internal support system—are a standard and are good to have around, especially if you are not an Adonis. Instead of plaid, buy one in matte black, for its slimming properties. Even more forgiving are surfer jams, with their loose, long legs, distracting prints, and adjustable drawstring waist. A newly popular hybrid suit has emerged from the depths of the sportswear sea and J. Crew and Patagonia: These are essentially cargo shorts made of nylon or microfiber with a drawstring waist, their advantages being that they are loose and casual, rugged and practical. You can stow things in the cargo pockets, on each leg, and you can wear them for other water sports, like kayaking and windsurfing. The neoprene rubber designs used by scuba divers are finding their way into the mainstream, thanks to the widening of water sports and the efforts of manufacturers like Body Glove. Pieces from wet suits and dry suits keep the wearer warm in freezing waters and have been widely adapted for use in kayaking, surfing, boogie boarding, and jet skiing. All of this is not to suggest that Speedo-type bikini briefs do not have their place. They are excellent for pool and health-club use, among other things, and they are a snap to pack.

AUTUMN ESSENTIALS

Transitional clothes include everything from sweaters and jackets to flannel shirts and corduroy jeans.

Fall fashions have a spirit and a texture all their own. They're burly, patterned, and earthy. Colors tend to be natural and multihued, like the dazzling deciduous backdrops they move around in. They are clothes for a season of transition, when the air turns crisp but not yet cold, and the temperature can vary widely in the course of a day. So autumn clothes have their own abrupt transitions: the smoothness of cashmere against the scratchy wool of a buffalo-plaid shirt jacket, the stiffness of leather hiking boots against the plushness of wide-wale cords. Everything comes out of mothproof storage—sweaters, flannel shirts, woolen scarves, and topcoats. In most places, it is sweater season. So a well-dressed man will need several, especially in smoothly knit wools. Cashmere is particularly useful, simply because it is light not bulky, warm enough for cool days but not so warm as to stifle when an Indian-summer sun emerges from the clouds. A car coat or waist-length outer jacket is certainly indispensable, in either gabardine, poplin, or tweed. Many men have discovered the advantages of a nylon jacket with Polartec fleece lining for in-between seasons: It repels rain and has good insulating ability but will not overheat. A more traditional option is the wax- or oil-treated Barbour jacket, which cuts the wind and rain but is much lighter than an overcoat. Suede and leather are key fall fashion components too. They are materials that hold their shape, enable texture to be introduced, and allow for artful cutting and designs, and their rich colors mirror the natural world. They cut the wind but offer very little insulating power (anyone who wears them on really cold days is foolish). Which makes them just right for fall.

Gloves. Sometimes, when it's not quite blustery enough for an overcoat but the wind is still sharp, a pair of simple leather gloves can add not only thermal comfort but a finishing touch. We're not talking black or neon ski gloves or woolen "daschermitts" for western wall assaults, just thin, fine soft leather in either black or brown. Goatskin is thin and fits well; deerskin is excellent and dries without stiffening. The brown often ages into a nice mahogany, full of character and memory. **Driving Gloves.** In the days of wooden steering wheels, driving gloves gave that extra purchase for control. Today, with most wheels leather wrapped, they're not as important, but for fall driving with the top down and the heater on, they're perfect.

It's often more comfortable if when layering you alternate textures—avoid wool on wool.

The "shirt jacket" is occasionally legitimized by the fashion industry as cycles return, but pairing a heavy wool shirt—whether it's a classic buffalo plaid from L. L. Bean or a cashmere derivative—with a cotton sweater adds both a layer of insulation and wind protection and an element of texture to any outfit.

STICKING YOUR NECK OUT

The turtleneck, with its high collar, serves both to warm the Adam's apple and to lengthen the neck. It also somewhat dressy. Though it originated in the 1890s, its moment was in the sixties and seventies, when turtlenecks were widely worn in lieu of a shirt and tie, a practice once again in vogue. Mock turtlenecks abbreviate the height of the collar, so it can't be folded down.

"I stick my neck out for nobody." *Humphrey Bogart in* **Casablanca**

Knitwear has returned to the fore-front of men's fashion. Its warm, fuzzy shapes represent a release from the restrictions of shirt and tie.

Sweaters. A fashion fixture among a new generation of men, sweaters are now sometimes worn instead of a jacket, sometimes against bare skin. As tailored garments have become more unstructured and sweaterlike, designers have focused on sweaters as an area of experimentation. This new emphasis can be attributed both to advances in the manufacture of yarns and to the trend toward natural, homespun, organic-looking clothing. Bulky, oversize sweaters with proletarian touches and lean, Lycra-blend body-contouring knits worn as a color accent under suit jackets are among the innovative looks pouring out of New York and Milan. The origins of the garment are not quite so chic. The sweater was originally designed to make a man sweat—hence the name. It was introduced in the mid-nineteenth century as a jersey worn by sportsmen (early sweaters were referred to as jerseys, after the sailors from the Isle of Jersey who wore them). It eventually was adopted by workingmen. Another version holds that the style comes from the practice of horse trainers who used heavy blankets called sweaters to keep their lathered horses warm after a run. V-necks and crewnecks (named for college crews) are the most versatile and easiest to wear; they can go with a shirt or without. Roll necks, so popular in mail-order catalogs, are like crew necks with a bit of a roll to the collar. Thick knits are also very much a part of the current scene. The short, bulky poorboy sweater, named for 1920s newsboys who hawked their product on windblown streets, has returned to fashion. Cable-knit sweaters, like the hand-knit fisherman's sweater, also remain popular for their distinctive textures and water-repellent qualities. A fad for vintage ski sweaters, with their close fit and graphic color-blocking, has inspired many contemporary spinoffs by retailers like the Gap and J. Crew.

KNIT PICKS

Lambswool. Sweaters made from lambswool, the first shearing from lambs seven to nine months old, is somewhat finer and softer than wool from older sheep. Look for it in simple V-necks and crewnecks in classic colors.

Merino. The wool from the Australian merino sheep is woven into a soft fabric resembling cashmere. Like cashmere, it can be worn against the skin. A simple dark merino T-shirt with long sleeves is a nice sweater to have.

Cashmere. Made from the woolly underbelly of the Kashmiri goat, cashmere sweaters provide exceptional warmth without bulk. It is often combined with wool to soften the expense. Even 10 percent cashmere has a luxurious feel, but 100 percent is heaven.

Fair Isle. The colorful, horizontal-patterned wool sweaters from Fair Isle, off the coast of Scotland, have become almost a generic term for the type of design. The real thing is hand-knitted.

Icelandic. The lanolin-rich wool from Icelandic sheep makes for the most water-repellent and wind-resistant of all knits. Handmade Icelandic sweaters typically have banded designs around the neck that mimic the beaded collars worn by the Eskimos.

two layers

Jacket Power. The relaxation of dress codes has increased the power and versatility of the sport jacket. As more attention is paid to what men wear instead of a dark suit, tailored jackets are used more and more as layering pieces to be combined with elements from the casual wardrobe. Layering has evolved for reasons of both style and function. Although we tend to associate layering with the onset of the "Annie Hall" look, the practice has a long history in cold climates: The Eskimos and other indigenous peoples in frigid places have always done it with furs. In Fall, when temperatures fluctuate throughout the day, you simply peel off and add layers as needed. A tweed jacket can be layered just as smoothly with a plaid flannel shirt and jeans as with a Shetland sweater, dress shirt, and suit trousers. Casual jackets are also part of the mix: Leather, suede, and plaid wool jackets are effectively layered, sometimes even with shirts and ties. Increasingly, men are exploring and experimenting with the interchangeability of their wardrobes.

Brisk clear days. A richly tinted landscape. The honk of migrating geese. In short, walking weather. First, a sturdy middle-weight jacket. To facilitate their perambulations in the countryside, English gentlemen turned to the tweed jacket and various other thorn-resistant garments. These tend to be in somewhat coarse patterns and fibers, including Donegal, saxony, and herringbone. Harris is considered the tops for tweed, primarily because of its sturdy hand-weaving and naturally dyed colors. This jacket does quite nicely on city streets. Tweed jackets can last for generations, so they make an especially fine investment. Another robust option is the field coat, also known as the barn jacket. Typically made of a tough canvas fabric, usually in tan or blue, with a contrasting corduroy or leather collar, these jackets are exceptionally durable and comfortable. Companies like L.L. Bean and Carhartt make them with a variety of linings, from cotton and wool to Primaloft and Thinsulate. Underneath, you've got your chamois or flannel shirt, robust and warming with an outdoorsy feel. Perhaps a nice Shetland sweater or Polartec fleece vest for layering. Trousers made of tweed are somewhat rare, since the coarseness of the fabric usually mandates that they be lined. The classic trousers for fall weekend expeditions would be a rough but refined cavalry twill, flannels, wool gabardine, or moleskin. But cords, jeans, and khakis (all of which can be purchased with flannel linings) make good sense too. A pair of deerskin gloves for the display pocket of your jacket and the picture's perfect.

WEEKEND: AUTUMN

Hacking Jacket. As the saying goes, the horse invented sports clothing. The term "hacking" can be traced to the hackney, a saddle horse used for everyday riding rather than for the more formal hunting and jumping. The more informal the ride, the more informal the style of the hacking clothes. Tweed was used for ordinary riding jackets, in place of the more formal wool melton or cavalry twill. The hacking jacket typically has three or four buttons, often leather; a throat tab on the collar; a long center vent and ample skirt to facilitate riding; and two side pockets and a ticket pocket, cut on a slant—and alll very dashing.

pipes

Something to Do with Your Hands

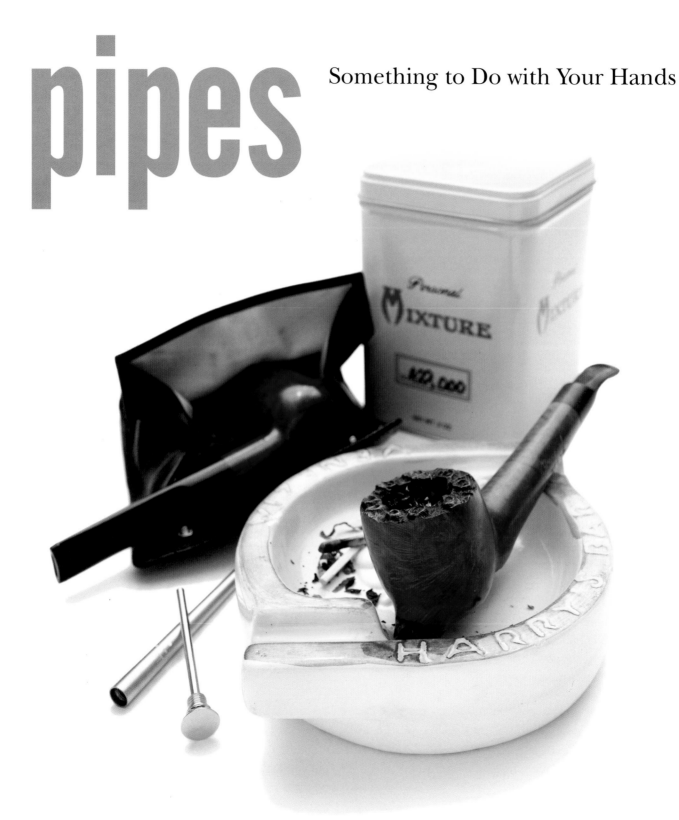

Smoking

Pipe smoking involves both ritual and high style. Unlike cigars, which have become a power accessory, as redolent of hubris and new money as overpriced suits and cars, pipes are a less obtrusive, more intellectual way to enjoy a smoke. Einstein smoked a pipe. Camus smoked. Great literary men like Mark Twain and William Faulkner smoked pipes. Many of Twain's characters, starting with Huck Finn and his corn cob, smoked religiously. Twain observed, "As an example to others, and not that I care for moderation myself, it has always been my rule never to smoke when asleep, and never to refrain when awake."

Pipes

Pipe smokers maintain entire wardrobes of pipes, tobaccos, and accessories. The pipes themselves can be works of art. There are many different styles: "bents" and "straights" and "sandblasts." Some of the finest pipes are made from hard Mediterranean briar, especially from the mountain plateaus of northern Greece, since this wood has a low flash point but carves beautifully. Pipes fashioned from meerschaum, a white, claylike mineral mined in Turkey, are among the most expensive and collectible. Instead of a Cubano cutter, pipe smokers have their tampers and picks. Settling on a favorite blend of tobacco can be an intricate, ongoing quest requiring a great deal of trial and error till the exact combination of taste and aroma are arrived at. And for this pipedreams were invented.

Tips

A few tips for those starting out: Pipes need to be broken in. Smoke slowly. Always pack the bowl evenly to avoid hot spots. If one side is too loose, use a tamp tool to push it down. Never smoke to the bottom of the first bowl. Never remove a stem from the shank while the pipe is still hot (it can cause the wood to split). Find a quiet reflective spot to kick back and smoke.

WINTER **ESSENTIALS**

When the big chill sets in,
the well-dressed man views driving snow
and pooling slush as challenges,
not affronts, to his sense of style.

Technology has changed the way we face winter. No longer does a man have to depend on wool overcoats and plenty of long underwear to see him through. Down-insulated garments have revolutionized our approach to the coldest days. Waterproof Gore-Tex finishes have altered our view of the wettest ones. Most men own a good winter parka with a generous wadding of insulation: if it's premium goose down, about ten to twelve ounces will do; if Thinsulate, about 200 grams. Others opt for the so-called systems approach in technical outerwear, which combines a waterproof outercoat or shell with either a down or Polartec fleece inner jacket or vest. So in addition to the classic winter overcoat—by no means obsolete, since it is needed for business and formal occasions—a man these days needs a technical garment or system for extreme conditions. (If you wish to wear your parkas and shells with a suit, wear the suit jacket for try-ons to be sure the outercoat is long enough to cover.) For deep winter weather, the best fleece is fleece pile, which is thicker than the ordinary variety but still breathable.

Scarves and Mufflers. Early in this century, mufflers were an integral part of men's wardrobes. They are an enduring feature of the masculine look that changes in shape and fashion to suit the times. These days more and more men are tying theirs in the hacking or ratcatcher style, which involves folding the scarf double and then slipping both ends through the loop formed in the center.

Wool. Long wool mufflers or reefers, popularized on campus, are usually worn throw-over style (a simple slip knot with the pulled-through end going over the top). They can be fringed, plaid, striped, or solid. The clan tartans of Scotland are especially desirable. Long overcoats usually call for long wool scarves.

Cashmere. Sumptuous against the throat, the oblong cashmere muffler is adaptable to almost any occasion, dressy or casual. Some elegant reversible scarves have cashmere on one side and figured silk on the other.

Silk. Silk dresses up most outfits. A paisley silk scarf worn ascot fashion can be tucked into a shirt or sweater. The white knitted or woven silk muffler is a finishing touch to formal evening wear. Black or gray silk also are appropriate for black tie.

Even if you have a closet full of fleece pullovers in their most up-to-date technical incarnations, you will want a few extra-thick wool sweaters, like a Norwegian or cable knit. The cable knit, so named for its overlapping knit strands that resemble cables, are made from worsted, long-staple wools and often come from small knitting mills in Ireland. In an age of high-tech, the Irish cable knit is the comfort food of the modern wardrobe. It makes even the coldest and most ruthless financial types seem snuggly and warm. (Cable-knit socks are also good to have in winter.)

Pendleton. Some of the finest flannel and wool shirts bear the blue-and-gold label of Pendleton Woolen Mills of the Pacific Northwest. Founded in 1863 by English-born Thomas Kay, who came to Oregon to establish a textile business, Pendleton became famous all across the West for its wool Indian blankets and shirts. Pendleton controls every phase of the manufacturing process, from selecting the wool to spinning, dyeing, weaving, and tailoring it. The distinctive plaids of the shirts and the bold Indian graphics of the blankets have made vintage Pendleton products collectibles. The company is still family-run.

"[Japhy] and I and Alvah drove to Oakland in Morley's car and went first to some Goodwill stores and Salvation Army stores to buy various flannel shirts (at fifty cents a crack) and undershirts. We were all hung-up on colored undershirts, just a minute after walking across the street in the clean morning sun Japhy'd said, 'You know, the earth is a fresh planet, why worry about anything?' (which is true) now we were foraging with bemused countenances among all kinds of dusty old bins filled with the washed and mended shirts of all the old bums in the Skid Row universe."

Jack Kerouac,
The Dharma Bums

Flannel & Wool

Flannel is not effete. It's a real-guy fabric, honest and cozy. Its tight, smooth weave feels right in winter, whether for shirts, underwear, pajamas, or suits. Flannel shirts usually have a smooth finish but a rugged look, especially when they are plaid. Also known as lumberjack shirts, they became the style emblems of the grunge-rock movement of the Pacific Northwest. In a larger sense, they symbolize the American man's rejection of overwrought fashion and corporate conformity. They come in either cotton, wool, or blends of both. Some flannel shirts are quilted with a polyester filling for greater warmth. Men who spend a lot of time outdoors wear these as jackets, often with a wool or cotton Henley underneath.

Wool remains the most important cold-weather fabric, simply because science has had a difficult time coming up with something as warming and water-resistant that also feels good against the skin. As casual dressing changes the look of American business, wool shirts with a rugged spirit are replacing fine cottons, particularly on winter Fridays. But a wool shirt could look incongruous with a shiny silk tie. In an era when many of us feel estranged from nature, a wool flannel shirt with a thick wool necktie sends a rugged, outdoorsy message.

WEEKEND: WINTER

The sleek Alpine look in winter wear is largely a thing of the past. Gone are the days when men gadded about in wool snowflake sweaters tucked inside worsted gabardine tapered trousers, topped by a Tyrolean hat. Contemporary cold-weather clothes have more of an expedition quality, like something you'd wear for a trek to the South Pole or an assault on Annapurna. Rugged, technically driven antistyle has become the style. The symbolism of inner-city survival dressing now includes the Michelin-man fat look, based on big quilted down coats, heavy Timberland boots, and knitted wool caps. In the city, where wind shears from the skyscrapers blast cold air into every seam, some of us want to be not only warm but almost scientifically toasty and impervious to the elements. The haute couture names in technical fashion are The North Face, Marmot, Patagonia, Helly Hansen, First Down, Bear, Eddie Bauer, and L. L. Bean. In the country, interestingly, the subfreezing style is somewhat more relaxed. The down vest paired with a flannel shirt and corduroy pants has become practically a uniform. When a jacket is worn, it is typically a ripstop nylon shell parka with excellent water-repelling characteristics. In addition to the flannels, corduroy, and down, country weekends also call for an all-terrain shoe called an approach shoe that can scramble, hike, and mountain-bike. Such shoes have hiking-boot soles with athletic cushioning.

Shell Parkas. Inspired by thrill-seeking endorphin addicts—ah, the joy of snowstorms at seven thousand feet!—technical outerwear has made great strides and now influences everything we wear. In the world of adventure skiing and mountaineering, the nylon shell parka has become as indispensable as crampons and sleeping bags. There are dozens of types: cycle shells and velocity shells for mountain biking: paddling and kayaking shells; breakwater jackets for ocean sailing; snowboarding anoraks; and so on. The principle remains constant: a lightweight, full-on storm protection jacket that allows your body moisture to escape (wick away) while simultaneously keeping you dry inside so the insulating layers can do their work.

Corduroy jackets are an autumn classic that look better the more they're worn. Make sure that you buy them large enough, since they can shrink and it's smart to have room for layers.

Fleece vests keep the torso warm while leaving the arms free to move. They are easier to layer than their ancestor, the down vest.

Shearling coats originated with cowboys and sheepherders who wore sheepskin with the insulating fleece on the inside for warmth and the skin or leather on the outside to repel the elements.

Approach shoes, named because they are what climbers wear walking to the mountain, are a new boot alternative.

Cold Comfort. The traditional flannel shirt and corduroys have obvious advantages, not least of which are their cozy textures and natural insulating abilities. Flannel's tight weave and corduroy's thick pile make them intrinsically good layering materials in cold weather. When the flannel shirt is paired with a down vest and a nylon shell, a new level of sophistication is obtained. Warmth is combined with flexibility, since the layers can be peeled off or added on as temperatures change. That is the beauty of technical layering systems. Ultimately, nature's own insulators can never be completely supplanted, simply because of the sensuousness and comfort of natural fibers. A shearling jacket—a western classic now refined—over a cashmere turtleneck provides ample warmth and something else besides—a beautifully rugged and handsome style.

The studded driving shoe, designed for sports-car driving, is a classy, comfortable shoe with a distinctly practical side: your feet won't ever slip on the clutch.

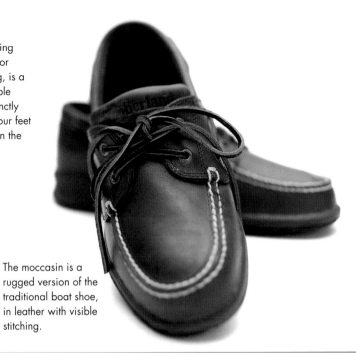

The moccasin is a rugged version of the traditional boat shoe, in leather with visible stitching.

Face it, those full-brogue wing tips look like oil tankers with jeans. Casual shoes gotta have sole.

The ornately tooled leathers and Western mystique of cowboy boots have made them a popular casual shoe around the world.

The reverse calfskin chukka, three-holed with leather soles, is an elegant variation on the desert boot. Suitable for dancing.

Not just for Pat Boone (especially now, in his heavy-metal phase), white bucks are a wonderful summer casual, good with flannels to khakis.

COOL SHOES

The American working boot went full fashion in the early nineties—along with England's equivalent, Doc Martens—but their proletarian origins insure comfort and security in whatever conditions.

Informal. Shoes have a way of telegraphing one's status and the degree of formality of an outfit. Avoid wearing casual shoes for business, unless they are part of the accepted dress code. To the sharp observer, they can be a dead giveaway that you are not part of the managerial class. The difference between shoes you wear for business and for casual, everyday use is comfort, freedom, and style. Moccasins are perhaps the most comfortable shoes. Boat shoes, or Top-Siders, a type of leather moccasin with a hard white slip-resistant sole, are an integral part of the off-hours uniform of the preppie class. Desert or chukka boots, made of unlined suede cowhide with thick crepe-rubber soles, were originally worn by polo players and adopted for general wear in the 1950s. Modern versions are considerably more structured than the famous Clark's version. Cowboy boots, high-heeled and made of highly tooled or appliqued leather with a dip top, look good with straight pants.

Driving. With their soft uppers and studded leather soles, driving shoes were specially designed for sports-car enthusiasts. They are classy shoes with a distinctly practical angle. Developed in the days of clutch driving, when you really did use your feet, the studded soles allow you to catch the edges of the pedals easily without slippage. But they are also very comfortable and make for stylish walking—as popular for strolls in Beverly Hills as they are at the track in Lyme Rock, Connecticut. They are versatile additions to any man's shoe wardrobe. Before you know it, you'll be gazing fondly at vintage Austin Healeys.

Inclement. A word about slush: Every prudent fellow will keep a pair of slip-on rubber overshoes at home and in the office for those days when freezing rain makes the sidewalks resemble the notorious Madison Square Garden ice. For casual wear, a good pair of mud shoes, in the L.L. Bean duck-shoe tradition, with full-grain-leather uppers and rubber outsoles, are in order. For extreme wear, you will need additional insulation: a pair of subzero, wool-pile-lined boots with soles so heavily lugged they are almost like all-terrain tires. Like Ford Expeditions for the feet.

get away

The First Rule of Travel: If you want to get away from it all, don't take it all with you. Never pack more than you can carry the length of Heathrow. You know that you'll need a toothbrush. But what else? You want to pack for the weather and social conditions you will encounter, but you don't want to lug a ton of stuff. Only pack things that work well together. Start with a sport jacket, preferably a solid blazer that can be used in several ways. Don't pack it, wear it. Ditto for a raincoat or topcoat—wear it or carry it on your arm. Pack a dress shirt that you also wear casually and a black knit tie. Bring a pair of gray flannels and khakis. Always bring a sewing kit and a Swiss Army knife. Never check your medicines or electronic paraphernalia. They go on board with you. If you are flying, your carry-on should meet the average allowable dimensions for domestic airlines: 10" x 14" x 22".

Cross trainers for walking or working out. Store in gallon freezer bags to keep the smell under control.

Black and white T-shirts go from the gym to a nightclub with a blazer.

River shorts are perfect for running, hiking, or swimming.

Leather Dopp kit. Be sure it's big enough for extras, shampoo, vitamins—whatever you travel with—and that it's lined with waterproof material.

Travel kit: for road hazards. Pack matches in waterproof case, a modem phone cord, a Swiss Army knife, Leatherman plier tools, and a Maglite flashlight.

Tie case, with **black knit tie** that will go with anything, either casual or dress-up, and a **silk dark gray tie**, perfect with all dark suits or blazers.

Black loafers can be both casual and dressy, accompany everything from denim to flannel.

Jeans, classic dark blue, which can go more places than old or faded ones (except the Ritz).

Black V-neck cashmere sweater provides lightweight elegant warmth, worn alone or under a blazer.

White athletic socks are fine for either working out or casual wear. Bring a pair of wool ragg socks and use them as shoe socks to protect the loafers and as protection against drafty hotel rooms.

Leather duffel bag, suitable for the trunk or the overhead in the train or plane—10" x 14" x 22".

"Travel is a vanishing act, a solitary trip down a pinched line of geography to oblivion."
Paul Theroux, **The Old Patagonian Express**

Weekend. The basic blue blazer, which goes with almost everything, can be indispensable on weekend getaways. It is dressy enough for dinner in a fine restaurant and can also be worn with jeans and a T-shirt. Cashmere or a wool-cashmere blend makes good sense for travel, since it will provide lightweight warmth and comfort en route and be dressy enough once you get there.

variations on a theme

Classic clothes don't have to be boring or predictable. Stylish men always manage to give the tried-and-true a new spin or wear classic clothes that have off-center personalities. For example, a traditionally cut blazer has a completely different mood in leather or suede than one in blue cashmere with brass buttons. Yet it is still classic. Or take the tuxedo, as irreproachable and safe as you can get—but it's also a uniform and therefore somewhat predictable. But a velvet dinner jacket with peaked lapels maintains the basic shape of the tuxedo with its own distinctive look. Indeed, the basic layout of the tuxedo has been twisted and reshaped in countless ways by fashion designers, especially Yves Saint Laurent, whose celebrated "le Smoking" designs adapt the tux to the feminine form. And for decades Saint Laurent has played notionally with the classic trench coat in his Paris collections ("trench dresses," for instance). Men's trench coats based on the World War I military model come in all different fabrics and colors. A suede trench adds a touch of luxury to what began as a humble, utilitarian style. The same principle applies throughout fashion. Masculine pinstripes, associated with the banking profession, can now be had in kelly green or bright rust on suits of four or five buttons with very experimental cuts. Wall Street meets Carnaby Street. Pinstripes are also commonly worn now as separates—that is, the pants or the vest worn alone—by poets, rock musicians, and other noncorporate types. They borrow the chic of striped tailored wool while negating its power connotations. Varsity or team jackets, conventional symbols of squeaky clean athleticism and American group spirit, have been widely adopted by even notoriously rebellious rock stars and their entourages on tour. Instead of thick wool, they come in leather, nylon, and suede, and carry the band's logo instead of a team's. Clothes can be traditional or transgressive, depending on how you wear them.

● **Soundtracks**
Entertaining

Perrey & Kingsley ● *The In Sounds from Way Out*
The Art Van Damme Quintet ● *More Cocktail Capers*
Getz/Gilberto ● *Getz/Gilberto*
Combustible Edison ● *Four Rooms*
Hank Williams ● *Twenty Greatest Hits*
Squirrel Nut Zippers ● *Hot*
Astrud Gilberto ● *Beach Samba*
Frank Sinatra ● *Songs for Swingin' Lovers*
Ray Condo & His Ricochets ● *Door to Door Maniac*
Louis Armstrong ● *Jazz 'Round Midnight*
Ray Charles ● *His Greatest Hits Vol. 1 & 2*
Classic Torch Singers ● *Sirens of Song*
Junior Vasquez ● *Live*
Charlie Parker ● *Swedish Schnapps +*

The suede of the trench coat works effectively with the cashmere of the turtleneck. This is a case of opposite textures complementing each other.

The monochromatic palette of gray adds a sophisticated backdrop to the mahogany richness of the leather jacket.

Dress boots are in keeping with the subtle rugged qualities of the leather jacket. These are dressy yet casual.

A gray flannel pinstripe slack worn casually works in the context of the rest of the clothes.

PEA COAT

The dark, monochromatic color scheme can take you from downtown to uptown, and to any party in town.

The watch cap—so named for sailors standing watch—is functional, warm, and always in style.

Velvet pants have limited versatility and should be added to your wardrobe only as an extra.

Making Waves. The hip-length pea jacket with notched lapels, slash pockets, and center vent in back has long been an item of reverse chic. Based on the heavy wool double-breasted jackets worn by sailors, pea coats can now be found in leather, suede, nylon, and cashmere. The name derives from the Dutch word pij, for a coarse woolen material. With turtleneck, jeans, and watch cap, today's pea coat is shipshape; with shirt and tie, it's a shore thing.

REVERSIBLE COAT

The nylon of the jacket is quilted for warmth. A common European look—influenced by hunting and activewear—it is growing in popularity in America.

Originating from game pockets in hunting jackets, the patch pockets add a sporty look.

A ranger set belt has an American heritage. A Western artifact, it is a work of art with hand-tooled leather and richly engraved buckle.

Switchbacks. Garments with reversible fabrics were once very popular. They were prized for their longevity as well as for their flexibility in varying weather. Perhaps now, with so many amazing fabrics available, not to mention shrinking closet space, they will return to favor. A rain-shedding treated nylon jacket surface can be alternated with a soft wool side, offering different looks: the nylon side for rainy days in town, the wool side for brisk, sunny days.

"No, thanks. I'm completely Gore-tex."

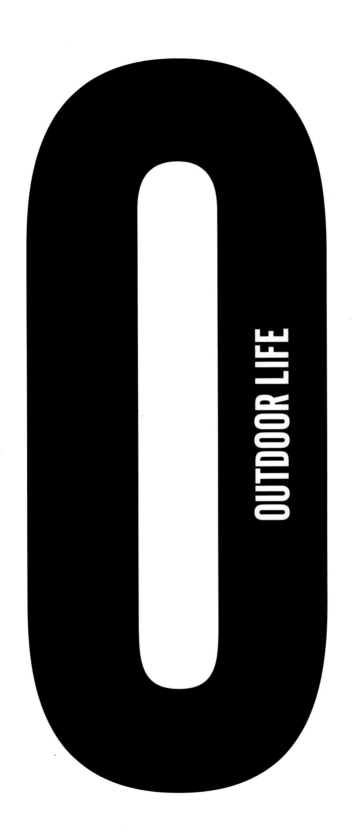

"There is also the matter of her clothes. Kristina is sensitive to the glamour angles of hunting and wants to look her best in the field at all times. She is a former fashion model and beauty-pageant queen, and wears tweed caps, occasionally a wide-brimmed felt hat for the sun, Hermès neckwear, expensive quilted shooting gloves, thick Scottish sweaters, thick Scottish socks. She likes her brush pants snug. To me, this makes her look like a rank amateur and lessens our chances of getting crucial access when we appear together in a muddy, cold and rainy, vehicle strewn, dog clamorous barnyard wanting to ask some startled young Norsky farmer's permission to kick out his irrigation ditches for birds. I myself strive for a less memorable impression in my hunting clothes, and from time to time I've even asked Kristina to 'dress down,' my wish being not to come on so strong, and for us to seem 'authentic'—though 'authentic' what I'm not sure: authentic hunters, maybe, and not authentic assholes. Her view on all this has, however, been unchanging: In an encounter with a dazzling huntress, stepping off the pages of the Abercrombie's wish list, no farmer would say no for fear of ruining his private and well-earned fantasy. So far she's been right."

Richard Ford, "Hunting with My Wife…and Others"

outside

Today we live more active lives, especially outdoors. The explosion in jogging, Rollerblading, cycling, hiking, climbing, golfing, and board sports has sparked a revolution in the technology of outdoor clothing. The active man now has an entire wardrobe of clothing manufactured with great specificity for various outdoor adventures. This is where practicality rules—and the rules of the workday world are left behind.

ATHLETE

instant

Working out. Traveling light. Modern mantras that actually can go together. On the road or simply commuting from country to city, a few easy pieces facilitate a quick lunch workout or a visit to the hotel gym after the flight. The choices should be as versatile and portable as possible. Classic cotton sweat clothes have given way to ultralight technical nylons and micro-fibers, which wick perspiration and dry quickly, helping to prevent the growth of bacteria. The essential four pieces, with optional running tights:

3 Cotton wicking socks.

1 Tank top and
2 running shorts with built-in brief; no need for a jock.

5 Lycra spandex running tights hold their shape.

4 Air-cushioned running shoes.

For dealing with the elements, layering is the way to go. The entire array of specialized new fabrics is organized around the principle of peeling off and adding layers as needed. Warmth and moisture management are the goal. With exertion, the body cools itself through perspiration. The layers in your activewear wardrobe act as second skins, enabling clothes to breathe with your body.

The technical outerwear of today relies on vapor-lock technology that allows moisture to move through clothes but discourages water from entering. A lightweight Supplex nylon jacket typically forms the first line of defense against wind and rain. A Polartec fleece shirt is next, an improvement over the traditional cotton sweatshirt, since it doesn't hold moisture and has a zip front to allow for selective ventilation. The high-zipped neck promotes the "chimney effect," which allows hot air to rise and moisture to evaporate.

But underneath it all, a white cotton T-shirt. It's still great to have the natural softness of cotton against your skin.

Orange nylon zippered jacket, microporous to allow moisture out.

Blue fleece zip-neck shirt, light enough for exercise, warm enough for most conditions with addition of nylon shell.

Sportwatch, with large easy-to-read numerals, a mini-computer on your wrist.

Microfiber jogging pants have reflective stripes, ankle zippers for ease in pulling on over shoes. Great for inclement conditions.

golf

The wayward white spheroid has had a dynamic influence on fashion, if not always an estimable one. Golf is one of the few sports in which the status clues of street dress and the functionality of sports clothing are tightly interwoven. At the beginning of this century, American golfers took their cues from the Scottish links, where golf originated: plus-fours, or knee breeches, with a tweed jacket, starched shirt, tie, and a tweedy cap. By the 1930s, an era associated with great masculine elegance, golfers had discovered the utility of generously cut flannel trousers, the elasticity of knitted shirts, and the cozy class of alpaca cardigans. But by the 1960s, with the advent of synthetics, golfing fashions took on a strange life of their own. Orange Ban-Lon knit shirts and pink plaid polyester slacks were par for the course. In the 1990s, with the introduction of designer golf collections and the involvement of sportswear giants like Nike and Reebok, golf apparel has become both more classic and more technologically sophisticated. Of course, "slacker hackers" have come up with a gonzo style all their own. But in a game were relaxation is of paramount interest, loud colors and personal expression are giving way, allowing comfort and casual elegance to play through.

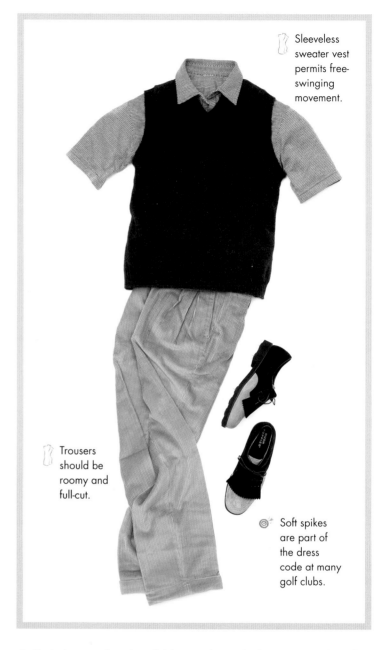

Sleeveless sweater vest permits free-swinging movement.

Trousers should be roomy and full-cut.

Soft spikes are part of the dress code at many golf clubs.

Golf clothes tend to be clubby, traditional (the sport *is* played at clubs). The knit cotton shirt is usually by Grand Slam (the original knit golf shirt from 1954), Lacoste, Ralph Lauren, or Bobby Jones, or, for luxury, a cashmere polo by Loro Piana. A sleeveless sweater and a pair of corduroy trousers, for ease of movement, complete the picture.

The checked silk golf cap is a cut above a baseball cap or visor.

Layering is a good idea, since you can peel off clothes as the day gets warmer.

Cotton argyle socks are perfect for golfing.

White acrylic knit cap for cold-weather golf.

A performance golf sweater is lined with nylon to keep moisture and wind out.

Leather Nike Air Max golf shoes resemble running shoes with spikes.

If in doubt, go for neutral colors rather than the wild, plaid confections that decorated country clubs for decades. Good, smart classics could include a light blue golf jacket and alpaca cardigan from Paul Stuart worn with khaki pants. Your concession to flamboyance and color can be your argyle socks (an English nod) or two-tone saddle golf shoes.

In colder weather, turn to more technical golf apparel and, of course, layer. The extra clothing can always be stowed in your golf bag as the sun gets higher. The black V-neck pullover above is made of polyester with a nylon lining—yet it has classic golf styling. The spiked leather golf shoes resemble running shoes, but they are built for walking the fairways.

tennis

A country club sport with a genteel image, tennis was originally played in white oxford or broadcloth shirts, with the sleeves rolled up; cream-colored flannel trousers; and perhaps a heavy white cable-knit sweater with club colors set in around the neck and waist. Players usually carried woolen blazers. Anything the least bit sartorially untoward was pooh-poohed by the crusty guardians of the game. In 1928, when an American player showed up at Wimbledon wearing white trousers with stripes down the sides, it became a cause célèbre. Many tennis tournaments had rules against any deviation from the all-white court costume. The turned-down-collar short-sleeved tennis shirt, known as a polo shirt, began to appear in the 1920s. William Tilden was the first to wear very full pleated trousers. In 1932, Bunny Austin wore shorts to Forest Hills, causing a sensation. By the mid-thirties, shorts were widely accepted. Everything outré eventually becomes old hat. In the sixties, the Peacock Revolution extended to the tennis court, with the usual dubious consequences. Today, the stars serve as prototypes for what people wear to play tennis. Players arrive at matches wearing two-piece nylon warm-up suits, and their on-court attire typically has more to do with the logotypes they are displaying to the television cameras than it does with any particular sense of style. Fortunately for the weekend player, the corporate sportswear giants focus on the ideal of performance. Tennis clothes today, with their Lycra blends and other high-tech synthetics, allow for superior moisture management and tremendous freedom of movement. The modern essentials remain constant: a knit short-sleeved polo shirt (with a small emblem of your choice); a pair of self-belted shorts with ball pockets; low-cut leather tennis shoes; and a visor.

The original polo shirt, a short-sleeved white pullover made of knitted wool, had a rolled collar that didn't flap around, which particularly endeared it to dashing gents on horseback. It also suited other sportsmen, including the French tennis star René Lacoste, known as "Le Crocodile" for his ruthless manner of play. Lacoste's version, which he began manufacturing with his signature crocodile emblem in 1933, comes down to us today in waffle-knit piqué cotton or mercerized lisle cotton (silky smooth) in forty colors. These days the logo appears only on the bona fide models made by La Chemise Lacoste of Paris. You can wear them anywhere, from the golf course to the office on Friday. Every wardrobe could use a few—or ten.

"Couldn't you see the [bleeping] ball? That cost me the [bleeping] set.
[Bleep] you, you [bleeping] [bleep]. Suck [bleep]." *John McEnroe*

TECHNICAL MATERIALS

More than anything dreamed up lately in Paris and Milan, clothing has been revolutionized by technology. You don't have to be a mountain guide to realize this; just look at the labels inside your clothes. While designer names have dominated fashion for decades, real closets at the turn of the century have been transformed by other kinds of names. Polartec. Gore-Tex. Nautex. Lycra spandex. Supplex nylon. Microfiber. Thinsulate. Velcro. Whether water-repellent, superlight, superwarm, or breathable, these futuristic fabrics have molded clothing to the active needs of wearers. Just as graphite rackets and metal woods have revolutionized tennis and golf, modern technical fabrics have changed the way we dress for sports and the outdoors, allowing us to be at the top of our game, increasing our comfort while we play, and, in extreme cases, enhancing our chances of survival. And, guess what, most high-tech fabrics can be thrown into a washing machine and tumble dried.

Lo-tech

WOOL is nature's great insulator, and its heat retention does not diminish when wet. However, wool can be bulky, and it is slow-drying compared to today's high-tech fleeces and polyester microfibers. DOWN is a terrific insulator when protected by a waterproof shell, but not much good when wet. OILED AND WAXED cotton originated among British hunting outfitters as a fairly low-tech way to water- and windproof outdoor clothing. BUSH POPLIN, a medium-weight fabric with a crosswise rib, usually cotton, offers excellent water and thorn resistance and is used in the classic belted bush or safari jacket.

COLD COMFORT

Capilene has an inner core that wicks moisture off the body.

A fleece shirt gives ultralight warmth, and keeps the wearer dry when exerting.

Black nylon athletic pants get their "give" from Lycra spandex. Good for winter sports from snowshoeing to cross-country skiing to lodge cruising.

Cycling gloves typically have breathable nylon mesh and a palm insert to cushion road shocks.

Synchilla is a synthetic fur made by Patagonia from post-consumer-recycled (PCR) polyester—80 percent of its fiber comes from recycled plastic bottles. It keeps you warm even in wet conditions.

Hi-tech

GORE-TEX started it all by creating a membrane small enough to allow vapor to pass through but too small for rain to enter. CAPILENE, a trademark polyester fiber made by Patagonia, is another membrane that permits moisture to be wicked from the body. SYNCHILLA, the Patagonia brand name for fleece, is lightweight, warm, and wicks vapor. THINSULATE, created in 1978 by 3M as a synthetic substitute for down, maintains its warmth even when wet. LYCRA SPANDEX provides an element of stretch to everything from running tights to bicycle shorts. POLARTEC, a polyester fleece made by Malden Mills, is brushed to create a thermal barrier of trapped warm air. ACTIVENT, a newer innovation from W. L. Gore and more breathable than regular Gore-Tex, is used in high-energy activities like trail-running or cross-country skiing.

WET COMFORT

Golf jacket of tightly woven polyester cuts the wind.

Striped golf shirt made of a water-resistant microfiber helps avoid the clamminess of cotton when swinging hard.

A "skin" shirt with a polyester core keeps cold out, while a fleece and neoprene vest keeps warmth in.

Khaki shorts with water-resistant nylon lining. Fall into the lake with a smile.

If Lloyd Bridges had only known—for warmth and comfort, neoprene, or wet suit material, is gaining as a swimsuit alternative. Especially in outdoor water sports—surfing, windsurfing, jet skiing—it adds a protective layer of padding.

"I don't think I'll ever be a real boat reporter. My Rolex isn't big enough. Also, I don't have the color sense. You have to wear orange Top-Siders and a pair of electric-blue OP shorts and a vermilion-and-yellow-striped Patagonia shirt and a hot pink baseball cap with the name of somebody's boat on it in glitter, plus Day-Glo green zinc oxide smeared down your nose and around your lips like a radioactive street mime." *P. J. O'Rourke,* **Holidays in Hell**

ski

The Norwegians invented skiing simply as a means to get around, and the clothing associated with it has always been geared to locomotion. Of course, as skiing evolved into a sport, it has had a major impact on fashion, from the plus-fours and Fair Isle sweaters of St. Moritz in the 1920s to the hip-length jackets and stirrup pants of Sun Valley in the 1940s. In the 1960s, the skiing racing circuit of America and Europe influenced the jet set. Robert Redford starred in *Downhill Racer* and the country was full of tight ski pants and bold striped racing sweaters—some even appeared on the ski slopes. Jean-Claude Killy swept the Olympics with élan and cool ski glasses, and Billy Kidd battled for the United States, its racing as well as its sartorial pride, bombing down slopes in his Stetson and Western cut wind shirts. Yeehaw!

Today there are ski fashions to suit every style of skiing, whether cross-country, telemark, alpine, or snowboarding. Baggy Norwegian knickers have been replaced by streamlined ski pants with internal gaiters. Fleece vests and microfiber anoraks have replaced wool jackets and sweaters. For "back-country", there are high-tech "helisuits" with water bladders and pockets for avalanche beepers. Snowboarders have driven a punk style of hip-hop onto the slopes in gear influenced by skateboarders. Then there is the retro influence, like a loden-wool jacket with Thinsulate lining from Prada (opposite), which combines technical and traditional fibers. From The North Face extreme-skiing parkas worn by urbanites to the racing-stripe sweaters of the 1960s, ski clothes have always been as much about fashion as functionality.

SLOPE

UNSLOPE

On the slopes: Loden-cloth jacket with Timberland's zippered polyester performance shirt.

Although they look like cavalry twill, the pants are microfiber, perfect for any snow conditions.

After the slopes: the Prada loden jacket worn with Pendleton wool plaid shirt, knit tie, and beige cords.

A hand-tied fly
resting on your
tweed lapel is
both a reminder of
memories and a
small piece of art.

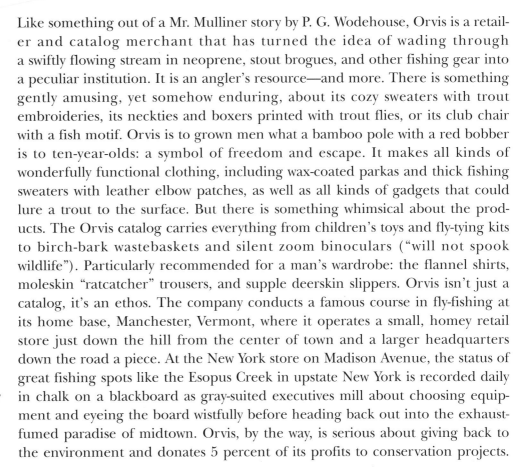

fishing = Orvis

Hunting Vests. Like the fisherman's vest, the shooter's vest meets particular needs of the sportsman but is also stylish in its own right. Made of sturdy leather or suede, it usually has an ammunition pocket, a decoy pocket, and a padded shoulder to protect the wearer against the rifle's recoil. It has become very popular for casual country wear under a sport jacket, but a lot of guys who are seen in them are just shooting the bull.

Like something out of a Mr. Mulliner story by P. G. Wodehouse, Orvis is a retailer and catalog merchant that has turned the idea of wading through a swiftly flowing stream in neoprene, stout brogues, and other fishing gear into a peculiar institution. It is an angler's resource—and more. There is something gently amusing, yet somehow enduring, about its cozy sweaters with trout embroideries, its neckties and boxers printed with trout flies, or its club chair with a fish motif. Orvis is to grown men what a bamboo pole with a red bobber is to ten-year-olds: a symbol of freedom and escape. It makes all kinds of wonderfully functional clothing, including wax-coated parkas and thick fishing sweaters with leather elbow patches, as well as all kinds of gadgets that could lure a trout to the surface. But there is something whimsical about the products. The Orvis catalog carries everything from children's toys and fly-tying kits to birch-bark wastebaskets and silent zoom binoculars ("will not spook wildlife"). Particularly recommended for a man's wardrobe: the flannel shirts, moleskin "ratcatcher" trousers, and supple deerskin slippers. Orvis isn't just a catalog, it's an ethos. The company conducts a famous course in fly-fishing at its home base, Manchester, Vermont, where it operates a small, homey retail store just down the hill from the center of town and a larger headquarters down the road a piece. At the New York store on Madison Avenue, the status of great fishing spots like the Esopus Creek in upstate New York is recorded daily in chalk on a blackboard as gray-suited executives mill about choosing equipment and eyeing the board wistfully before heading back out into the exhaust-fumed paradise of midtown. Orvis, by the way, is serious about giving back to the environment and donates 5 percent of its profits to conservation projects.

Fishing Vests. Fishing, the most contemplative sport, requires a bit of thoughtful planning with regard to dress. Among the staples of the angler's kit: waterproof rubber waders, a vented soft hat with medium brim, and, of course, a fisherman's vest. The classic angler's vest has multiple mesh pockets for storing various items and a patch of shearling at the top to hold one's flies. The good ones, like those made by Orvis, come in processed polyester, for water-resistance. Fisherman's vests also do double-duty for hiking and have become popular among photojournalists.

HUNTER'S HERITAGE

Two hunting jackets that have stood the test of time: the Norfolk jacket (lower right), which has bellow pockets, a box pleat at each side in front, two similar pleats in back, a bi-swing back and an all-around belt; and the bush or safari jacket, a belted, single-breasted jacket with four patch bellows pockets. The Norfolk jacket, the forerunner of all sport jackets, was named for the Duke of Norfolk, who held shooting parties on his Victorian estate. The design of the jacket allowed for the easy swing of a gun, as well as providing ample pockets for carrying cartridges. The safari jacket was made for white hunters in the 1920s and 1930s who needed coats durable enough to survive the bush but lightweight enough to be comfortable in the heat. The style was revived in the 1970s by less predatory sorts, including suburban dentists and accountants, who simply liked its look. Safari jackets, with their tightly woven cotton shell, remain functional and versatile warm-weather outerwear.

Barbour Coat. A classic hunting overcoat, in oiled thornproof cloth of Egyptian cotton. Indestructible, water-resistant, replete with pockets—from moleskin-lined handwarmers to cavernous interior game pockets—great for rabbits and quail but also handy for airplane tickets or agendas. The oilcloth has a smell that can rival Proust's madeleines for evoking memories.

The Flask. A fine flask is as much a fashion accessory as a mainstay on cold days in the woods—or on the 50-yard line. The object itself and the gesture it represents can be as important as the nip. Like the swank snap of a handsome cigarette case or the elegant blaze of a fine lighter, there is something ineffably chic about a leather- or canvas-covered flask produced at the right moment.

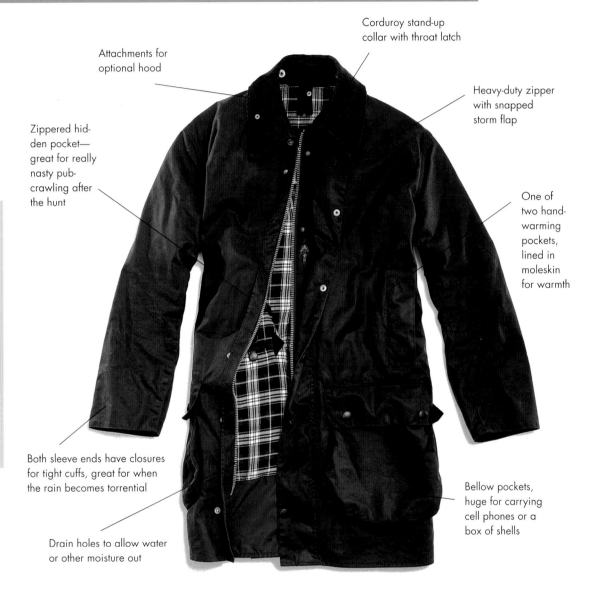

Corduroy stand-up collar with throat latch

Attachments for optional hood

Heavy-duty zipper with snapped storm flap

Zippered hidden pocket—great for really nasty pub-crawling after the hunt

One of two hand-warming pockets, lined in moleskin for warmth

Both sleeve ends have closures for tight cuffs, great for when the rain becomes torrential

Bellow pockets, huge for carrying cell phones or a box of shells

Drain holes to allow water or other moisture out

"Next morning Brideshead wore scarlet; Cordelia, very smart herself, with her chin held high over her white stock, wailed when Sebastian appeared in a tweed coat: 'Oh, Sebastian you can't come out like that. Do go and change. You look so lovely in hunting clothes.'" *Evelyn Waugh,* **Brideshead Revisited**

"The bar is brief, furtive. It allows you a long sweet expectation through the day, then you go and hide in the shadows among the leather chairs: at six in the evenings there's nobody there, the sordid clientele comes later, with the piano man. Choose a louche American bar empty in the afternoon. The waiter comes only if you call him three times, and he has the next martini ready.

It has to be a martini. Not whiskey, a martini. The liquid is clear. You raise your glass and you see her over the olive. The difference between looking at your beloved through a dry martini straight up, where the glass is small, thin, and looking at her through a martini on the rocks, through thick glass, and her face broken by the transparent cubism of the ice. The effect is doubled if you each press your glass to your forehead, feeling the chill, and lean close until the glasses touch. You can't do that with martini glasses.

The brief hour of the bar. Afterward, trembling, you await another day. Free of the blackmail of certainty." *Umberto Eco*, **Foucault's Pendulum**

While formal dressing has become considerably more relaxed, it is better to bend the rules rather than break them. The time-honored rituals, everything from tying the bow tie to offering a proper toast, are part of what makes formal affairs fun. But how do you personalize the look so you don't end up looking like one of the waiters? Should you own a tuxedo or are you better off renting? How expressive should you be in your accessories, footwear? Going out to dinner after work—tie or no tie? The solutions beckon. Turn the page.

● **Soundtracks**
Getting Ready

The Dave Brubeck Quartet ● *Take Five*
Serge Gainsbourg ● *Couleur Café*
Curtis Mayfield ● *Superfly Deluxe*
Max Roach ● *To the Max*
Camille Saint-Saens ● *Symphony No. 3 in C Minor, Op. 78*
Ella Fitzgerald ● *For the Love of Ella*
Amarcord ● *The Soundtrack*
Fred Astaire ● *Steppin' Out*
Various Artists ● *The Last Temptation of Elvis*
Charlie Parker ● *The Complete Charlie Parker on Dial*
Al Green ● *Let's Stay Together*
Jimi Hendrix ● *Electric Ladyland*
Ruby Braff & George Barnes Quartet● *Salutes Rodgers and Hart*

LOOKING GOOD

The day is over; work, Saturday chores, whatever, are finished and now you are going out. The goal is to feel good, look good. From a casual dinner with a friend or friends to a charity ball, an opening night gala, or visiting the club scene, the modern man has many more options than ever before. The traditional dinner jacket has its place, but even at black-tie affairs it is being reconfigured to suit a more casual time. When real formality is called for, simplicity and elegance are the watchwords of the age.

Matchless. Even if you do not smoke yourself, you may want to carry a beautiful lighter for those auspicious moments when a stunning woman is fumbling for matches or the boss is patting his pockets in search of a flame for his stogie. Any excuse will do. Perhaps it is simply a matter of illuminating your program at the theater. In terms of absolute style, the gold Dunhill Rollalite is the ultimate tool on such occasions and a splendid accessory in its own right. A direct descendant of the legendary Dunhill Rollagas (discontinued in 1958 with the advent of butane), the modern Rollalite comes with the same famous slender ribbed body plated in fourteen-karat gold, with the same marvelous methodology. Lighting it requires you to flick up the top with one finger and then roll the striker along the side with the same hand to spark the flame into life—a very elegant movement, like something out of an old John Gielgud film. The beauty and utility of such a lighter command attention, especially in situations like openings, black-tie evenings, and meeting damsels, when style itself is the star.

"To judge by the glittering pile, this had been, or was, a rich man. It contained the typical membership badges of the rich man's club—a money clip, made of a Mexican fifty-dollar piece and holding a substantial wad of banknotes, a well-used gold Dunhill lighter, an oval gold cigarette case with the wavy ridges and discreet turquoise button that means Fabergé." *Ian Fleming,* **From Russia with Love**

appropriate behavior

The flexibility of a classic sport jacket—the houndstooth pattern becomes dressy with the simplicity of a white shirt, single-pattern tie, and wool slacks.

The same jacket can cruise art galleries, bars, or a neighbor's get-together with a cashmere polo sweater and a pair of textured corduroy pants.

It's the details that make up the whole—here the French cuffs add a note of evening to the outfit.

Another detail is the crocodile wristband on the vintage watch—it adds a gentle statement of individuality.

When the sun sets, women seem to know how to dazzle, but men are frequently in the dark. Once out of the nine-to-five uniform, they are like fish out of water. We're not talking black-tie here, which is its own sort of uniform and does not require any great feats of the imagination. Nor do we mean strictly laid-back casual clothes, your routine jacket, jeans, and sneakers act. There are many occasions of intermediate formality, from a dinner date to a concert to a night out at a club, that can be challenging to the masculine psyche and closet. What's needed are a few good fashion pieces and a dash of nonchalance. You want to look fabulous but not too fabulous. For starters, the man doesn't have to upstage the woman, so it is not at all necessary to dress like a peacock. The original after-six black-tie formula was designed to provide a neutral backdrop for the woman's more glamorous presentation. The principle still makes sense. So, by analogy, stick with dark colors. Blues and black go well together, as do blues and brown, black and tan, black and gray. Dress for the situation. Like impeccable manners, appropriate dress will be quietly respected and appreciated by anyone you step out with, unless maybe you're dating Courtney Love. If you are dining at a first-rate restaurant, shirt, tie, and jacket are logical (if not required). You can loosen up a bit by wearing a sport jacket. Or, to take a different approach, you can wear a suit but substitute a turtleneck or knit T-shirt for the shirt and tie. If you are going to an art opening, rock show, or some other event with a creative edge, you might want to try half-boots instead of lace-ups, a dark-colored iridescent dress shirt, open at the collar, instead of a white one, and so on. For events that border on formality but have a strong avant-garde ambience, it is nice to have a strong piece of clothing that works for you in that situation. This is where so-called designer clothes can make a lot of sense. A jacket with some off-center detailing or an interesting cut may be what you need. Or, then again, you can be like Ahmet Ertegun, the Atlantic Records honcho, who throughout his decades hanging backstage with the Rolling Stones and other transgressive rock acts has always worn beautifully tailored Savile Row suits. His hipness has been in his heart, not on his sleeve.

"The whole world is about three drinks behind." *Humphrey Bogart*

A leather-collared wool jacket by designer John Bartlett, with a cashmere turtleneck and Glen plaid trousers, combines the colors of the night, black and gray, with hip styling.

Is it corny to have the bow tie and cummerbund match? Not a bit. Tie and cummerbund should definitely match, unless they happen to be in some horrible high-school-prom color (like metallic cherry red), in which case they should not be worn at all.

black tie

Nothing is more elegant—and more unassailable—than a well-cut and perfectly accessorized dinner jacket. While the words "black tie" engraved on the bottom of an invitation can strike terror in the hearts of some, there is absolutely no cause for alarm. Black tie is your friend, not your enemy. Ever since a rebellious young dandy named Griswold Lorillard wore an abbreviated black formal jacket, without the usual tails, to an exclusive country club in Tuxedo Park, New York, in 1896, the tuxedo, as his ensemble came to be known, has been the mode by which any man can achieve a high level of sophistication and chic. While leaving some room for judicious experimentation, the dinner jacket, or tuxedo, is actually a uniform, and if one observes a few ground rules, the look is difficult to screw up (although plenty of guys manage to do so). A classic dinner jacket is one of the best wardrobe investments a man can make. Whether it is purchased in a traditional Anglo-American or Italian cut, your dinner jacket should be limited to one of only four viable styles: single- or double-breasted peaked lapel, with satin or grosgrain facing on the lapels; and single- or double-breasted shawl collar, with satin or grosgrain lapels. Black or midnight blue are the most acceptable colors. This can easily be a lifetime investment so take your time. Go for an enduring look, with perfectly matched accessories, and you will never have anything to fear.

"In a tuxedo, I'm a star. In regular clothes, I'm nobody." *Dean Martin*

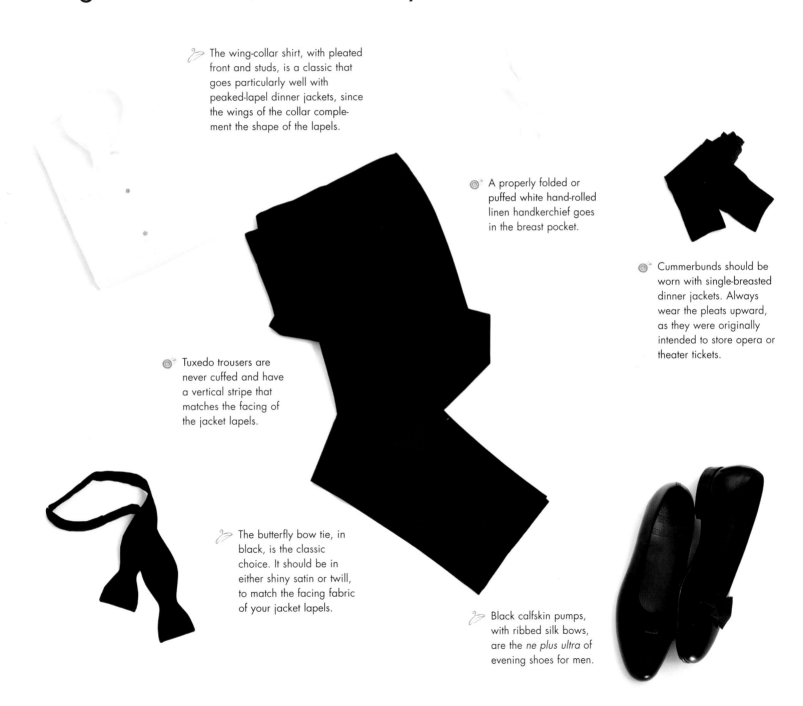

The wing-collar shirt, with pleated front and studs, is a classic that goes particularly well with peaked-lapel dinner jackets, since the wings of the collar complement the shape of the lapels.

A properly folded or puffed white hand-rolled linen handkerchief goes in the breast pocket.

Cummerbunds should be worn with single-breasted dinner jackets. Always wear the pleats upward, as they were originally intended to store opera or theater tickets.

Tuxedo trousers are never cuffed and have a vertical stripe that matches the facing of the jacket lapels.

The butterfly bow tie, in black, is the classic choice. It should be in either shiny satin or twill, to match the facing fabric of your jacket lapels.

Black calfskin pumps, with ribbed silk bows, are the *ne plus ultra* of evening shoes for men.

tux

"Is Bob Dylan wearing a tux?

A band-collar shirt with a single collar stud is one hip variation on black tie.

A splash of color with black tie is great if it goes with your personality.

Evening can be a time to wear a different look in eyeglasses— darker rims are more dramatic.

Personalize Your Basic Tuxedo.

While black tie by definition calls for sartorial conformity, there is certainly room for individual expression. For starters, the tie itself needn't be black, and at some black-tie events, like music awards, the tie is frequently dispensed with altogether. A few very elegant men have always gained a kind of fashionable notoriety by wearing sandals or oxford button-down shirts, Levi's, and cowboy boots (Ralph Lauren) or Converse HighTops (Woody Allen) with their tuxedos. Waistcoats, shoes, and other accessories can be varied to give your basic black tie a distinctive personality. It is up to you, the individual, to exercise some restraint. At most formal affairs it is preferable to be quietly chic rather than stridently fashionable.

More men are wearing non-traditional vests in place of a formal waistcoat. Exercise caution here, though.

Soft, tasseled Belgian loafers are an acceptable (and comfortable) alternative to patent leather dress shoes. A vintage wristwatch or pocket watch also enhances the presentation.

 Never let your clothes speak louder than you do.

That's it, the sixties are over." *Michael Kinsley, editor,* **Slate**

All black, even without a bow tie, is a look that says evening.

Polished black Beatle boots finish a black-tie look that is low on stuffiness and high on attitude.

If you still haven't made the leap and are renting your tux, then rent it one size too small. It instantly instills ownership (if the fly zips only half-way it's a clincher you own it).

Tying the bow tie: Begin with one end, approximately one and one-half inches below the other, and bring the long end through the center. Form a loop with the short end, centering it where the knot will be, and bring the long end over it. Form a loop with the long end and push it through the knot behind the front loop. Adjust the ends slowly. This is where the battle of the bow tie is won or lost.

MASTERING YOUR BLACK-TIE PRESENTATION

Fine Points:

💡 If your social calendar includes numerous affairs, buy several different type of shirts in assorted fabrics and collars to add some variety—cheaper than different bow ties and cummerbunds and simpler.

There is really no substitute for the hand-tied bow tie, which requires a bit of practice. (If you are experiencing difficulty, try tying it around your thigh first, just to get the hang of it.) If the tie is black, its texture should relate to the fabric of the lapels (satin finish if the lapel is satin faced, etc.). Formal dress shirts come in two basic types: wing collar with piqué front, or turndown collar with pleated front. The latter is slightly less formal, considerably more comfortable, and goes well with shawl-collared jackets. The stiff piqué front or pleated bosom of the shirt should never extend below the waistband of the trousers. In a pinch, it is not at all beyond the pale to wear a regular white dress shirt, preferably with French cuffs, to a black-tie affair—assuming all the other elements are impeccably turned out.

EVENING CHROME

"A cocktail party is what you call it when you invite everyone you know to come over to your house at 6 p.m., put cigarettes out on your rug, and leave at eight to go somewhere more interesting for dinner without inviting you." *P. J. O'Rourke,* **Modern Manners**

Since the basic uniform looks pretty much the same on everyone, how does one look distinctive without looking out of place? How do you bend the rules without breaking them? Begin with the tie itself. "Black tie" doesn't mean the tie itself has to be black. A midnight-blue or beautiful brocade paisley tie is perfectly acceptable as well as chic. A small black-and-white check pattern can also be extremely elegant. In each case, make certain that the cummerbund is in a related or complementary pattern. A great pair of braces, particularly in black satin or white, also sets the sartorially sophisticated apart (belts are not worn with tuxedos). When it comes to studs and cuff links, keep them simple. Black onyx, silver, and gold are the obvious choices. Mother-of-pearl is typically worn with white tie or in the summer with an ivory dinner jacket. To acquire fine stud sets with a different look, shop in antique stores and vintage jewelers. Finally, an elegant dress watch, vintage or modern, completes the look.

CAN MAKE OR BREAK A BLACK-TIE ENSEMBLE

The shawl-collared ivory dinner jacket is a warm-weather classic.

A horizontal-stripe formal shirt gives graphic snap to the ensemble.

(faQ)

What do you wear when the invitation says "black tie optional"? In nearly every case, do not wear a tuxedo, especially in summer. A dark business suit (not seersucker or khaki) is appropriate for such occasions. Otherwise you will usually look more like the waiters than anyone else.

Whimsical suspenders enliven a summer formal look.

summer formal

The ivory dinner jacket has long been a favorite for formal affairs between Memorial Day and Labor Day as well as for resort wear in the tropics. The look projects an aura of coolness (Bond, James Bond) and comfort in contexts that we associate with stuffiness and formality. The classic shawl-collared versions are readily obtainable in second-hand clothing stores (check carefully for excessive yellowing of the fabric).

A double-breasted dinner jacket provides an extra layer of warmth.

Note that a cummerbund is never worn with a double-breasted dinner jacket, as it would be redundant.

A dark velvet smoking jacket is an elegant alternative.

If you wear velvet or patent-leather evening slippers in winter, keep a careful eye on the weather forecast. Slush is their downfall.

winter formal

The heavy barathea wools that once characterized most fall-winter evening clothes have been largely replaced by tropical-weight fabrics, making most black dinner jackets virtually seasonless. Nevertheless, in the interest of warmth, a double-breasted model places an extra layer of fabric across the body. And a soft velvet smoking jacket is both a stylish change of pace and a winning ticket to wintertime elegance.

pumped

While considerable latitude has crept into the realm of formal footwear for men, the shoes should still be black and the spirit somewhat luxurious. Keep in mind, you are no longer at work. The most traditional and proper styles are two: black patent-leather oxford lace-ups or patent-leather pumps with a dull ribbed-silk bow at the toe. Velvet evening slippers with gold-crest embroidery are a smart alternative, as are the aforementioned Belgian shoes, incomparably soft loafers that now come in patent leather for evening. In the same vein, cushy black suede loafers or lace-ups can be stylish if casual black-tie options. Highly polished ankle boots and dressy black lace-ups also make the grade, but tread lightly here—black-tie events are special occasions, and one doesn't want to detract from the special magic with mundane, everyday attire.

A plain pair of black leather cap-toe dress shoes is sufficient (if a tad unexciting) for most black-tie affairs—as long as they are in good condition and well polished. Avoid at all costs shoes with perforated saddles or wing tips. They spoil the whole effect.

"For me, a tuxedo is a way of life." *Frank Sinatra*

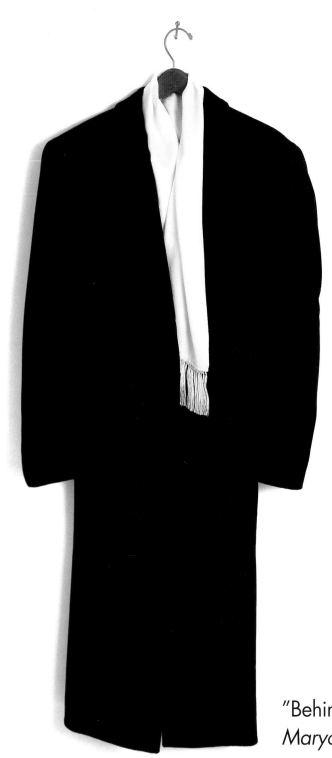

ELEGANT

An evening scarf, usually in white or ivory fringed silk, is the proper complement to the evening coat but can also be worn with just the tuxedo.

The velvet chesterfield coat, in dark blue or black cashmere, is specifically appropriate for black-tie occasions. But it can be worn more casually too.

Topcoats need to cover the knee to balance the look, but they should never be so long that they drag on a long flight of steps, like those at the Metropolitan Museum of Art and countless other black-tie venues.

"Behind every great man there is a surprised woman."
Maryon Pearson

TOPPER

Many men prefer to leave their coats at home on formal evenings to avoid the coat-check crush. But in frigid weather, you will want a topcoat to finish off the look. There is nothing more suitable than the fly-front chesterfield, in black or blue, with velvet collar. The velvet facing on the collar is a vestige from the time of the French Revolution, when gentlemen in other countries expressed their disapproval of the executions by adding black velvet as a sign of mourning. No need to be gloomy, though. Out on the town, the style today just seems a bit dashing and debonair.

A pair of gray mocha leather or suede gloves is a traditional finishing touch, and whether you smoke or not, a sleek silver cigarette lighter (to fire up your date's cigar) is the kind of sophisticated accessory that separates the men from the boys.

 Letting a woman enter a taxi first is one of those unwritten laws that seems to be elementary, a simple matter of urban chivalry. In actuality, it depends on the place. In New York or Paris, for example, where traffic is perpetually whizzing on the street side of the cab, it is usually far more considerate for the man to enter first and then slide over, saving the woman from the hosiery-destroying process of wriggling across a tightly spaced rear seat. In less frenzied environs, the man should let the woman enter first at the curb, and then go around to the other door and seat himself on the far side. In the rain, or other ambiguous circumstances, it is a good idea for the man to open the door and then suggest, "Shall I go in and slide over?"

Should you leave the band on a cigar? Traditionally the English in their clubs took off the band before smoking—this was to prevent embarrassment to any fellow smoker whose smoke wasn't of the same caliber.

If you don't smoke enough to justify a traditional humidor, consider a travel humidor. Depending on the size you favor, it can hold five to ten cigars in an enjoyable state, and it's great for being on the road.

a quiet night

"Fresh air makes me throw up. I can't handle it. I'd rather be around three Denobili cigars blowin' in my face all night." Frank Sinatra

There you are by the fireplace. Logs of seasoned oak or green ash coaling up nicely in the grate. A symphony by Brahms or Charlie Parker with Strings on the hi-fi. A snifter of cognac or a single malt, neat, twinkling in the firelight. Sometimes you are your own best company. (Okay, on the whole, you'd much rather be out chasing chicks or watching very tall men stuff balls into hoops.) You could simply hang here in your old sweat clothes. But why not live it up a little? You don't have to be Noël Coward to put on some elegant loungewear: that silk foulard robe from Sulka— perhaps the leather slippers from Brooks Brothers. Sometimes after all the buzz of the business day, you don't need any companionship except yourself and a fine cigar. Now, publicly, the cigar has become a widely abused, somewhat noxious yuppie power accessory, a walking Freudian slip. At parties, cigars can be intrusive and silly. For one thing, they stink. However, alone in the privacy of your own parlor or den, the cigar can be a civilizing pleasure—the lengthening ash measuring the fullness of each passing moment and the magnitude of your thoughts. Perhaps you should write a play... Start a mergers-and-acquisitions department... Read Melville... Run for office... or just... go to bed...

"It is awfully easy to be hard-boiled about every-thing in the daytime, but at night it is another thing." *Ernest Hemingway,* **The Sun Also Rises**

good night.

p.m.

⊚⁺ The shawl-collared silk foulard smoking jacket, usually in a rich paisley pattern, can be worn for a satisfying solitary smoke or for entertaining at home. Some men even venture out in them to black-tie affairs.

first aid.

A final guide, a radiant burst of helpful hints and pieces of practical information for you guys out there who want to get your domestic lives together, but don't know where to start. Taking care of your clothes, strengthening your body, knowing where to find that one suit jacket that really fits—we've done all the initial research to get you that much closer to a life less complicated. Now use it.

LAUNDRY AND DRY CLEANING

Washing

Get ahead of the laundry-sorting dilemma by hanging mesh laundry bags in the closet or bathroom for whites, colors, darks, and garments that must be dry-cleaned or washed by hand. • Be sure to unbutton garments before putting them in the washing machine. • Wash dark colors, anything with lettering, and fleece garments inside out. • Anything elastic, and undergarments of all kinds, should be hang-dried or dried in a machine on a no-heat setting. • Hang-drying is better than machine-drying for preserving the richness of dark-colored clothes. • Always remove clothes promptly from the washer and dryer. • If clothes are forgotten in the wash overnight and smell musty, rewash them immediately (with bleach if the clothes can tolerate it) to prevent mildew.

Bleach

Use to whiten white fabrics. Check the care label on colored and synthetic fabrics before washing with bleach. • Never bleach garments containing silk, wool, or other specialty hair fibers. Spandex, leathers, and some nylons must not be bleached. • Always use bleach with a detergent, in the hottest water allowed for that item of clothing.

Starch

For men who get their shirts professionally laundered, there is only one consideration: starch. While it may make the shirt look stiff and smooth, it can also be treacherous for the material. The simplest precaution is to starch only the collars and the cuffs, and not every time you have the shirt laundered. If you insist on having a stiff collar, try some spray starch. As for boxing versus hangers: Shirts that are laundered and put on hangers are usually more expensive and don't come back with creases. But shirts that are boxed make sense for the man who travels. They pack beautifully when boxed.

Dry Cleaning

Always dry-clean all pieces of an outfit of the same material at the same time, even if one part is not dirty. • Be sure to check with your dry cleaner before cleaning precious items (getting your money back for a ruined garment is something you can't count on). Items known to be troublesome include sequins, metallics, decorative buttons, and permanent pleats.

If Your Clothes Come Back Shining

Dry cleaning doesn't make clothes shine, but when clothes are pressed incorrectly at too high a heat, the cloth becomes glazed. Some fabrics, such as dark gabardines, can become glazed by wear alone (especially at stress points such as the seat and the elbows). The only way to correct the situation is for an expert to work over the garment with a very fine grade of sandpaper to restore a more matte appearance. Unfortunately, this remedy is only temporary.

How to Check for Colorfastness

To check for color bleeding on dyed fabrics, run this simple test. Find an inconspicuous area on the garment (inside hems are a good place), wet the fabric, and blot it with a white cloth. Allow it to air-dry to determine if the dye and sizing are disturbed. If any color bleeds onto cloth, or the fabric seems damaged once it's dry, dry-clean only.

Stains

Success in stain removal is determined by the degree to which dyes and sizings (the finish applied to fabric in its manufacturing) are colorfast when wet. Do not try to remove a stain yourself if the care label says DRY CLEAN ONLY or if the garment is not colorfast. Because dyes and sizings tend to discolor with moisture, attempting to remove stains with water is not recommended without first testing the garment for colorfastness. Try to absorb stains before they set by using the tip of a white paper towel to soak up excess liquid. Never scrub or press; doing so could ruin the fabric's texture. To assist in the professional removal of stains from nonwashable fabrics, take a stained garment promptly to the dry cleaner, and tell him what caused the stain. The recommendations below are mostly for washable fabrics. When in doubt, take the stained garment to the dry cleaner for professional attention.

chewing gum and tape. Carefully scrape off as much as possible without damaging the fabric (harden it first with an ice cube and it will come off more easily), apply dry-cleaning solvent, and peel off the stain; then launder. If stain persists, try using a grease solvent.

combination stains. These stains include chocolate, gravy, ice cream, and milk. First apply a dry-cleaning solvent, then air-dry. Treat the protein component of the stain by applying liquid detergent and rinsing with cool water. Then use a prewash stain remover. Wash with detergent in the hottest water the garment can withstand. If stain persists, wash again with detergent and appropriate bleach.

grass. If the stain is fresh, try an enzyme presoak, a heavy-duty detergent, or white vinegar on washable fabrics; then rinse. If the stain has already set, try a cleaning fluid.

grease. Typical grease stains are caused by oils, butter, margarine, crayon, mayonnaise, medicines, candle wax, and oil-based cosmetics. Dabbing on talc right away (allow to sit at least a half hour) will help lift the stain. Brush off talc, apply a stain remover, and wash in the hottest water the garment can withstand. For stubborn stains on synthetic fabrics, your dry cleaner can usually handle the problem.

lipstick. For washable fabrics, first use dry-cleaning fluid, then soap and water.

mildew. Treat as soon as possible. Wash mildewed items thoroughly (make sure they are washable) and dry them in the sun. If the stain persists, try chlorine bleach (if care label allows). Take non-washable items to the dry cleaner.

paint. Read the paint-can label carefully. If the paint is water-based, use soap and water if the paint is still wet. If the paint is dry, or it's oil-based, try turpentine. Take nonwashable items to the dry cleaner.

perspiration. The longer it remains, the harder it is to remove. Silk is especially vulnerable. Dry cleaning removes only the oily component of the stain; an expert should administer detergent with a little added water, bleach, or acid or alkaline solutions. If you're concerned about damaging a garment, sew in protective underarm shields.

protein stain (water-borne). These stains include blood, baby formula, deodorant, diaper stains, egg, meat juices, perspiration, and urine. Apply detergent to stain and soak in cool water, then launder. If the stain persists, wash again in an appropriate bleach and the hottest water the garment can withstand. Enzyme presoaks can also help.

tannin. These stains result from coffee, ketchup, tea, wine, vegetables, soft drinks, fruit juice, and mustard. Soak the garment in cool water. Put detergent and white vinegar on the stain, flush with water, and allow to air-dry. If the stain persists, wash with detergent and appropriate bleach in the hottest water the garment can withstand.

REMOVING WRINKLES AND PILLS
Ironing
A man and his iron should never be at odds with each other. • Use a plant mister to dampen the clothes you intend to steam-iron. • A little spray starch can work wonders for cotton shirts. • Iron items that require a cooler iron, such as silk, first. • When in doubt, start with a low setting. • Iron non-showing parts of garments (underside of cuffs and collar) first. • Pull fabric taut as you go along; it makes for smoother ironing. • Iron around buttons, not on top of them. • Pay special attention to the placket. It may be obscured by the tie, but it will make the shirt look crisper.

Wrinkle Remover
The movement and shifting of your packed clothing are the major cause of wrinkling. Fill empty spaces in your suitcase or bag with rolled-up socks, T-shirts, underwear, or wads of tissue or crumpled plastic dry cleaner or grocery bags.

When Traveling
Most hotels can do laundry in a matter of hours, but the charges can leave you feeling wrung out. Hanging especially wrinkled clothing in a bathroom made steamy by letting the hot water in the shower run should do the trick. Socks and underwear can be cleaned in your bathroom sink, using shampoo—just rinse well.

Pilling
Pilling is caused by abrasion during regular use; it often develops on elbows, on the seat of pants, and in areas rubbed by a bag or briefcase. • Unfortunately, it's impossible to tell when buying a sweater or other garment whether it's going to pill. Good-quality clothes should be made of superior fibers that are less likely to pill; soft fuzzy surfaces are more susceptible than others. • To remove pills, manually pick them off (very time-consuming) or invest in a small hand-held electric shaver specifically designed for depilling.

QUICK FIXES

The One-Minute Hem
Use safety pins to reattach hem or cuff to pant leg—just be sure to prick the inside of the cuff or hem and catch a few threads—otherwise your hasty alteration will be visible. • Other options: a few pieces of packing tape, or heavy-duty masking tape. Staples are especially good for khakis, or any lighter-colored pants. (They're not really recommended for black or navy blue slacks—the metallic staples will be sure to stand out on top of a dark background.)

French Cuffs
Improvisation. It's gotten McGyver out of more binds in one episode than most of us get into in a lifetime. Think of the smallest, most insignificant little objects: paper clips, rubberbands, bread bag fasteners. Paper clips can be bent out of shape and twisted together to cuff holes together. Rubberbands and those little twisties can be tied together to do their job, and remain discreetly covered—just make sure you tie them together from the inside of the cuff. These makeshift cuff links may not be entirely attractive, but they do work. Remember, "desperate times call for desperate measures." Think practical and keep your dinner jacket on.

Collar Stays
Collar stays can easily be replaced with cardboard pieces, roughly cut into the shape of collar stays. Look for the cardboard backs of notepads, the TV channel listings sitting atop the hotel television set, empty tissue boxes, etc.—you get the idea.

SHOE AND FOOT CARE

Promoting Shoe Longevity
Leather breathes, and it needs a day or two after being worn to dry out. The same shoes should not be worn day after day. Alternate shoes if you want them to last. Polishing leather helps to keep it from cracking; shoe trees maintain shape. Disposable inner soles cushion each step and absorb odor and sweat. Reheel and resole when necessary. Avoid wearing down heels by having taps placed on them immediately after buying (this costs a lot less than having to fix the heels later).

polished leather. Place shoes on a sheet of newspaper. Brush off surface dirt with a rag, paper towel, or soft brush. • Apply a thin layer of cream polish in appropriate color or neutral. Use circular strokes, rubbing in the polish as you go. Do not leave an excessive amount on the surface. • When shoes are dirty, buff them with a brush of soft cloth. • If not satisfied, repeat. • Between polishes, you can rebuff with a soft cloth. • If there is a grease stain on polished leather, first blot with a dry cloth;

if the stain persists, try lifting it with a little white vinegar.

patent leather. Wipe shoes clean with a soft cloth. Use shoe products made specifically for patent leather to prevent cracking.

suede. Spray suede shoes with silicone spray before wearing them for the first time. Be aware that the spray will waterproof but may dramatically darken the color of the shoes. Silicone spray is best suited for black or hiking shoes. Fluoropolymer, nonsilicone spray also waterproofs, repels stains, and preserves the color and look of the shoe, and is well suited for dress shoes. Consider reapplying either spray frequently if shoes are worn often. If you develop a bald spot on a shoe, use a very fine grade (00) sandpaper gently on the area until the nap lifts. You can also lift the nap by holding shoes over a boiling kettle and brushing them gently with an old toothbrush.

low-tech canvas sneaker. Machine-wash in warm water—mild soap, no bleach. • Sneakers will be protected in the spin cycle if washed with a towel. • For best results, place in the dryer immediately after washing. • Machine-dry for approximately forty-five minutes on highest heat setting. [Courtesy of Keds]

western boots. Use saddle soap according to directions. Allow to dry a full day between wearings.

STORAGE

Ideal Storage Conditions
The ideal environment for storing fabric is a stable 70 to 72 degrees Fahrenheit, with 50 to 55 percent relative humidity. There should also be adequate ventilation. Extreme fluctuations in temperature are harmful. If you live in a warm climate, beware of particle-board shelving. Particle board, which is made of chopped-up bits of wood, expands in high humidity and may cause boxes stacked on top to become glued there. This will not happen with ventilated shelving.

hangers. Generally, the heavier the garment, the heavier the hanger. Wire hangers are less sturdy and more likely to snag clothes. Uniform plastic hangers are sturdy, as are contoured wooden suit hangers. Padded hangers work well for delicate fabrics like linen and silk, and cedar hangers can help repel moths. Two-piece suits save horizontal space if they are hung together. Pants, unless they are knit, should always be hung. Make sure dress shirts and jackets are partly, if not completely, buttoned. Pants, however, should not be buttoned; fold them along creases.

cleaning before storage. This is recommended, as fresh stains that may not yet be visible will oxidize and become fixed during storage. Furthermore, storing clothes without first cleaning them is like curing food for moths.

seasonal items. Storing off-season items makes selecting from your closet each morning easier by affording more space for your current wardrobe and cutting down on visual distraction. Exposure to air, dust, moths, and sun can damage fabric. Zippered fabric garment bags protect antique or delicate clothes best. Remove all dry-cleaner plastic. Wrap in acid-free tissue or cotton muslin if clothing is made of silk or other delicate fabric. Try to store off-season items in remote areas. Space can be created with collapsible garment racks or rods installed in alcoves. • Put in boxes on wheels under the bed • in clear plastic boxes stacked on closet shelves • in a dresser or trunk in an extra room • in an old suitcase or trunk.

storing with plastic. Natural fibers, especially silk and linen, need to breathe. Storing white fabrics in cellophane will cause them to yellow from oxidation. Keep them uncovered, or cover with a cloth. Dry-cleaner plastic keeps dust away, but beware of moisture if the climate is humid or storage is likely to be long-term.

fading. Many brightly colored fabrics fade from exposure to sunlight or artificial light. Some blue and green dyes fade exceptionally fast, especially on silk. Store garments in closets away from light.

moth protection. Moths have a discerning palate; they feast only on natural fabrics. Mothballs (naphthalene) and cedar chips are standard protection from moth infestation of woolens. Mothballs work best in small, tight spaces. The parachlorobenzene they give off can leach color from fabrics and cause respiratory problems in people, so be careful how you use them. Cedar doesn't kill moths—it only repels them—but it is a natural substance without the chemicals used in mothballs. Cedar strips nailed inside a closet are an alternative to the cedar chest or cedar-lined closet. Cedar blocks do not have to be replaced; they require only standing to freshen their smell. However, according to Jeeves of Belgravia, a luxury dry cleaner in New York City, the most certain protection against moths is naphthalene; it's sold under different brand names in hardware and housewares stores.

Storing Accessories
belts. Do not store belts in pants, as this can damage the fabric or shape of the garment. The best way to store a leather belt is to let it hang from its buckle on a mounted rack, on a hanger-shaped rack, or from a hook. Coiling it inside a shoe caddy also works well.

hats. Hang hats on hooks or pegs along a wall, stack on a closet shelf, store them in hat boxes, or hang them from a coat tree. For obvious reasons, do not leave hats sitting on chairs or beds—besides, as Matt Dillon noted in the movie *Drugstore Cowboy*, it's bad luck.

dress shoes. Always store leather dress shoes on a wooden shoe rack, or leave them flat on the floor, stuffed with newspaper or tissue paper to preserve the shape of the shoes as they dry after wearing. Never store near a heat source because it will dry out the leather. Leather can mildew, so store your shoes in a dry place. The area should also be ventilated; don't store shoes in an airtight container, or with mothballs. • An organizational tip: stack shoes inside their respective boxes (with a packet of salt to absorb any moisture), and tack a photograph of the shoes or a label to the box.

dress codes.

Clothes can be functional gear or a mark of individuality, or simply something to wear. Right or wrong, impressions are made, according to communications consultant Roger Ailes, in the first seven seconds. Making the most of your clothes means knowing what to do with them and where. Here's how:

OFFICE

Before you start shopping, ask yourself these questions: What kind of office do I work in? • What is my role? • What is my day like? • What kind of image is the company trying to project? • What kind of image do I want to maintain? • Whether you work in a traditional corporate setting or one that is more relaxed, there are several things you can count on, especially if you're on a budget. • The blazer, in navy or black, is a staple for less formal corporate wear; the blazer is flexible in that you can wear it to the office, as well as to nonwork-related social gatherings. • For suits, it's better to choose neutral colors like charcoal gray, black, and navy—they are extremely versatile. Serious business attire calls for a single-breasted black suit. • Every man should own at least three suits. • Dress shirts—it's best to invest in white (which is the most formal dress shirt color), cream, and light blue. • You should ideally own at least seven or eight shirts to ensure that you always have something clean to wear. • You should also own at least one pair of gray wool or dark navy trousers—they'll take you everywhere. • To finish, two pairs of black or brown shoes —laced cap toe or split toe, with coordinating leather belts. • If you find yourself attending two or more formal events a year, it's also a good idea to invest in a tuxedo. • Other basic items: a dark-colored raincoat, a camel topcoat, and an assortment of ties that can be coordinated with your dress shirts. • If budget allows, the one thing that should be changed with some frequency is the tie. Tie styles and patterns are very timely. Buying ties every season will help keep your look current. • For dress-down Fridays, pick out a few striped dress shirts with bright, bold colors—to be worn without a tie; spread collars and French cuffs are a nice touch.

Personalizing Your Look at the Office
If you want to add a kick or create a unique personal style, add vests, different shoes, any number of colored dress shirts (such as dark blue). • Also try varying color combinations and your choice of colors. • Colored shirts, ties, and knit wear also add variety.

Casual
Dressing for casual affairs is a little easier than dressing for the office. Recommended basics include dark washed jeans, cuffed slacks, khaki trousers or tan chinos, a high-quality sport shirt (one that does not resemble a dress shirt without a tie), at least one navy blazer or sport coat (tweed), and finally, suede-finished shoes or loafers. • Dark colors and earth tones are more flexible than bright primary colors or pastels. • One of the easiest things you can do is to stick with black. Black is easy and flexible. There's nothing as simple and as versatile as a black mock turtleneck, black trousers, and a black blazer. You'll be zipping out the door in seconds flat.

THE JOB INTERVIEW

You have two objectives here: Survive the interview and get the job. A few words about living through the experience: • Look your best. You will act more confident. • Play it safe—wear something you don't have to worry about—no wrinkle-prone fabrics. • It's fine to be overdressed at the interview, but serious trouble if you're too casual. • Single-breasted suits in charcoal, gray, navy, or black are always safe. • Avoid clunky or flashy shoes. • Stick to subdued solid-colored ties or ties with small prints—nothing loud or overbearing.

Traditional Fields
Business, law, medicine, insurance, banking: Tailored conservative outfits are best. Nothing should distract from your main purpose: to do the job well and efficiently.

Creative Fields
Journalism, publishing, multimedia, advertising, graphics, art galleries: Your own style is more important here. You are being hired for your creative talents, so show them off in a subtle way, by dressing with personal flair. While on the job, journalists in particular should learn to match their wardrobe to their assignments.

Service Oriented Jobs
Retail, restaurants: These jobs are all about looking presentable. Try and get a sense of what the company's style is before you go in for your interview. Then adapt your own.

PUBLIC SPEAKING AND TELEVISION

People often form their impression of you within the first seven seconds of your meeting, so think about what your clothes are communicating and whether it's helping you get your message across. • Wear comfortable clothes that you feel look good on you. You will appear comfortable with who you are. • Wear safe colors: neutrals like navy and beige look good on television. White shirts are too bright for television. Stick with blues, dusty pinks, off-whites, subtle stripes • Beware of patterned fabrics—they may create a moiré pattern on the television screen. • Wear glasses with a nonglare coating. • Dress the part. Don't wear something that distracts from what you are saying. When delivering your message, always consider who your audience is.

travel.

Pete Townshend sang about "Going Mobile" twenty years ago, and what a prophetic line that was as we all spend more time getting from here to there than we spend either here or there—below are tips on arriving if not unwrinkled at least not frayed at the edges.

WHAT TO WEAR EN ROUTE

Airplanes, trains, taxis, and hotel lobbies can get hot and stuffy. Wear lightweight clothes while you're on the road. Stick with wrinkle-free, breathable, comfortable clothes.

Packing and Travel Tips

Before you even start packing, put together a checklist of all the things you're going to need on your trip—that way, you'll be less likely to forget something. • Pack as lightly as possible. • Stick with neutrals—they're just more versatile. • To prevent wrinkling, place tissue paper or a plastic dry cleaner's bag between each layer of clothes. • Pack your small camera, film, personal stereo, or travel alarm clock into shoes for protection. • Always take more socks and underwear than you think you'll need; also, they can take up space to keep clothes from shifting. • Pack more pants than sport coats. • Bring a light sweater for the airplane. • Always bring a pair of thick wool socks—at some point your feet will get cold. • Pack a collapsible bag for items acquired on the trip. • It's hard to tell if a checked shirt is wrinkled. • Khaki pants and black jeans will save you over and over. • The best way to pack less is to buy a smaller suitcase—a reasonably sized travel bag is one that you can carry at least half a mile. • A photocopy of your birth certificate can speed the replacement of a lost passport. • Travel with wool, if possible—it is one of the most forgiving of fabrics. Also stick with microfiber fabrics and wrinkle-resistant cottons. • Be aware of developing weather patterns before you set out for your destination.

jackets. Start by emptying all the pockets. • Hold the jacket facing you by placing your hands inside the shoulders. • Turn the left shoulder (but not the sleeve) inside out. • Place the right shoulder inside the left shoulder. • The lining is now facing out, and the sleeves are inside the fold. • Fold the jacket in half, put it inside a plastic bag, and place it in your suitcase.

pants. Check to make sure all pockets are empty, since keys or change may damage the fabric once the pants are packed. • Pants should always be the first item packed in a hard case, so place them on the bottom, with the waistband in the middle of the suitcase and the legs falling outside the bag. (If you are packing two pairs, place them waistband-to-waistband, with the legs extending in opposite directions.) • Pack the rest of your things on top, and then wrap the pants legs over the pile, placing one last remaining item over the legs to hold everything in place. • Interlock your belts and run them along the circumference of the suitcase—never pack them in the belt loops, or both pants and belt could change shape.

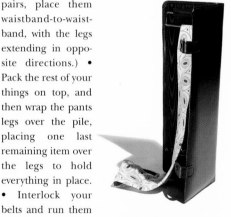

shirts. Button all buttons, noting which front button falls below your waist. • Lay the shirt face down on a flat surface and fold the sleeves back at the shoulder seam. • Fold the tail up from the point of the button that is below your waistline. This will prevent the unpacked shirt from having a crease across your stomach. (Note: If you can plan ahead, have your shirts cleaned and folded at the laundry before your trip.)

shoes. Shoes should always go in a bag—either cloth ones that can be laundered or disposable plastic bags. • Place shoes along the edge of a hard case to keep your folded clothes from shifting. In a duffel, shoes get packed first, at the bottom. • Shoes can carry socks, a coiled belt, extra eyeglasses, or overflow from the toiletry kit, like a tube of sunscreen (to be safe, wrap it first in a plastic bag). *Tip*: Always wear your heaviest shoes for traveling, since they are probably heavy because they're comfortable and sturdy—also, you won't have to carry them.

ties. Fold the tie in half, then place it on a sheet of tissue paper or plastic. • Roll it up, and secure it loosely with a rubberband.

Packing a Duffel Bag

Tissue paper is especially useful in duffel packing to avoid wrinkles. • Roll up cottons and knits, including underwear, sweaters, T-shirts, and pants, and pack them as bumpers against one another. • Pack shoes at the bottom and hard items, like books or an umbrella, along the edges.

Traveling by Plane

computers. When checking a computer through airport security, always send it with your carry-on luggage through the X-ray machine, which won't damage your equipment in any way. Taking it through the magnetically charged metal detector, however, can cause the contents of your computer's hard drive to be erased.

shopping.

Department stores, outlets, thrift stores, and specialty shops. Today, the number of places to shop can be overwhelming. This section should ease some of your shopping angst and help you distinguish the good, the bad, and the truly ugly.

GENERAL TIPS

Wear clothes that you can easily slip in and out of, and put on shoes you plan to wear with the garment you're looking for. • Bring along someone who can provide you with an honest opinion—someone who will tell you straight out if the color's not right, or if something doesn't fit correctly. • Shop for who you are now, not who you will be five pounds from now. • Don't be afraid to try on different silhouettes, particularly if you're buying a suit. For example, if you are looking to buy a single-breasted suit, it's a good idea to try on a double-breasted suit, just to get a feel for other styles and fits. • Pick out the suit you like—one that fits into your budget reasonably. Also pick a suit that is of exceptional quality—regardless of price. Take both suits into the fitting room and then try them on. The superior suit becomes your standard—it should embody all the qualities you are looking for in a suit—take mental note of its fit, its draping abilities, its detailing, etc., and when trying on any other suit in the future, the high-quality suit will act as the comparative model. • Before you buy, check yourself in a three-way mirror in as many positions as you can—sit down, stretch, etc. Make sure you can move with ease, and that your clothes move with you. • Key times to hit the stores: summer clothes, sales after Memorial Day; winter items, after Christmas. However, for a variety of economic reasons, the number of sales held during the course of a year has increased. • When you find a salesperson who speaks your language, stick with him or her. If they're really good, think about helping them out by dropping a line to their manager. • Beware of sales if you're prone to impulse buying. Before you go out, reassess what you have and make a list of what you need; then try to stick to it.

Shopping at a Thrift Store

Thrift stores often reflect the personality of the neighborhood they're in. Affluent areas usually have a lot of evening wear and designer clothing. • Trendy areas usually have more hip clothes; however, designer vintage stores are ridiculously overpriced. • For the best finds, go to no-frills thrift shops, like the Salvation Army, and large warehouses, such as The Garment District in Cambridge, Mass., and Domsey's in Brooklyn, where clothing is sold by the pound. • Look for recognizable labels—particularly if you are familiar with a brand's fit, quality, and sizing. • Remember, this is a thrift store; you're probably not going to be able to find your exact size. Considering the amount of money you save buying secondhand clothes, it's worth taking these not-so-perfect finds to your tailor. Be sure to check for holes and stains, especially in the crotch and armpit areas, and in a jacket's lining. • Look at the underside of clothes for worn-thin fabric and weak seams. • If the garment has a zipper, make sure it runs up and down smoothly. • Check for loose buttons, and inspect the buttonholes. Loose threads surrounding the hole indicate a weak buttonhole. Buttons will slip out of these holes too easily. • Clean everything before you wear it.

Mail Order

It can be more expensive, and a mistake may cost you some postage (not to mention the hassle of going to the post office), but the advantages are many: • You can try things on in the privacy of your own home and take as long as you want in deciding. • You can try things on with other pieces in your wardrobe and see what works. • You can see things in lighting and mirrors you trust. • You can order as much as you want and then return the rejects. • If you find a mail-order catalog whose sizes and styles work for you, stay with it. Each company tends to stick to a consistent overall style, year after year.

HOW TO FIGURE OUT YOUR SIZE AND FIT

To arrive at your true dimensions, all you need is a little patience, a tape measure, and maybe someone else to help.

belts. Same as pants waist sizes. If your waist is an odd number of inches, buy the belt in the next larger size.

chest. Make sure to measure around the trunk at its broadest points: keep the tape measure high under the arms and be sure to encompass shoulder blades and chest.

gloves. Measure around the whole hand at its broadest point (do not include the thumb; be sure to measure your right hand if right-handed, your left if left-handed). The size equals the number of inches.

hats. Measure the crown of the head just above the eyebrows. Convert inches to hat size.

inseam. The easiest way to measure is to take a pair of well-fitting pants (down to the ankle) and measure from the crotch seam to the end of the pants leg. Round up the measurement to the nearest half-inch. The number of inches equals the size.

shirt collar. Measure the collar of a well-fitting shirt you already own. With the collar flat, start at one end (from the middle of the collar button) and measure to the other end of the collar (at the buttonhole). The number of inches is the size. Always allow for shrinkage.

shirt sleeves. With the shirt on, have someone measure from between the shoulders down the shoulder to the elbow (which should be bent). The number of inches is the size. Allow for shrinkage.

waist. While wearing a shirt, measure around your waist, adding a finger's width between you and the tape. The size equals the number of inches.

Suits

Check the fabric. The cheaper suit will be made of cheaper fabric. It may be adequate, but it will not have been chosen especially by the designer for its drapability, hand, strength, or softness. And it may not have as good a memory—the ability of a fabric to hold its shape after multiple wearings—as pricier fabric. The expensive suit, by contrast, is designed in the best fabric the designer could find to realize his or her vision, with little regard for cost. The best thing to avoid when shopping for clothes is cheap fabrics. They lack durability, they are difficult to clean, and, most important, they probably won't work with your body to bring out the look you want. **Look at the detailing.** Machine detailing is not as strong, luxurious, or subtle. It cannot allow for the irregularities of the human form the way hand detailing can, so the cheaper suit may not fit as well as the more expensive one.

Jackets

There are several things you should watch for in a jacket: • **Unnatural ripples or gatherings in the fabric.** A well-made jacket will have no unnatural lines or gathers, as long as it fits well. Jackets that are too tight will start to gather at the shoulder blades and the back. • **Fabric.** Higher-quality fabric is soft to the touch. Lining should be made from a satiny material and should be loosely cut to allow for body movement. Most of the finer jackets are made from wool, or a wool blend. Advantages of wool jackets are that they don't wrinkle easily and they drape well. Polyester or any of the microfiber jackets also drape well. Linen and cotton are limited to spring and summer wear. They are hard to care for, as they wrinkle and fade. Synthetics like nylon, rayon, and triacetate are sturdy and inexpensive. • **Seam and stitching quality.** Check the sides and under the arms of the jackets for straight seams. Also check the back seam. Look for signs of handwork in the shoulders, lapel, and collars—hand-stitching signals finer craftsmanship. Hand-stitched garments tend to drape with a more natural shape. You'll know when a garment has been worked on by hand when you notice uneven, but tighter stitching. • **Interfacing.** All jackets have an inner chest piece, known as the interfacing. It gives the front of the jacket shape and rigidity—but note that too much stiffness can give your jacket a slightly unnatural look. In a quality jacket, the interfacing has been sewn in by hand. Another way manufacturers add the interfacing is to apply intense amounts of heat to the jacket—this fuses the chest piece into the jacket lining. To determine which method was used on your jacket, take one side of its lapel between your fingers and rub. If you can feel the interfacing moving, it's been sewn in rather than fused. • **Collar.** The collar of a jacket can tell you a lot about the overall quality of the jacket. Check the underside of the collar—wool under the visible side of the collar indicates fine craftsmanship. Jackets made well have collars that sit comfortably at the back of your neck—not too loose and not too tight. • **Shoulders and sleeves.** Beware of shoulders that are too round or too boxy. Instead, look for firm shoulder pads. Once you put the jacket on, stand in front of the mirror and make sure that shoulder pads are equally positioned and of the same size. At the junction where sleeve and shoulder meet on the jacket, watch for rippling, or unnecessary gathering. Sleeves should conform to the arms naturally. The sleeve should fall about five inches above the tip of your thumb. • **Lapels.** Check both sides of the lapel to make sure they are equal in size. When you put on the jacket, also check to see how both sides of the lapels are distanced from each other. Too wide a distance indicates that the jacket is too tight. • **Buttons and buttonholes.** Make sure buttons are firmly attached to the jacket and are evenly spaced. Buttonholes should be stitched evenly, with no loose threads.

Dress Shirts

Quality dress shirts are of lightweight, finely woven cotton. The most luxurious are made from superfine cottons, such as **long-staple Egyptian cotton** and **Sea Island cotton**, which, because of longer fibers, create a sheer and satiny texture, at a price. **Cotton poplin** and **broadcloth** are suitably smooth weaves for city shirts. The less formal shirt takes a rougher weave such as **oxford cotton**, the fabric of the Brooks Brothers button-down, which remains perfectly businesslike. **Linen and cotton batiste**, both sheer and lightweight, are comfortable in warm temperatures. • The collar should be evenly stitched around the edges. • Make sure buttons are attached with firm cross-stitches and no loose threads. • Also check for single-needle stitching—it's a more costly and time-consuming method of machine-sewing because it uses one needle to sew one side of a garment at a time rather than two. However, it proves to be a more careful and consistent stitch. Double-needle stitching works at both sides of a garment at once, but there's a greater likelihood that puckering will occur. • A vertical seam down the yoke of the back of the shirt is a sure sign of quality. • Also check the placket—a count of fourteen stitches per inch on a shirt's placket indicates quality. Fewer than eleven per inch signals less quality. • Collars should sit evenly on the neck. A well-made turndown collar will have a line of stitching around the edge, as well as interfacing—a separate fabric insert, not a joined "fusible"—to give it shape. Puckering, in either stitching or fusing, is not a good sign. • Collars should fit snugly and should accommodate neckwear knots. In a cuff, tapering the sleeve into a cuff is a tailoring shortcut. The better-made shirt retains the blousiness of the sleeve by joining it to the cuff with careful pleats and gathers. • The anachronistic detail of a gauntlet button, sewn into the sleeve placket on the slit along the forearm, also signals quality.

Ties

Details are everything in a tie. • A silk tie should feel smooth, not coarse or brittle. • Hold the tie over your hand and let it fall. The narrow end should fall directly in the middle of the wide end. • A high-quality tie, constructed from three pieces of fabric, should lie perfectly flat, without bumps or ripples. Lesser ties are constructed from two pieces of fabric and do not lie as flat. • Make sure that the bar tack is securely attached to the back of the tie, and that it is on straight. • Pull on the back slip stitch—one that has been sewed on correctly helps maintain the shape of the tie and gathers together when pulled. • Tie width fluctuates all the time, but 31/4 inches mark a safe middle ground.

Trousers

Look for a lining sewn inside the pants where the crotch seams meet, to disperse stress and reduce chafing. • There should be a fully constructed, cotton-lined waistband that doesn't curl on itself. • Genuine horn buttons denote quality.

glossary.

This section will help clear up any confusion about a balmacaan coat being the native costume of the Balmacaan nations or a four-in-hand being a sexual technique for Siamese twins. And you will smugly know that Cooper collars aren't barrel maker's shirt collars.

General Terms

BELLOWS PLEAT: Deep fold of fabric along an article of clothing to allow for more flexibility.

BIAS ("Cut on the bias"): Woven fabric cut on a diagonal; when expertly done, it produces an ideal drape.

BOX PLEAT: Double pleat used on shirts and jackets.

CORDOVAN: Refers to men's leather goods, dark burgundy in color, constructed from horsehide. Characteristically smooth and nonporous in appearance.

CUMMERBUND: A waistband worn as an accessory to the tuxedo. Standard colors are black and red. The pleats on the cummerbund always face up, originally to hold theater tickets.

DART: Small pleat along body of garment to make a cleaner fit.

DRAPE: Refers to how the fabric of a garment hangs when worn.

DROP: The chest measurement minus the waist measurement. The longer the drop, the trimmer one has to be to wear the garment well.

EPAULET: A decorative shoulder piece—a strip of fabric or a military ornament indicating rank.

FLY FRONT: When buttons are hidden by a placket.

FROGS: Decorative Chinese closures made out of intricately knotted cord or fabric.

GORGE: The seam that connects the collar and the lapel.

GUSSET: A piece of fabric (usually triangular in shape) placed inside the seam of a garment for reinforcement.

HANDPICKED: Refers to the hand-stitching at the edges of a jacket, lapel, or pocket. It's usually a sure sign of fine craftsmanship, but always double-check to make sure that the stitches aren't sloppy.

MEMORY: The ability of certain materials to return to their original shape after being stretched or deformed in some way.

PLACKET: A fabric strip placed at the area of closure (on a jacket, shirt, or pants) that hides buttons from view.

SILHOUETTE: The line and outer shape of a garment. A European silhouette has a tailored, narrow fit, emphasizing the shoulders. A soft-shouldered, boxier look is more characteristic of the American silhouette.

SINGLE-NEEDLE STITCHING: A single needle is used to sew one side of the garment at a time. It produces durable seams that fit better against the body than double-stitching.

Shirts

CAMP SHIRT: Typically rayon or linen; some camp shirts fall under the bowling shirt, golf shirt, or Hawaiian shirt category. Sleeves are generally cut loose to the elbow. Best suited to complement shorts or khakis.

CREW NECK: Pullover neck opening without a collar.

POLO SHIRT: A collared pullover shirt once worn exclusively by polo players, now very much the everyman's shirt.

RAGLAN SHIRT: Fabrics range from cotton to cashmere. These loose-fitting shirts come in long sleeves and short sleeves and are popular on golf courses and in casual workplaces.

SPLIT-SHOULDER YOKE: A yoke made of two pieces. Allows for movement in the shoulder. This feature is usually found only in the finest (often custom-made) dress shirts.

YOKE: The specially designed part of a garment from which a curved waistband or the back of a shirt's shoulders hang.

Sweaters

CARDIGAN: A button-down sweater, without a collar or lapels, named for the Earl of Cardigan, who led the Charge of the Light Brigade.

FAIR ISLE: A sweater, often yoked, with multicolored geometric design, named after one of the Scottish Shetland Islands, where it originated. In the twenties, the Prince of Wales played golf while wearing sweaters of this design.

TURTLENECK: The turtleneck's characteristic long neck makes this sweater perfect for cooler weather. Average neck length in a turtleneck is 41/2 to 5 inches. Mock turtlenecks have shorter necks and are considered more formal—you can wear these with a suit.

V-NECK: As its name implies, this sweater's most obvious trait is the V-shaped neckline that falls right above the pecs.

Collars and Cuffs

BANDED COLLAR: At one time, collars on standard dress shirts were made detachable for easy cleaning and starching. Dress-shirt manufacturers simply added a strip of fabric that encircled the neck and buttoned at the front. With the inception of the collared dress shirt, the banded collar declined in popularity. Even so, some men still wear the banded collar shirt as a tieless yet dressy alternative. Note that this style is considered inappropriate workwear—even on casual Fridays.

BARREL CUFFS: Shirt cuffs that close with a button. More casual if there are two buttons.

BRITISH SPREAD COLLAR: Like the regular spread collar, but broader and more formal. Best suited for men with narrow faces.

BUTTON-DOWN COLLAR: Collars that are held in place by two small buttons at the collar's points.

COLLAR PIN: A decorative pin for the collar. Fred Astaire wore one with a button-down shirt, but most men wear them with long-point or rounded collars. It's perfectly okay to make holes in your collar if your shirt doesn't come ready-made with them. The hole you make will disappear when you wash it.

COLLAR STAYS: Plastic support pieces that fit snugly into a collar's stay pockets to define and stiffen the shape of the collar. Finer models are constructed out of thin metal covered with cloth, silver, or gold.

CONVERTIBLE CUFFS: Cuffs that can either button or take cuff links.

COOPER COLLAR: The Gary Cooper–inspired spread collar

with tips that point at an angle rather than straight out. Also boasts a soft, unconstructed back that can be worn up or down. Paul Stuart has adopted it as the label's signature collar.

CUTAWAY COLLAR: See spread collar.

ETON COLLAR: A rounded collar with pinholes or eyelets at the corners through which a pin is inserted to hold the wings of the collar together and bump up the tie knot. Popularized by Eton schoolboys of the early twenties and thirties.

FRENCH CUFFS: The dressiest kind of shirt cuffs; they fold over on themselves, away from the wrist, and require cuff links.

NOTCHED COLLAR: A design characterized by a triangular notch at mid-lapel.

SHAWL COLLAR: A rolled collar and lapel that curves from the back of the neck down to the front closure of the garment.

SPREAD COLLAR: A formal shirt collar. Spread wider apart than regular shirt collars to allow for the larger Windsor tie knot. Also known as the cutaway.

STRAIGHT COLLAR: The most common and traditional of all dress-shirt collars. The collar points downward, parallel to the drop of the arms. Collar length is about three inches and is usu-

ally accompanied by a relatively small tie knot.

TAB COLLAR: Collars that can be held in place with two small tabs that lie underneath the collar points. When hooked together, the tabs draw the collar close to the collarbone. Once a tie is put on, the tabs are hidden from view.

Shoes

ANKLE BOOT: Usually a two-eyelet boot with a leather sole. Comes in a dressier leather than its chukka counterpart.

BROGUE: A low-heeled oxford shoe with perforations and wing tips. At one time, brogues were tough, untanned leather shoes worn in Scotland and Ireland.

BUCK: Low, casual shoe with a rubber sole and simple construction. Different colors and materials make it an extremely versatile shoe.

CAMP SHOE: Casual shoe with rawhide laces and visible cut-and-stitched leather.

CAP-TOE: Low, lace-up shoe resembling an oxford with an extra piece of leather sewn over the toes.

CHUKKA BOOT: Also known as the desert boot. A sturdy, two-

eyelet ankle boot with a rubberized sole.

ESPADRILLE: A shoe with a cloth upper and rope sole. They are traditionally flat but now can be stacked. Comfortable, but not terribly durable.

EYELETS: Circular rustproof aluminum pieces that reinforce lace holes.

GALOSH: A kind of raincoat for your shoes. Easy to slip on. Fastened by zipper or buckles.

GILLIE: An oxford that is laced though loops rather than eyelets.

INSTEP: The upper shoe surface area from the ankles to the tips of the toes.

LAST: The wood or metal form around which shoes are shaped; also refers to the final shape of the shoe.

LOAFER: The ultimate slip-on casual shoe; low-heeled, with tassels or stitching (to hold the penny) in front.

LUG SOLE: Soles with rubber cleats or treads for added traction. Lug soles dress down many otherwise formal shoe designs.

MONK STRAP: Casual, plain shoe that fastens with one side buckle and strap.

NUBUCK: Typically made from cowhide through a process that abrades the hide's outer grain to make it mimic the look and feel of buckskin.

ORTHOTICS: Specially designed inner soles for the shoes of those suffering from chronic foot pain.

OXFORD: A flat, lace-up shoe with thin sole and a narrowed toe.

PADDOCK: Lace-up boot for adjustable ankle support; used for horse riding. The sole of the authentic paddock boot is always sewn, never glued or bonded.

PUMPS: Perhaps derived from the word "pomp." Comes in patent or matte leather, with a grosgrain bow. Plain-toe oxfords, in calfskin or patent leather, are an alternative. Both take calf-length black socks in silk or lightweight wool.

SADDLE OXFORD: An oxford with an extra piece of leather sewn over the shoe's mid-section, often in a different texture or color.

SPECTATOR: Also known as the correspondent's shoe. It's a two-toned shoe; the style first became popular in the twenties but has had many revivals since.

TONGUE: A retractable leather piece under a shoe's laces. Protects feet from the elements and also makes it easier to put your shoes on.

VAMP: The part of the shoe that covers the toes and instep.

Signs of Quality Tailoring: Shirt

SINGLE-NEEDLE STITCHING
A more costly and time-consuming method of machine sewing that uses one needle to sew one side of a garment at a time, providing a consistent, careful stitch. The faster, less expensive method is to sew with double-needle stitching, working both sides of the garment at once, with a greater likelihood of puckering.

BUTTONS
Cross-stitched and made of mother-of-pearl.

GAUNTLET BUTTON
An anachronistic button on the sleeve opening, above the cuff.

FRENCH CUFFS
To be worn with cuff links.

LONG TAILS
Long enough to come together between the legs.

COLLAR
Evenly stitched around the edges.

FIT
Sufficient blousiness in the sleeve. Where it joins the cuff, fabric should be gathered into pleats, not tapered.

SPLIT-SHOULDER YOKE
A vertical seam down the yoke on the back of the shirt.

PLACKET
A count of fourteen stitches per inch on a shirt's placket—the strip of fabric on which the buttons are sewn—indicates quality. Fewer than eleven per inch signals lesser quality.

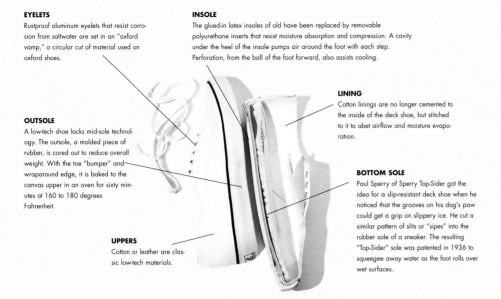

EYELETS
Rustproof aluminum eyelets that resist corrosion from saltwater are set in an "oxford vamp," a circular cut of material used on oxford shoes.

INSOLE
The glued-in latex insoles of old have been replaced by removable polyurethane inserts that resist moisture absorption and compression. A cavity under the heel of the insole pumps air around the foot with each step. Perforation, from the ball of the foot forward, also assists cooling.

OUTSOLE
A low-tech shoe lacks mid-sole technology. The outsole, a molded piece of rubber, is cored out to reduce overall weight. With the toe "bumper" and wraparound edge, it is baked to the canvas upper in an oven for sixty minutes at 160 to 180 degrees Fahrenheit.

LINING
Cotton linings are no longer cemented to the inside of the deck shoe, but stitched to it to abet airflow and moisture evaporation.

UPPERS
Cotton or leather are classic low-tech materials.

BOTTOM SOLE
Paul Sperry of Sperry Top-Sider got the idea for a slip-resistant deck shoe when he noticed that the grooves on his dog's paw could get a grip on slippery ice. He cut a similar pattern of slits or "sipes" into the rubber sole of a sneaker. The resulting "Top-Sider" sole was patented in 1936 to squeegee away water as the foot rolls over wet surfaces.

VIBRAM SOLE: Lightweight, rubbery outsole that adds spring and slip resistance.

WELLINGTONS: A classic rubber boot, originating on British battlefields.

WELT: Extra pieces of fabric or leather that reinforce seams. A welt on a shoe is usually an extra piece of leather between the upper and the sole.

WING TIP: Classic men's dress shoes with decorative toe tip in the shape of a flying bird. Suede wing tips are slightly less formal than those in leather.

Ties

APRON: There are two aprons to every tie. The front apron is the visible wide end of the tie; the rear apron is the hidden narrow side.

ASCOT: A formal day scarf or wide tie, looped and knotted around the collar in such a way that the ends lie flat, one on top of the other at the front of the neck. Often held in place with a stickpin.

BAR TACK: A short horizontal fabric piece on the back of the broad end of the tie that helps maintain the tie's structure.

BATWING: A square-shaped bow tie.

BOW TIE: A small necktie knotted into a bow. Clip-on bow ties are available, but hand-tied bow ties are a mark of elegance. See page 183 for a step-by-step illustration. See also Batwing, Club, and Thistle.

BUTTERFLY: A bow tie with flared ends.

CRAVAT: A term loosely used to describe any kind of neckwear.

CLUB BOW TIE: A straight and wide bow tie.

CLUB TIE: Silk tie with a repeating pattern of small emblems.

DIMPLE: The indentation directly under the knot.

DOT TIE: Simply, a tie with a dotted pattern. The smaller the dots, the more formal the tie. Large, polka-dotted ties are more spirited, but are sometimes clownish.

ENVELOPE: The visible surface of a tie; contains a wool inner lining.

FOUR-IN-HAND: The knot was named after the eighteenth-century coach and four drivers who were the first to tie their neck cloths in this manner. It is now the most common method for tying a necktie, largely because it produces a simple, straight knot, and it works well with all fabrics—especially knits and bulky wools.

HAND-ROLLED TIE: All tie edges are rolled over and stitched—otherwise the frayed edges of fabric would be visible. Tie edges that are hand-rolled and hemmed have a superior shape to that of a machine-hemmed tie.

KNIT TIE: The most versatile tie, especially in black. Wool is more casual than silk.

REGIMENTAL TIE: A specific type of striped tie whose colors pertain to a particular British regiment.

REP(P) TIE: A diagonally striped tie made of corded silk with a crosswise weave—its roots come from the regimental tie. See also striped tie.

SLIP STITCH: The stitching (it may be either a loop or a loose thread) inside the envelope of a tie. Helps the tie maintain shape and stretch.

STRIPED TIE: Also known as the rep(p) or regimental tie. Evolved from displaying the colors of British clubs or army regiments on ties. In England, the stripes run from high left to low right, but in the U.S., it's the other way around.

THISTLE BOW TIE: A straight and narrow bow tie.

TIE BAR: Typically, a chain or pin that sits at the knot of the tie. Used to hold the tie in place.

TIE CLASP OR CLIP: A decorative device used to keep the two ends of a tie attached to the front of the shirt. It's especially useful for architects, or anyone who leans over a lot.

TIE TACK: An ornamental pin that holds tie and shirt in place.

WINDSOR KNOT: A decorative, protrusive knot popularized by the Duke of Windsor, who liked his ties to jut forward from a spread collar. A full or half Windsor knot requires many more twists and turns than the four-in-hand.

WOVEN TIE: A woven tie, such as a silk grenadine, is usually produced in a solid color. The texture of the weave serves as the pattern.

Jackets and Coats

BALMACAAN COAT: Single-breasted, loose-fitting coat in which sleeves are cut generously and are attached to the main body of the coat by a seam that extends from the armholes to the neck. Buttons extend to the neck for full body closure.

BARN JACKET: For generations, a utilitarian roomy jacket. Traditionally in canvas duck, or, more recently, a microfiber. Comes with corduroy collar, large patch pockets, flannel or wool lining, and big buttons.

BELLOWS POCKET: An expanding pleated jacket pocket.

BESOM POCKET: A jacket pocket with a stitched fold on the upper and lower sides.

BLAZER: Traditionally, the blazer comes in navy blue; double-breasted with six metal buttons, only two of which, on the lower right, actually function. Side vents, two flap pockets, a breast pocket, and peaked lapels characterize this classic navy-inspired jacket.

BOMBER JACKET: Leather U.S. Air Force pilot jacket with sheepskin lining and elastic waist.

BOUTONNIERE: A flower placed on the lapel of a jacket for adornment.

BRITISH WARMER: Double-breasted overcoat; knee or slightly above knee length, and flared at the bottom.

Signs of Quality Tailoring: Tie

SLIP STITCH
When the slip stitch is pulled, the tie should gather together, which helps maintain its shape.

LINING
It allows the tie to knot easily and prevents it from wrinkling. Should be made of 100 percent wool.

BAR TACK
This supplements the slip stitch and keeps the two ends of the tie from separating.

HAND ROLLING
A tie that is rolled and hemmed by hand has the best shape to it.

FABRIC
A silk tie should feel smooth; brittleness is usually a sign of inferior material. Three pieces of fabric—cheaper ties use two—allow it to lie better.

BUSH JACKET: See safari jacket.

CHESTERFIELD COAT: Named after the British Earl of Chesterfield. Single- or double-breasted. Its straight-cut, dark or herringbone wool fabric and velvet collar are qualities most appropriate for formal occasions or business situations.

CUTAWAY: A single-breasted formal coat with peaked lapels. The back tail extends and tapers at the knee.

DENIM: To its great benefit, the jean jacket has never shaken the brooding aura of James Dean. Like all Western work wear, it has risen above fashion by being outside it: functional, unaffected, proletarian clothing made for dusty surroundings.

DINNER JACKET: Also referred to as a tuxedo jacket. For semiformal or formal wear. Single- or double-breasted, most typically in black or white, with peaked lapels or shawl collar.

DOUBLE-BREASTED: A kind of jacket or coat in which a few inches of fabric flap over and close the opening of the jacket; also, the two rows of buttons at the front are usually a telltale sign.

DUFFEL COAT: Originally an overcoat worn by seamen during cold weather conditions. Toggle fasteners close the front and a large hood sits in the back of the neck for extra protection.

FLAP POCKET: The piece of material that hangs over a pocket opening.

HACKING: The tweed hacking jacket is the most widely worn sport jacket. Side vents and angled flapped pockets were originally designed for sitting in the saddle. It still has a slightly flared skirt and the three-button closure common to all jackets in the twenties.

HUNTING JACKET: A type of sport coat with a throat latch for Highland chills. With a bi-swing back for easy movement, in a warm tweed that hides dirt. Elbow patches decorate and reinforce the sleeves of the jacket.

LAPEL: In a coat or a jacket, it's the fabric that folds back at the front and connects to the collar. It traces down the chest, eventually forming into a V-shape.

LONG ROLL LAPEL: A lapel that extends beyond the usual point of closure.

MODERN COAT: A refined version of the British warmer. Simplified styling with minimal amounts of detailing, single-breasted, often with three buttons or a fly front.

MOTORCYCLE JACKET: See The Perfecto.

NORFOLK: The grandfather of sport clothes, the Norfolk jacket introduced the idea that a jacket and trousers didn't have to match. It takes its name from the shooting parties held on the Duke of Norfolk's estate in the nineteenth century. The jacket provides for mobility with box pleats down the back, a band of fabric around the waist, and bellows pockets for carrying cartridges.

PATCH POCKET: A pocket made from a piece of fabric stitched onto the outside of a jacket. The most casual of pockets—best reserved for sport jackets.

PEA COAT: Heavy wool short coat styled similarly to the reefer. The difference lies in the pea coat's nautical background, as the buttons' anchor insignia indicates.

THE PERFECTO: The indestructible biker's leather jacket worn by Marlon Brando in The Wild One—the classic rebel uniform, made to be beaten up. Designed in 1927 by Schott Bros., it provides bikers with body cover in the event of accident and was distributed directly to them through Harley-Davidson Motorcycles. The thick belt across the back protects the kidneys.

POLO COAT: In the late 1800s, polo players wore a long, robe-like coat made of camel hair while resting between periods. The comfort and warmth, combined with polo's prestige as an elegant rich man's sport, turned the camel-hair polo coat into a classic in the 1920s.

RAGLAN: Named for the first Baron Raglan, commander of British troops during the Crimean War, this is a loose-fitting coat with full-cut sleeves and a seam that extends from each armhole to the collar in both the front and the rear.

REEFER: A single- or double-breasted overcoat, often made from heavy wool or cashmere. Its narrow silhouette is ideal for those who prefer a slim fit. A reefer could also refer to a long oblong wool muffler or a marijuana cigarette.

SAFARI JACKET: Also known as the bush jacket, the safari was not commonly available until Abercrombie & Fitch distributed it during the 1920s, at a time when expeditions to the African continent were the rage. Usually khaki-colored, it's outfitted with four flap pockets, epaulets, and a belt; an alternative to a sport jacket or cardigan.

SLASH POCKET: A pocket set into a jacket with either a vertical or diagonal slash.

SMOKING JACKET: An elegant, loose-fitting wrap jacket with a shawl collar and ties at the waist. Usually in velvet, wool, brocade, or another heavy, thick material. Smoking jackets are meant to be worn only at home and usually by men when relaxing with a pipe or cigar.

SPORT COAT: The sport coat was invented when King George IV ordered a jacket without matching trousers to wear while shooting at the Duke of Norfolk's estate. Today, it might be better called the spectator coat; climate control has obviated the need for a lapel closure and lightened the weight.

SWAGGER BACK: A jacket back that is unfitted and drapes straight from the shoulders.

TRENCH COAT: Designed for trench warfare during World War I. Today, its epaulets, D-ring belts, and wide lapels serve only decorative purposes.

VARSITY JACKET: By popular demand, the archetype of high school and collegiate athletic jackets has shaken off its "retro," frat-house image. Formerly a vintage item stocked in second-hand clothing shops, the varsity jacket is now widely manufactured, and is worn as a contemporary classic.

VENTS: The slit(s) at the back of the some jackets and blazers. Comes in single or double.

WAISTCOAT: Basically, it's a vest, waist-length, sleeveless, and worn over a dress shirt.

WELT POCKET: A breast pocket.

WHITE TIE: Also known as tails, usually worn at state dinners or by members of a wedding party. Elements include a tailcoat with matching trousers, trimmed with two braids running down the outside leg, white piqué tie, white piqué single- or double-breasted waistcoat, etc.

WRAP COAT: A loose-fitting, over-the-knee coat. The original wrap coat comes without buttons and must be belted closed.

ZOOT SUIT: Super long jacket with padded shoulders and tapered waist put together with full-cut trousers with high rise and pegged bottom. Popularized by the Harlem swing kids of the 1930s, most notably Cab Calloway. Often accessorized with a long watch chain and wide-brimmed fedora.

Trousers

BELT LOOPS: Fabric loops constructed to hold belt in place. Normally, trousers with expandable waists do not have belt loops.

BRACES: More commonly referred to as suspenders.

BREAK: The horizontal ripple in the trouser leg where it touches the top of the instep. A break could also refer to the crease across the vent of a shoe.

CUFF: The folded end of a trouser leg, usually 1½" wide—no less.

INSEAM: The length of the inside of the leg, cuff to crotch.

FLAT FRONT: Pleatless trousers. Though generally informal, flat-fronted trousers happen to be favored for suits by traditional men's wear tailors.

GRIP: A piece of fabric in the inside part of the waistband that holds the shirt in place.

KHAKIS: When the British imperialists occupied India during the nineteenth century, Commander Harry Lumsden insisted that his troop's white military uniforms be dyed a yellowish-brown to blend in with the dusty Indian climate. The Indians referred to the resulting uniforms as khaki, a Hindi word meaning "dust-colored." Today, khaki pants are worn by virtually everybody, popular for their relaxed fit and comfort.

OUTSEAM: Measures from the top of the waistband to the bottom of the cuff.

PEG: The tapering or narrowing of pants at the ankles.

PLEATS: A fold, usually on the front of trousers, created to allow for more flexibility. In trousers, pleats can be "reverse" (folded inside) or "forward" (folded outside). Reverse pleats can create a slender appearance—unless the pants are too tight, in which case the bulging pleats can actually make you look heavier.

RISE: Measurement from the crotch to the top of the waistband. This is the one feature on a pair of trousers that cannot be altered by a tailor. Because most pants are cut to a "medium" rise, many tall men have difficulty finding pants with a comfortable rise.

SUSPENDERS: Adjustable strips or bands of fabric attached to the waist and worn over the shoulders to hold up trousers. They are a more formal alternative to the belt.

WAISTBAND: On casual trousers, they're softer, less constructed, and can either be non-roll with expandable side tabs or have hook closures.

Hats

BERET: Central to French style, it is one of the easiest hats to wear. It has lots of Bohemian attitude but remains flexible on all counts. It adapts to almost any hair style and packs well.

CAP: Originally worn by workmen, the cap has been popular with sporty men since the turn of the century. In the sixties, it appeared in flamboyant sizes and colors and was worn by both men and women.

CROWN: The top of the hat where the head fits inside.

DERBY: Also known as a bowler. With hard round top and curled brims. Usually in felt.

FEDORA: Although this felt hat with a soft brim hails from the Austrian Tyrol, its name derives from Fedora, a play performed in Paris in 1882.

HOMBURG: A felt hat with a dented crown and a curled brim; originally hailing from Homburg, Germany. Worn most

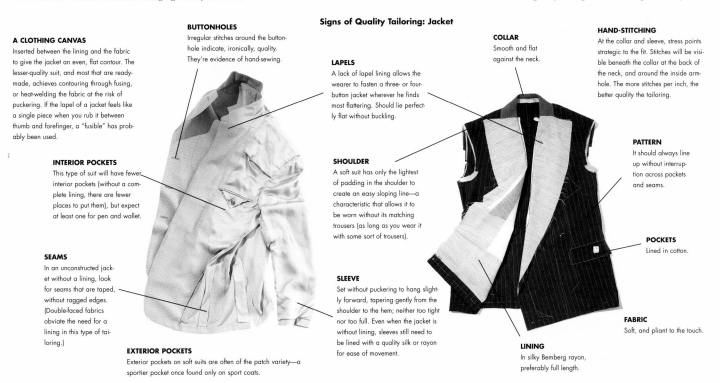

Signs of Quality Tailoring: Jacket

A CLOTHING CANVAS
Inserted between the lining and the fabric to give the jacket an even, flat contour. The lesser-quality suit, and most that are ready-made, achieves contouring through fusing, or heat-welding the fabric at the risk of puckering. If the lapel of a jacket feels like a single piece when you rub it between thumb and forefinger, a "fusible" has probably been used.

INTERIOR POCKETS
This type of suit will have fewer interior pockets (without a complete lining, there are fewer places to put them), but expect at least one for pen and wallet.

SEAMS
In an unconstructed jacket without a lining, look for seams that are taped, without ragged edges. (Double-faced fabrics obviate the need for a lining in this type of tailoring.)

EXTERIOR POCKETS
Exterior pockets on soft suits are often of the patch variety—a sportier pocket once found only on sport coats.

BUTTONHOLES
Irregular stitches around the buttonhole indicate, ironically, quality. They're evidence of hand-sewing.

LAPELS
A lack of lapel lining allows the wearer to fasten a three- or four-button jacket wherever he finds most flattering. Should lie perfectly flat without buckling.

SHOULDER
A soft suit has only the lightest of padding in the shoulder to create an easy sloping line—a characteristic that allows it to be worn without its matching trousers (as long as you wear it with some sort of trousers).

SLEEVE
Set without puckering to hang slightly forward, tapering gently from the shoulder to the hem; neither too tight nor too full. Even when the jacket is without lining, sleeves still need to be lined with a quality silk or rayon for ease of movement.

COLLAR
Smooth and flat against the neck.

LINING
In silky Bemberg rayon, preferably full length.

HAND-STITCHING
At the collar and sleeve, stress points strategic to the fit. Stitches will be visible beneath the collar at the back of the neck, and around the inside armhole. The more stitches per inch, the better quality the tailoring.

PATTERN
It should always line up without interruption across pockets and seams.

POCKETS
Lined in cotton.

FABRIC
Soft, and pliant to the touch.

appropriately with a dinner jacket in a black or a midnight blue for evening wear.

KNIT CAP: The knit cap is of simple handmade origins dating back to the invention of the knitting needles. These hats have been worn the world over by skiers, fishermen, nightclub ravers, and burglars—a true global vernacular.

PANAMA: The best Panama hats are Ecuadorean. Fine straw and a tight weave are marks of quality.

SENNIT: A boater or sailor hat with a flat top and brim.

TIBETAN WASHA HAT: The name derives from the Tibetan word for fox (the typical fur used to edge the hat). The crown is often made from colorful silk and ties in the back for a snug fit.

Patterns

Patterns relax suits and stir up color, but even they must act within certain guidelines. Patterns are most effectively combined

Signs of Quality Tailoring: Trench Coat

WOOL-LINED COLLAR
Turns up to protect the neck.

BUTTONED-DOWN EPAULET
Served to secure a rifle over the shoulder.

LINING
Detachable, made of wool.

SEPARATE BACK YOKE
For rain protection.

STORM FLAP
Buttons over the chest.

CLOTH BELT
Usually worn tied, not buckled, it has metal rings from which to hang grenades and canteens.

BUCKLED CUFF
Battens out the wind.

when they are of different scales. A broad-striped tie works best with a fine-striped shirt; a Glen plaid sport jacket can take a boldly striped shirt. The point is to avoid competing patterns; let one dominate.

ACCENT STRIPES: Colored stripes on a shirt or jacket that replace or appear in addition to the traditional white or gray pinstripes.

BIRD'S EYE: A semiformal cotton or linen weave characterized by tiny alternating light and dark threads. Notable for its absorbent qualities and its geometric dot pattern; each dot is equally spaced apart from each other on a solid-colored background. The "dots" are not circular at all—they are more diamond shaped, resembling the eyes of birds.

CHALK STRIPE: Broad stripes running vertically along a shirt or suit fabric. With shirts, the broader the stripes, the more informal.

HAIRLINE STRIPE: Vertical stripes falling consistently against a lighter background color. Hairline stripes are thicker than both the pinstripe and the pencil stripe, but is not quite as wide as the chalk stripe.

HERRINGBONE: A twill weave or fabric with small adjoining, slanted lines forming a V-like pattern. This pattern continues down vertical rows.

HOUNDSTOOTH: Wool twill weave with a checkered pattern of four dark threads and four light threads.

NAIL'S HEAD: Small dotted design, usually reserved for sharkskin and worsted fabrics.

PAISLEY: A pattern born in the 1800's as an attempt by the mills of Paisley, Scotland, to imitate the spade pattern of Kashmiri shawls.

PENCIL STRIPE: Generally reserved for dress shirts. Narrow stripes, not quite as fine as a pinstripe.

PINCHECK: Small check pattern that is popular for suits and outerwear.

PINSTRIPE: A fine line, usually white or gray, running vertically along a shirt or suit. Pinstripes should line up along pockets of jackets.

PLAID: Overlapping multicolored stripes running horizontally and vertically. Of Scottish origin.

TATTERSALL: Checked pattern formed by vertical and horizontal stripes in one or two colors on a light-colored background. First associated with waistcoats and horse blankets worn (by sportsmen and horses) at the London horse market founded in 1766 by Richard Tattersall.

WINDOWPANE: Lines on a fabric that form continuous box-like patterns. The thin lines that frame a broad area of solid color suggest a windowpane.

Fabrics

It all begins here. Fabric provides the original link between skin and clothing and, as such, is the key to comfort. Subtlety is fabric's triumph, pulled off in tone-on-tone weaves, surface pattern, textural contrasts, and gradients of touch.

ACETATE: Acetate was invented in 1869, but wasn't used commercially until after World War I. Acetate drapes nicely and dries well, but is not very colorfast, is prone to melting, wrinkling, and stretching, and requires dry cleaning. Satins and sateens for lining suits and coats are often made from acetate.

ACRYLIC: Orlon acrylic was developed by Du Pont during World War II, but wasn't marketed until 1950. This synthetic fabric resists wrinkling and is machine-washable, but can pill, absorb oil-borne stains, and shrink under heat. Acrylic is typically made into knits and fabrics resembling wool.

ALPACA: Fleece from an animal related to the camel. Soft and shiny, much like mohair; made into jackets and coats.

ANGORA: Soft, warm, delicate fabric made from the hair of Angora rabbits; used in coats and often blended with wool. See also Wool.

ARAN: A knit associated with the people of the Aran Islands, off the west coast of Ireland. Coarse, handspun wool, usually in a natural, off-white color. Knitted in cables, twists, and bobbles down the front and sides of a sweater. Often the designs take on symbolic meanings; they are the Irish equivalent of the Shaker quilt.

ARGYLE: Multicolored diamond pattern knitted in the style of a Scottish tartan; most often appears on socks and sweaters.

BARLEYCORN: A small tweed or woolen pattern used in suits and sport coats.

BEDFORD CORD: A heavy and durable textile with pronounced vertical ribs. Once produced in worsted, it is now made in cotton, linen, and wool in an assortment of shades and colors.

BEMBERG: A trademark name for a type of treated rayon, usually used in jacket linings, that is stronger than silk and requires less maintenance.

BLEND: Fabrics of combined fibers—for example, cotton and polyester, or cotton and linen.

BOUCLÉ: Decorative nubbly knit, appropriate for colder weather.

BREATHABILITY: Refers to the ability of the fabric to release body heat. Loosely woven, highly "breathable" fabrics like linen feel good in the summer. The more waterproof the fabric, the less breathable; the more breathable, the less waterproof.

BROADCLOTH: When technology first allowed for larger

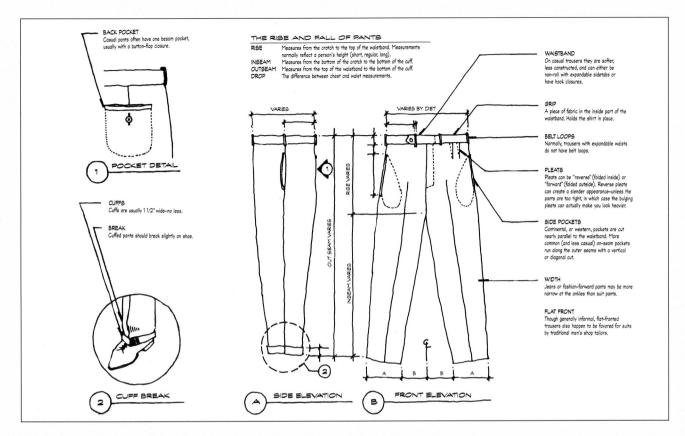

BACK POCKET
Casual pants often have one besom pocket, usually with a button-flap closure.

① POCKET DETAIL

CUFFS
Cuffs are usually 1 1/2" wide—no less.

BREAK
Cuffed pants should break slightly on shoe.

② CUFF BREAK

THE RISE AND FALL OF PANTS

RISE	Measures from the crotch to the top of the waistband. Measurements normally reflect a person's height (short, regular, long).
INSEAM	Measures from the bottom of the crotch to the bottom of the cuff.
OUTSEAM	Measures from the top of the waistband to the bottom of the cuff.
DROP	The difference between chest and waist measurements.

VARIES

VARIES BY DIET

RISE VARIES

OUT SEAM VARIES

INSEAM VARIES

A B B A

① ② ⓐ SIDE ELEVATION ⓑ FRONT ELEVATION

WAISTBAND
On casual trousers they are softer, less constructed, and can either be non-roll with expandable sidetabs or have hook closures.

GRIP
A piece of fabric in the inside part of the waistband. Holds the shirt in place.

BELT LOOPS
Normally, trousers with expandable waists do not have belt loops.

PLEATS
Pleats can be "reverse" (folded inside) or "forward" (folded outside). Reverse pleats can create a slender appearance—unless the pants are too tight, in which case the bulging pleats can actually make you look heavier.

SIDE POCKETS
Continental, or western, pockets are cut nearly parallel to the waistband. More common (and less casual) on-seam pockets run along the outer seams with a vertical or diagonal cut.

WIDTH
Jeans or fashion-forward pants may be more narrow at the ankles than suit pants.

FLAT FRONT
Though generally informal, flat-fronted trousers also happen to be favored for suits by traditional men's shop tailors.

looms, the fabrics produced were dubbed broadcloths. Today the term refers to plain- or twill-woven wool or cotton (usually preshrunk and/or mercerized).

BROCADE: A formal fabric woven with a detailed embossed pattern, often with metallic threads.

BURLAP: A thick and extremely coarse weave, brittle in texture, made out of jute or hemp. Don't wash or wet burlap.

CAMEL HAIR: Formally classified as a kind of wool; often blended with other wool fibers. Camel hair comes from the undercoat of the two-humped Bactrian camel, which is collected after the animal sheds or has been sheared. Color ranges from a light tan to a deep brown. The fur of these seven-foot-tall, 1,500-pound desert dwellers produces soft, high-quality textiles, most commonly used for coats and jackets. Because 100 percent camel-hair products are so expensive, many coats called camel-hair actually come in wool or cashmere blends. See also Wool.

CANVAS: A thick cotton, hemp, or linen weave often used for sneakers, caps, and bags. Easy to clean and quite durable.

CARDED: The technological process of separating raw fibers. Smooths and softens rough fibers with a combing technique.

CASHMERE: Extremely soft wool fabric from Tibetan, Mongolian, or Iranian goats; worsted cashmere is stronger and purer than carded cashmere. See also Wool.

CAVALRY TWILL: A sturdy medium-weight, slightly elastic wool weave or cotton fabric originally used for riding apparel and country suits, later used for military uniforms.

CHALLIS: A soft, nappy twill fabric (made of wool, rayon, or cotton), usually with a small pattern. Available in light summer fabrics, yet most commonly used for cold weather garments. The name derives from the Hindi word shalee, meaning "soft of the touch."

CHAMBRAY: A plain-weave fabric (made of cotton, rayon, silk, or linen) woven from white and colored threads to create a muted, frosted appearance. Most frequently used in cotton and linen sportswear and nightwear.

CHARMEUSE: Originally, lightweight silk worked in a satin weave in France. Now the term also refers to easily draped fabrics made of cotton, rayon, and other synthetics, with a shiny face and matte back.

CHENILLE: Textiles woven or knit from very narrow strips of pile fabric (cotton, silk, or synthetics). The word is derived

from the French for caterpillar.

CHEVIOT: Most often, a twill weave made out of the wool of the Scottish cheviot sheep. Its textured surface, resulting from the weave's finishing process, creates a napped effect. Cheviot can also refer to shirting textile, in a twill weave with a striped pattern; usually in cotton, a blend of cotton, or manufactured fiber.

CHIMNEY EFFECT: When ventilation is built into the design of a garment by means of zippered necks, high collars, open cuffs, or vents that allow hot air to rise and moisture to evaporate.

CHINO CLOTH: Like khakis, chinos are a smooth all-cotton twill. They come in a range of colors—black, gray, white, khaki.

COLOR-BLEEDING: Refers to dyes on fabrics unable to withstand the procedures listed in the care instructions without fading or bleeding. Articles labeled as dry-cleanable will sometimes contain dyes that bleed when dry-cleaned. Deep colors may transfer onto lighter areas. Garments labeled as washable may also bleed and lose color, especially darker colors. If an article is multicolored, test it for colorfastness before washing, and do it separately in cold water.

COLORFAST: Maintaining color without fading or running.

CORDUROY: From the French phrase cord du Roi, meaning "cord of the king." Characterized by its vertical ridges. The ribs that stick out of the fabric are called wales. They are cut with a special machine after the fabric has been woven on the loom and then fluffed. You can find corduroy in cotton or velvet, in all weights, qualities, and colors, the wales thin or wide.

COTTON: A vegetable fiber, coming from the seed hairs of the cotton plant. It takes about six months for a cotton boll to mature. The highest-quality cottons are Sea Island and Egyptian because they are made from the longest, thinnest fibers, or staples, and are slightly sheer. Pima cotton is also made from a long-staple cotton, but is not as expensive. As a fabric, cotton is absorbent and comfortable in hot weather, feels good against the skin, irons well, is moth-safe, and doesn't produce static. It does, however, wrinkle easily. Cotton knits fade easily and are not very durable, so it doesn't make sense to spend a lot of money on them.

CREPE: A lightweight seasonless fabric with an irregular, textured appearance, made out of wool, cotton, silk, or other fibers. Basically, it's fabric that's been forcibly crinkled. Ideal for day-to-day wear.

CREPE DE CHINE: A lightweight fabric (made of silk or a synthetic) that is woven from twisted yarns to create a slightly textured, lustrous surface. Less wrinkle-prone than broadcloth, but more expensive.

DENIM: A sturdy, twill cotton fabric woven from white and colored threads (traditionally indigo blue). Although denim is considered the world over as American as apple pie, its name derives from de Nîmes, or "from Nîmes," a town in the south of France.

DONEGAL TWEED: Tweed named for the northernmost county in Ireland, characterized by thick twists of multicolored yarns.

DOUBLE KNIT: In contrast to the single knit, the double knitted fabric has two finished sides and thus is reversible. The double knit goes through a machine with two sets of needles, one for the front side of the fabric and one for its opposite side. Because of its two-ply nature, it is especially durable.

FLANNEL: A soft fabric, usually made of cotton or wool. Wool flannel produces high-quality suits; cotton flannel is more often used for casual shirts and pajamas.

FOULARD: A lustrous, delicate twill fabric originally made of silk and now acetate and other synthetics. Most commonly used for pocket squares, ties, and dress scarves.

GABARDINE: A tightly woven diagonal twill with a matte finish; comes in many weights and fibers; multiseasonal. Gabardine dates back to the Spanish Middle Ages, when gabardina, a wool fabric, was used for making protective capes.

GAUZE: Lightweight, elastic cotton in a loose weave. Used for summerwear and curtains.

GROSGRAIN: Literally "large grain" in French, this is a type of heavy, stiff, ribbed cloth or ribbon (made of silk, rayon, or synthetics). A grosgrain bow adorns classic men's evening pumps.

HAND: The characteristic quality of a textile: how it feels to the touch.

HARRIS TWEED: Trade name for an imported tweed handwoven on Harris and other Outer Hebrides islands.

HIGH-PERFORMANCE WOOL (SUPER 100s): Superlight worsted wool fabric developed in Italy and used for suits.

IRISH LINEN: Tight-woven linen used in solid-color summer suits; heavier, stiffer, and less easily creased than Italian linen.

JACQUARD: Fabric in which the pattern has been woven on a special loom, rather than printed on. The original loom was created by the French inventor J. M. Jacquard (1757–1834).

JERSEY: A lightweight, fine knit, with a slight rib on one side. Invented on the Isle of Jersey.

KHAKI: First originated as a heavy wool blend with cotton and linen for military wear, but soldiers complained that such a fabric was much too hot and stuffy to wear. Consequently, the wool was removed from the fabric and a lighter cotton weave was used to create the khaki material. Khaki can range from a dark olive green to a dusty light cream color. See also Khaki under Trousers.

KNITS: Unless the fabric is of high quality or hand-knit jersey, knit garments tend to be casual and less expensive than woven garments. Knits are easier to clean and pack than woven fabrics because they're more porous, less rigid, and less likely to wrinkle. Overweight men should avoid knits, as they easily stretch out of shape and drape close to the body.

LAMBSWOOL: Wool shorn from a young sheep (under seven months old). Much prized for its softness and for the ease in which these strands can be spun.

LEATHER: Most commonly made of pig, lamb, or cowhide, although leather specialists consider English or Italian lamb leather to be the finest. As to texture, leather comes in Napa, a smooth finish; Buffed, or nubuck, appearing somewhat like a matte suede; and Distressed, a rough, "wrinkled" leather finish.

LIGHTWEIGHT WORSTED SUITING: A fine wool weave with a silky finish.

LINEN: A vegetable fiber woven from the stems of flax. It's lightweight and comfortable in hot climates. It's more absorbent than cotton, but it's not durable, does not retain dye well (especially on shinier varieties), and wrinkles very easily. Linen tends to become whiter with use. Unless the air is very polluted, line-drying in the sun will whiten it further. Linen can also yellow with age, especially if it's been stored in plastic garment bags.

LODEN CLOTH: A heavy twill weave made with coarse wool that is sometimes blended with mohair. It is water-repellent and especially suited for outdoor use.

MACCLESFIELD: Fabric with rough open silk weaves with a small, compact allover pattern. Generally used for ties.

MADRAS: By law, only the handwoven madras from Madras, India, can be so named. The madras shirt peaked in popularity in the late 1930s, thanks to the Hathaway company. It became synonymous with style and preppiness. Real madras is vegetable-dyed on fine cotton in plaids, stripes, and checks. Everything from pants to watchbands has been made of madras.

MATTE: A dull finish—any surface that lacks gloss or shine.

MELTON: Tightly constructed, heavy cloth, finished with a smooth face, concealing the weave. Most famously used in pea coats.

MERCERIZED: Cotton that has been processed to become mildew-resistant and stronger, with additional sheen and dye-absorption properties. The process derives its name from John Mercer, a nineteenth-century calico painter.

MICROPOROUS: Outerwear surface of finely woven microfiber that allows vapor to escape but keeps water droplets from entering.

MODACRYLIC: This fiber, also known as dynel, was first put on the market by Union Carbide in 1949. Modacrylic is lightweight, warm, and abrasion-resistant. Typically made into pile clothing and fake furs.

MOHAIR: Shiny, soft hair from the Angora goat, usually used in long-hair sweaters or woven into summer suits.

MOISTURE TRANSPORT: See Wicking.

MOLESKIN: A durable fabric with a suedelike nap, usually in cotton, that resembles mole fur. Traditionally used for sportswear and work clothes, but in recent times popular in avant-garde men's wear.

NATURAL FIBERS: Natural fibers have wonderful luster, feel, and general appearance. They tend to be more stain-resistant than synthetics. They also breathe well, allowing for comfort in a variety of climates. On the other hand, natural-fiber clothing often does not last as long, may fade and wrinkle more easily, may require more careful (and costly) maintenance (especially for some wool and silks), and tends to be more expensive than clothes made of synthetic fibers.

NUBUCK: Nubuck is typically made from cowhide through a process that abrades the hide's outer grain to make it look and feel like buckskin, but it feels tougher than suede.

NYLON: Originally, Du Pont launched nylon in the form of stockings; marketing on a large scale didn't begin until the 1940s, when nylon was marketed to replace silk that was needed for parachutes during World War II. Nylon is strong, does not easily abrade, and resists staining and wrinkling. It also washes and dries easily, doesn't need ironing, has good "memory"; doesn't absorb moisture. Its drawbacks are that it tends to pill, can feel clammy, and generate static (though this effect can be minimized by new finishes). When a small percentage of nylon is mixed with natural fibers, it can greatly enhance the durability of the garment. From nylon, manufacturers can produce swimwear (knits), hosiery, lingerie (knits, satins, sateens), various blends and twill fabrics.

OMBRE: Fabric woven or dyed in a gradation of shades.

PILE: Fabric with a surface made of cut yarns (like velours and velvets) or uncut yarns (like terry cloth), so that it has a plush, "furry" texture.

PILLING: Small beads of fibers that build up on worn fabrics, usually at stress points under arms or at cuffs.

PIQUÉ: Usually made from mercerized cotton, piqué fabrics have a raised appearance, typically a waffle design. It is characteristic of many cotton polo shirts and men's evening shirts. Piqué is from the French verb piquer, meaning "to pierce."

PLY: The thicknesses of yarns that have been twisted together to be knit or woven into fabric. The term is most commonly used when describing the thickness of cashmere.

POLYESTER: Polyester was developed by Du Pont in 1951 and is now the world's most widely used fiber. It holds shape well; resists shrinking, stretching, and wrinkling, and adds these qualities to whatever fiber it's blended with. It's also tough and durable, can withstand abrasion and rubbing, is easy to maintain (it's usually machine-washable), and dries quickly. In addition, polyester is fade-resistant (especially an asset for blacks and other dark colors) and is inexpensive. Sometimes it can develop oil stains from other clothes in the wash. Pills develop easily, and are tenacious because of the strength of the fiber. When added to cotton and wool, it reduces wrinkling and weight, and adds strength. Chlorine bleach turns polyester gray. Washing Tip: To get rid of the gray tint, soak garment overnight in a solution of dishwashing detergent in warm water. Machine-wash garment before drying.

POLYESTER PILE: The insulation layer in fleece, or bunting fabric with "loft" or height for warmth.

POPLIN: A sturdy ribbed fabric, usually of cotton, silk, or rayon, used in suits and raincoats.

RAYON: Rayon was called artificial silk when it was invented in 1891, and although it is made from organic components such as plant fibers (cellulose, wood chips, cotton linters), it is considered the first artificial fiber. Viscose is a type of rayon, so named for the viscous solution from which the threads are spun. Rayon can mimic wool, silk, linen, and cotton. As a crepe, it's lightweight and seasonless. Rayon is also ideal because it's inexpensive, absorbent, and comfortable. However, rayon is not a durable fabric; it wrinkles and pulls easily, and doesn't hold its shape well. When blended with acetate, it holds its shape better—a good attribute for fitted clothing. Seasonless

garments like suits and pants are made from wool and rayon blends.

SANFORIZED: The trademarked name of a fabric that has been specially processed to prevent shrinkage.

SEERSUCKER: A striped cotton fabric (often white alternating with a light blue) with the colored stripe being permanently crinkled or blistered. The word derives from the Persian term shir-o-shakur, meaning "milk and sugar."

SERGE: A twill, made of wool, cotton, rayon, silk, or blends, created in a variety of weights, textures, and finishes to achieve great hand and drapability. Often used for business suits.

SHARKSKIN: The term refers to two different fabrics with a durable, sleek, pebbled texture. When made of acetate, rayon, or blends, it has a duller appearance. When made of worsted wool, it is a fine twill, often used for suits.

SHETLAND: A fine wool originating from a breed of sheep on the Shetland Islands. Today the term is generally applied to a type of wool yarn producing a similar surface.

SILK: It is said that silk was discovered when a cocoon from the larva of a Bombyx mori moth fell from a mulberry tree into the teacup of the Chinese empress Hsi Ling-shi in the third millennium b.c.; she opened it and found a glistening thread. Cultivated silkworms must eat thirty thousand times their weight in mulberry leaves; their cocoons, which are made from secretions from the worm's head, make up the silk fiber. Wild silkworms eat oak leaves and produce a silk of a coarser and less lustrous quality. If the worm's natural gum is not cleaned from the fiber, it is known as "raw silk." Pongee, tussah, and shantung are all unevenly woven, undyed, raw, naturally tan silks, with pongee being the palest and lightest, and shantung the heaviest. Silk is a very fine fiber and is the strongest of the natural ones (it is as strong as nylon, and is often compared to iron wire of the same thickness). It's also wrinkle-resistant, and holds shape well. At the same time, it's very elastic—it can stretch up to 120 percent of its length before snapping, it retains pleats and color well, it's lightweight, and although it can be warmer than wool, it is a year-round fabric. On the downside, silk is expensive, it's high-maintenance, it can burn while being ironed, and it can be damaged by the aluminum chloride in antiperspirants. When metallic salts are added to pure silk, the silk drapes better, but may deteriorate sooner. When rayon is blended with silk, the fabric attains the elasticity that rayon lacks. "Washable silk" is silk that has been washed throughout its production process—as a result, it's preshrunk and can be safely washed by the consumer at home. Sewing Tip: Always use silk or cotton thread on silk garments; the thickness of a polyester thread can cause puckering.

SUEDE: Leather whose flesh side is buffed to a velvet finish; the name is derived from the French word for Sweden, where the process originated.

SYNTHETIC BLENDS: When synthetic fibers are added in small quantities to natural fibers, the quality of the fabric can

actually be enhanced. Too much or too little of a particular fiber in a blend can determine the whole outcome of that blend—a cotton T-shirt with 2 percent Lycra has a sexier shape than a 100 percent cotton shirt. In the case of a cotton-polyester blend where the polyester content is high (over 35 percent), the garment can feel uncomfortable—more like polyester than cotton.

SYNTHETIC FIBERS: Man-made fibers tend to be incredibly durable, wash-and-wearable, and wrinkle-resistant. They dry quickly, have good pleat and color retention, are mothproof, and are less expensive than natural fibers. With new technological developments, man-made fibers are improving in feel, or "hand," and appearance. But, compared with natural fibers, synthetics tend not to breathe very well, which can cause some discomfort, especially in warm weather. We should point out, however, that synthetic fabric technology is rapidly improving. Many of the newer synthetics are even superior to natural fabrics; they wick away moisture and insulate more effectively than natural fibers. Man-made fibers may be highly heat-sensitive (don't allow them to dry close to heat sources like radiators or fireplaces) and sometimes discolor in sunlight. For the most part, the cons have diminished enormously, while the pros are gaining.

TARTAN: A Scottish plaid fabric; from the Gaelic tarstin ortarsuin, aptly meaning "across" in reference to the stripes that run across each other; warm, but tends to shed.

TERRY CLOTH: An absorbent fabric made from looped, predominantly cotton yarn. Most often used in bathrobes and beach coverups.

THERMAL INSULATION: Fabrics that keep you cool (such as Coolmax) or warm (such as Thermax), in part by keeping you dry through the wicking of perspiration. Some thermal fabrics are woven in a 3-D manner, often called "waffle weave," designed to trap the body's natural heat and keep you warm in cold weather; often made into long underwear.

TRICOT: French for "knit," tricot generally refers to fabric that has been knitted to produce ribbing.

TROPICAL: Lightweight wool, best for summer and tropical weather, sometimes blended with mohair.

TWEED: Coarse wool cloth, in a variety of weaves and colors. First woven by crafters near the Tweed River in Scotland; its name is derived from tweel or tweed, the Scottish word for "twill."

TWILL: Characteristically diagonal wool or cotton weave; the classic blue blazer is one famous example. Sometimes blended with silk, for summer.

VELVET: Formerly silk, now usually cotton weave, prepared with extra threads, which are clipped short.

VICUÑA: A soft, rare fabric, much like camel hair, woven from the hair of a mammal native to the upper Andes; but bear in mind that vicuña must be trapped for their pelts.

WARP: In a weave, the threads that traverse lengthwise.

WEAVE: Tighter weaves are more durable and less likely to shrink. The higher the thread count per square inch, the more durable the fabric. Before buying a garment, note whether the weave is straight and whether there are any broken yarns. • Warp: The taut lengthwise yarns on a loom; also known as the "end." • Weft: These yarns traverse the warp; also known as "filling" yarn. • Plain: This weave is where it all began: simple vertical threads holding threads running horizontally in place. Easy to launder and dry-clean, drapes well, is comfortable, and is usually inexpensive. Loose weaves (especially basket weaves) are more prone to shrinkage than close ones. • Satin: A shiny, slippery fabric (made of acetate, rayon, nylon, or silk) with loosely interwoven threads that are widely separated to create its smooth finish. It is not a durable fabric and is most appropriate for women's evening wear, and linings. • Twill: A sturdy weave (made of any fiber) characterized by diagonal ribbing. "Broken" twills are those whose diagonals are manipulated into different patterns: herringbones, zigzags, diamond patterns, and so on.

WEFT: In a weave, the threads that are woven up-and-down.

WHIP CORD: Twill weave with a diagonally ribbed surface.

WICKING (HIGH-TECH FABRICS): The ability of a fabric to disperse moisture away from the body. Fibers are treated to be either hydrophilic (to draw water) or hydrophobic (to repel water). "Push/pull" fabrics do both.

WOOL: Wool is made from the fleece of animals. Pulled wool is from slaughtered animals. Worsted wool is wool that has been combed and tightly twisted; it's so named for the city of Worstead, England, where it was first made in the Middle Ages. Lambswool comes from animals sheared at seven to nine months old. Angora is made from the fur of Angora rabbit. Mohair comes from Angora goats. Camel hair is really from camels but may be mixed with wool and/or cashmere. Cashmere is from the soft undercoat of goats that live on the cold high plateaus of inner Asia. Cashmere is finer, lighter, and stronger than other wools, and more expensive. The finest cashmere comes from the Tibetan mountain goat. The number of plies (hairs twisted together) indicates the weight of thickness of the cashmere—the higher the number, the thicker the fabric. What affects its softness most is the length and fineness of the fibers. Cashmere is prized for its softness because, unlike other wools, it feels great against the skin. Because of wool's natural crimp, it has built-in elasticity and resiliency; it can be wrinkle-resistant and is naturally water-repellent, stain-resistant, and soil-resistant. Wool is warm because its fibers trap air, creating an insulating effect; it also retains color well. Wool requires careful maintenance and storage to hold its shape and to prevent it from becoming food for moths. Quality wools are smooth and springy to the touch, usually "virgin" (never made into clothes before). Low-quality wool is stiff, abrasive to the touch, and lackluster; it may also be "reprocessed," meaning that it's been recycled from scraps or old clothing. Lightweight wool can be worn year-round, but heavier weights are appropriate only for colder weather.

WORSTED: Manufactured in Worstead, England, since the eighteenth century. Worsted is a closely woven, smooth-surfaced fabric made of yarn spun from combed, long-staple wool fibers. The fabric's tight weaves inhibit creasing and maintain the line of a suit well. Its light weight makes it the preferred fabric for hot-weather suits and sportswear.

YARN-DYED: Fabrics that are dyed before they are woven. Yarn-dyed fabrics retain color better.

High Tech Fibers

ACTIVENT: A newer innovation of Gore-Tex, with greater breathability. Used in high-energy sports like cross-country skiing.

CAPILENE: Capilene is a trademark Patagonia polyester fiber, worn by space and wilderness explorers—it is the astronaut's fabric of choice. An inner core attracts moisture to wick it off the body; an outer layer distributes moisture so that it dries quickly. Capilene is, however, flammable.

ENTRANT: An elastic, waterproof coating of polyurethane. The more layers of entrant that are applied, the more waterproof and the less breathable the fabric becomes. Like all coatings, it tends to be more breathable than a laminate. Used for winter outerwear.

GORE-TEX: A synthetic laminate that comes in many forms—as thin insulation, and as a waterproof coating applied to the outside of fabrics. It is also a microporous membrane sandwiched between the outer shell and its lining. Gore-Tex is unusual in that it provides both waterproofing and breathabil-ity. Typically, if a laminate is on the outer layer of clothing, it may stiffen in the cold; Gore-Tex, however, remains supple. A lot of outerwear, rainwear, and sportwear is made from Gore-Tex.

MICROFIBER (MICROWEAVE): Finely woven synthetic fibers; brand names include Super Microft, DRI-F.I.T. by Nike, Versatech, and Microsupreme Mesh by Ralph Lauren. Unusual for synthetics, microfibers breathe and offer warmth, can have a great feel, and a sueded or sand-washed silk texture.

NEOPRENE: A nylon-coated, four-way stretchy rubberized material. It is highly insulated, offering warmth and protection from below-body-temperature conditions. This is especially important for divers—hence, most wet-suit manufacturers produce their products with thickly padded neoprene material.

POLARTEC FLEECE: Made by Malden Mills from shredded plastic bottles. Comes in different weights—polyester pile, two-sided microfiber, and Lycra stretch. Synchilla is Patagonia's brand name for Polartec fleeces. Polartec fleece is not only lightweight and warm, but also breathable. It is not, however, good for windy conditions. For garments worn in place of sweatpants, sweatshirts, sweaters, and vests.

SCOTCHLITE: Scotchlite is a trademark of 3M, but is manufactured and marketed by the Nike company for jackets and sportsgear. Scotchlite is unique in that it reflects light back to the original source—individuals wearing Scotchlite garments are more visible in otherwise dark or hard-to-see areas.

SPANDEX: Spandex was first manufactured in the United States in 1959; by now, it has replaced rubber in many fabrics. Lycra is the trademarked name of the spandex produced by Du Pont. The fabric's excellent elasticity means it holds its shape well and resists shrinking, stretching, and wrinkling. Tough and durable (even stronger than rubber), it can withstand abrasion and rubbing—it does, however, generate static. Spandex is fade-resistant (especially an asset for blacks and other dark colors). Spandex requires little maintenance. Do not, however, wash it in strong detergent or bleach; hand-washing in Woolite is recommended to preserve the fabric. Always drip-dry or use nonheat setting on dryer.

SWAY: Developed by Toray in 1989, this is coated nylon that changes color when temperatures change. More recently, the fabric has declined in popularity.

SYNCHILLA: A synthetic fabric made by Patagonia from post-consumer-recycled (PCR) polyester—80% of its fiber comes from recycled plastic bottles. It is lightweight, warm, and wicks vapor.

TEKWARE: Developed by The North Face clothing company. A superior synthetic for its soft, cottonlike feel, its wicking abilities, and its resistance to shrinking and fading. Moisture dries up quickly against the Tekware synthetic fabric, and helps keep skin dry. Its light weight encourages greater mobility and more extensive physical activity.

THINSULATE: First introduced by the 3M Company in the 1960s. Accessories and apparel were not, however, being marketed until 1978. Since then, Thinsulate microfiber has appealed to winter sports enthusiasts for years—particularly for its light weight and its incredible warmth. It insulates one and a half times more effectively than down and other synthetics.

WINDSTOPPER: The latest in Gore-Tex related technology, the Gore-Tex windstopper is a highly breathable, ultra-light high-performance fabric coated with the patented Gore-Tex windstopper ePTFE membrane. This membrane prevents wind penetration and provides greater amounts of warmth with less bulk. It is not however, waterproof.

our favorite "where"s.

Shopping shouldn't be just about consuming but also about learning. A good men's store is a place of refuge and information. It is a place where questions are welcomed and the store's pride is your satisfaction. Whether the establishment is cutting edge or traditional, the only attitude should be one of service. It should be a place of discovery and comfort. Below are some of our favorite shopping places, both in selection and in what you can learn from visiting. Many of these stores have catalogs and some—like Zegna and Louis, Boston—even publish magazines that reflect their personal sense of style.

20 FAVORITE MEN'S WEAR STORES IN ALPHABETICAL ORDER

ALFRED DUNHILL OF LONDON, INC.
450 Park Avenue
New York, NY 10022
212/753-9292
(This Park Avenue store is a shrine both to the pleasures of smoking and to fine classical men's wear with a definite British sense of fabric and style.)

BARNEYS NEW YORK
660 Madison Avenue
New York, NY 10021
212/826-8900
(In New York's sepia days it was a bargain store in lower Manhattan, where a young boy got his first suit while Dad got a great deal on his. Now it's a complete global showcase of men's fashion, uptown to downtown.)

BERGDORF GOODMAN MEN
754 Fifth Avenue
New York, NY 10019
212/753-7300
(A true emporium that sedately and tastefully allows you to explore an amazing cross-section of the pleasures of dressing.)

BIGSBY & KRUTHERS
1750 North Clark Street
Chicago, IL 60614
312/440-1750
(A bold city with beautiful architecture deserves this store. Smart, intelligent, brash, and not afraid to strut—from its annual information guide, Suitbook, to its mix of traditional and European men's wear.)

BROOKS BROTHERS
346 Madison Avenue
New York, NY 10017
212/682-8800
(The store the man in the gray flannel suit emerged from, this old-line institution has reinvented itself. It carries the best selection of well-made, reasonably priced shirts, including the quintessential standard-bearer of modern man, the white button-down oxford shirt.)

ERMENEGILDO ZEGNA
743 Fifth Avenue
New York, NY 10022
212/751-3468
(A tribute to the wonder of Italian mills, this understated store showcases the sensual side of classic elegance with a true continental flair. Not a huge breadth, just a wise selection of suits in either soft or traditional cuts that are always flattering. Jeff's favorite favorite.)

ALAN FLUSSER CUSTOM SHOP
Saks Fifth Avenue
New York, NY 10022
212/888-7100
(On the sixth floor of Saks is a shrine to the drape suit, a marvelous classic cut that has a soft, sloped shoulder and a slight gathering at the waist, imparting a tapered overall look. Its creator, Alan Flusser, with his encyclopedic knowledge, ranks with Stanley Marcus as one of the great shamans of style.)

HARRISON JAMES
5 West 54th Street
New York, NY 10022
212/541-6870
(A newcomer to the scene, it encapsulates men's wear with nearly cinematic precision. It's the kind of place within whose walls it suddenly makes perfect sense to wear a hat. It also offers bespoke suits.)

HOLLAND & HOLLAND
50 East 57th Street
New York, NY 10022
212/752-7755
(Men's wear for the outdoor country gentleman with bifold vents aplenty. Hunting classics, and the romance of over-and-under or double-barrel appeal.)

LOUIS, BOSTON
234 Berkeley Street
Boston, MA 02116
617/262-6100
(There are great stores that are institutions and there are stores that are reflections of their owners. This store—in its taste, ambience, vision, and service—is the embodiment of a personality.)

L'UOMO
1452 Rue Peel
Montreal, Quebec
514/844-1008
(Some men drive—or dream of driving—Lincoln Town Cars; others dream of Jeep Cherokees. Still others prefer Ferraris, and this is indeed a Testarossa kind of place—high-powered, European, and confident.)

MAXFIELD
8825 Melrose Avenue
Los Angeles, CA 90069
310/274-8800
(The kind of store where you share a dressing room with Elton John. The clothes are cutting-edge, selected with an eye for beautiful design. Like a titanium bike, Maxfield is rare and powerful.)

NEIMAN MARCUS
400 NorthPark Center
Dallas, TX 75225
214/363-8311
(Neiman's credo of being a place where you can choose among the best prepares you for the breadth and depth of the NorthPark store. As is true of all great men's stores, the service here is legendary. Each sales associate is a knowledgeable guide both to clothes and to what will work best for you.)

NEW REPUBLIC
93 Spring Street
New York, NY 10012
212/219-3005
(The downtown classics of today; here slouches the perfect rethought waistcoat or black leather blazer, instantly cool yet elegant, along with updated antiques. It feels like a well-kept thrift store of the next century.)

PAUL STUART
Madison Avenue at 45th Street
New York, NY 10017
212/682-0320
(This store has always seemed to be the Cary Grant of clothiers: its unruffled sedateness doesn't rule out meeting Eva Marie Saint in the bar car en route to Mt. Rushmore. The suits are modified American classic mixed with pleasant English detailing.)

POLO AND POLO SPORT
867 Madison Avenue
New York, NY 10021
212/606-2100
(Ralph Lauren's two stores are across the avenue from each other. In the clothes they carry and their differing decor, the two represent both sides of Lauren's vision. In the old Rhinelander mansion, you wander into his anglophile paradise, lost in cinema moments from Gary Cooper to Rex Harrison. Across the way is Lauren's salute to Modernism in its American mode, capturing the new active lifestyle and its micro-fibered Lycra stretch clothes in sleek environs that mirror both a marina and a mountain lodge.)

PUCCI
333 North Michigan Avenue
Chicago, IL 60601
312/332-3759
(Hand-tailored clothes that stand on their own—heartland elegance in beautiful fabrics, as classic as a '57 T-Bird.)

SAKS FIFTH AVENUE
611 Fifth Avenue
New York, NY 10016
212/753-4000
(One of the finest department-store selections of quality men's furnishings. Recent expansion makes shopping a stress-free exploration of every major designer—the store exudes comfort in a big city way without pretension.)

SULKA
301 Park Avenue
New York, NY 10017
212/980-5226
(Civility is the salient experience in entering this refuge of silk and leather, cashmere and linen. From handkerchiefs to dressing gowns, it is always quality and classic style, with shirts that would have made Daisy weep.)

ULTIMO
114 East Oak Street
Chicago, IL 60611
312/787-0906
(Clothes as coolness. Ultimo helps educate with an exciting mix of fashion-forward and classics, from Ermenegildo Zegna to Issey Miyake. If you have been hesitant about being adventurous, this is a great place to start.)

WILKES BASHFORD
375 Sutter Street
San Francisco, CA 10017
415/986-4380
(Reentering this store feels like a homecoming. It's not really home but it feels so good to be here again—from the first floor, with refreshments in the back, to the exquisite displays throughout. Everything is carefully edited, just the best—with laid-back but comfortable sales associates.)

no boundaries. In today's world the choices are overwhelming.

Where do you start? Sometimes the answer is only as far away as your phone or modem—more and more designers, stores, and manufacturers are diminishing distance with catalogs and web sites. We've listed some of our favorite places—some best to visit in person, others to cruise to on the Net or just a phone number away.

PHONE NUMBERS & WEB SITES

ADIDAS
800/4-ADIDAS
(Sports shoes and apparel)

ALFRED DUNHILL OF LONDON INC.
212/888-4000
(Classic men's wear)

AIRWALK
800/AIRWALK
http://www.airwalk.com
(Sneakers and casuals)

ARMANI A/X
212/570-1122
http://www.ArmaniExchange.com
(Giorgio Armani basics)

BANANA REPUBLIC
888/277-8953
(Casuals and classics)

BASS/WEEJUN
800/777-1790
http://www.ghbass.com
(Shoes)

BILL'S KHAKI
800/43-KHAKI
http://www.billskhakis.com
(Comfortable, affordable khakis)

BLOOMINGDALE'S
800/777-4999
http://www.bloomingdales.com
(Upscale department store)

BOBBY JONES
800/295-2000
(Casuals and sportswear)

BROOKS BROTHERS
800/444-1613
(Classic men's wear)

BURBERRY'S LTD.
800/284-8480
(Outerwear and clothing)

CARTIER
800/CARTIER
(Fine jewelry and watches)

CHAMPION
http://www.champion.com
(Athletic wear)

CIGAR WORLD
http://www.cigarworld.com
(Cigar-related news and updates)

CLUB MONACO
800/383-9096
http://www.clubmonaco.com
(Casuals and classics)

COACH
800/262-2411
http://www.coach.com
(Bags and leather goods)

COLE-HAAN
212/421-8440
(Shoes)

CONSUMER REPORTS
800/234-1645
http://www.consumerreports.org/
(Consumer Reports magazine on-line)

COUNTRY ROAD AUSTRALIA
888/844-2045
(Casuals and classics)

THE CUSTOM SHOP
800/867-5985
(Custom-tailored shirts)

DAFFY'S
201/902-0800
http://www.Daffys.com
(Discounted men's wear)

DAYTON HUDSON/MARSHALL FIELD
800/292-2450
http://www.shop@.com
(Upscale department store)

DIESEL
http://www.diesel.com/
(Sportswear and casuals)

DKMEN
212/572-4200
(Designer clothes)

DOCKERS
800/DOCKERS
http://www.dockers.com
(Khakis and sportswear)

EASTERN MOUNTAIN SPORTS
603/924-6154
http://www.emsonline.com
(Activewear)

EDDIE BAUER
800/426-8020
http://www.eddiebauer.com
(Casual and outdoor wear)

FASHION MALL
800/859-1440
http://www.fashionmall.com
(Convenient shopping on-line)

FIRST VIEW
http://www.firstview.com/
(Preview designer collections)

THE GAP
415/777-0250
http://www.gap.com
(Clothing basics)

THE GENUINE SWISS ARMY KNIFE CO.
800/447-7422
http://www.genuineswissarmy.com
(Knives and watches)

GHURKA
203/866-7447
(Luggage and leather goods)

GIORGIO ARMANI
201/570-1122
(Designer clothes)

GRATEFUL DEAD NECKWEAR
http://www.deadties.com
(Ties by the late Jerry Garcia)

GUCCI
800/234-8224
(Leather and clothing)

HANES
800/994-4348
http://www.hanes.com

HARLEY-DAVIDSON MOTORCYCLES
800/443-2153
http://www.harley-davidson.com/
(Clothing and accessories)

Stores—In General
All over the world are stores that help light the way in the quest for wardrobe enlightenment. Here is a partial listing—by no means complete—from accessory experts to classic designer shops.

HERMÈS
800/441-4488
(Leather and clothing)

HUSH PUPPIES
800/433-HUSH or
800/313-5699
http://www.netpad.com/hushpuppies
(Shoes)

JACK PURCELL/CONVERSE
800/428-2667
http://www.converse.com
(Sport shoes and apparel)

J. CREW
800/782-8244
http://www.jcrew.com
(Casuals and classics)

JC PENNEY
800/222-6161
http://www.jcpenney.com/
(On-line department store)

J. PETERMAN
800/231-7341
http://www.jpeterman.com
(Casuals and classics)

JOE BOXER
http://www.joeboxer.com/
(Boxers, games, and more)

JOHNSTON & MURPHY
800/424-2854
http://www.johnstonmurphy.com
(Formal and casual shoes)

KENNETH COLE SHOES
800/KEN-COLE
http://www.kencole.com
(Shoes)

LANDS' END
800/356-4444
http://www.landsend.com
(Clothing basics)

LEVI STRAUSS & CO.
800/USA-LEVI
(Jeans and sportswear)

L.L. BEAN RETAIL STORE/CATALOG
800/543-9071
http://www.llbean.com
(Outdoor wear and gear)

LOUIS VUITTON
800/458-4136
http://www.vuitton.com
(Designer clothes)

MACY'S/BULLOCK'S/AÉROPOSTALE
800/45-MACYS
amy+@macy's.com
(Department store)

NAUTICA
212/496-0933
(Activewear)

NEIMAN MARCUS
800/937-9146
http://www.neimanmarcus.com
(Upscale department store)

NIKE
800/250-7590
http://www.nike.com
(Sportswear and shoes)

NORDSTROM
800/285-5800
http://www.nordstrom/pta.com
(Upscale department store)

THE NORTH FACE
630/990-0303
(Activewear)

OLIVER PEOPLES
310/657-5475
(Eyeglasses)

ORVIS
800/541-3541
http://www.orvis.com

OXFORD CLOTHES
888/4-OXFORD
(Fine tailored clothing)

PARISIAN
205/940-4000
(Upscale department store)

PATAGONIA
800/336-9090
http://www.patagonia.com
(Activewear)

PAUL STUART
800/678-8278
e/mail/pscatalog@aol.com
(Classic men's wear)

PENDLETON WOOLEN MILLS
800/841-7202
http://www.pendleton/usa.com
(Wool garments)

PERRY ELLIS
http://www.pemenswear.com
(Casual classics)

POLO/RALPH LAUREN
212/606-2100
http://www.poloralphlauren.com
(Designer clothes)

QUICKSILVER
888/222-2272
http://www.quicksilverusa.com
(Sportswear)

RAFFI LINEA UOMO
212/307-1416
(Knits and sweaters)

REEBOK
800/307-2356
http://www.reebok.com
(Activewear)

REI
800/426-4840
http://www.Rei.com
(Activewear)

ROCKPORT
800/ROCKPORT
http://www.rockport.com
(Shoes)

SAKS FIFTH AVENUE
212/753-4000
http://www.dreamshop.com/saksfifthavenue
(Upscale department store)

SEARS
847/286-5188
http://www.sears.com
(On-line department store)

SEBAGO
800/365-5505
http://www.sebago.com
(Shoes)

SONY
800/222-7669
http://www.sony.com
(Electronics)

SLATES
800/SLATES-1
http://www.slates.com
(Men's dress pants)

TARGET STORES
800/800-8800
http://www.target.com
(Basics)

TEVA
800/FOR TEVA
http://www.teva.com
(Sandals)

TIMBERLAND
800/258-0855
http://www.timberland.com
(Activewear and shoes)

TIMEX
800/367-8463
http://www.timex.com
(Watches)

TOMMY HILFIGER
212/840-8888
(Casuals and classics)

TSE
212/472-7790
(Cashmere clothing)

URBAN OUTFITTERS
215/569-3131
(Casual wear)

VANS
800/750-VANS
(Sport shoes)

WATERMAN PENS
800/523-2486
(Fine custom pens)

WATHNE
800/942-1166
(Elegant activewear)

ZIPPO
408/720-7620
http://www.zippo.com
(Lighters)

AUSTRALIA

COUNTRY ROAD
Pitt Street Mall
142 Pitt Street
Sydney
2/282-6299
(Classic sportswear)

DAIMARU
21 La Trobe Street
Melbourne
3/660-6666
(Upscale department store)

DAVID JONES
Elizabeth Street
Sydney
2/266-5544
(Upscale department store)

GEORGES
162 Collins Street
Melbourne
3/283-5535
(Upscale department store)

FRANCE

A. CRISTIANI
2 rue de la Paix
Paris
1/42-61-12-34
(Custom suits and tailoring)

ARNYS
14 rue de Sèvres
Paris
1/45-48-76-99
(Classic menswear)

AGNÈS B.
3–6 rue du Jour
Paris 75001
1/40-03-45-00
(Clothes and accessories)

AU PETIT MATELOT
27 avenue de la Grande-Armée
Paris
1/45-00-15-51
(Classic sportswear)

AU PRINTEMPS
64 boulevard Haussmann
Paris 75009
1/42-82-50-00
(Department store)

BERLUTI
26 rue Marbeuf
Paris
1/43-59-51-10
(Custom-fitted shoes)

CERRUTI
3 place de la Madeleine
Paris
1/42-65-68-72
(Sportswear and menswear)

CHARLES BOSQUET
13 rue Marbeuf
Paris
1/47-20-56-59
(Custom-tailored suits)

CHARVET
28 place Vendôme
Paris
1/42-60-30-70
(Custom-made dress shirts)

CIFONELLI
31 rue Marbeuf
Paris
1/42-25-38-84
(Classic tailor)

CRIMSON
8 rue Marbeuf
Paris
1/47-20-44-24
(Knitwear)

DANIEL CREMIEUX
6 boulevard Malesherbes
Paris
1/42-66-27-78
(Sportswear)

FACONNABLE
9 rue du Faubourg-Saint-Honoré
Paris
1/47-42-72-60
(Classic sportswear)

GALERIES LAFAYETTE
40 boulevard Haussmann
Paris 75009
1/42-82-34-56
(Department store)

GELOT
15 rue du Faubourg-Saint-Honoré
Paris
1/44-71-31-61
(Classic haberdasher)

HERMÈS
24 rue du Faubourg-Saint-Honoré
Paris 75008
1/42-17-47-17
(Clothing, accessories, jewelry, and luggage)

HONEST
37 rue Marbeuf
Paris
1/42-25-87-27
(Sportswear)

INÈS DE LA FRESSANGE
14 avenue Montaigne
Paris 75008
1/47-23-08-94
(Classic clothing and accessories)

ISLAND
place des Victoires
Paris
1/42-61-77-77
(Traditional sportswear)

HOBBS
45 rue Pierre-Charron
Paris
1/47-20-83-22
(Cashmere sweaters and socks)

JOHN LOBB
51 rue François-1er
Paris
1/45-61-02-55
(Classic custom-made shoes)

LOFT
12 rue du Faubourg-Saint-Honoré
Paris
1/42-74-44-02
(Chic sportswear)

MARCEL LASSANCE
17 rue du Vieux-Colombier
Paris
1/45-48-29-28
(Classic menswear and sportswear)

MASSARO
2 rue de la Paix
Paris
1/42-61-00-29
(Custom-fitted shoes)

METTEZ
12 boulevard Malesherbes
Paris
1/42-65-33-76
(Sportswear)

MOTSCH
42 avenue George-V
Paris
1/47-23-79-22
(Classic haberdasher)

OLD ENGLAND
12 boulevard des Capucines
Paris
1/47-42-81-99
(Classic department store)

RHODES & BROUSSE
14 rue de Castiglione
Paris
1/42-60-86-27
(Menswear, specializing in custom-made shirts, ties, and hosiery)

ROBERT CLERGERIE
5 rue du Cherche-Midi
Paris 75006
1/45-48-75-47
(Designer shoes)

VICTOIRE HOMMES
10-12 rue Colonel Driant
Paris
1/42-97-44-87
(Sportswear)

GERMANY

BRAUN
Bergstrasse 17
20095 Hamburg
40/33-44-70
(Designer menswear)

JIL SANDER
Milchstrasse 13
2000 Hamburg
40/5530-2173
(Designer clothing)

LADAGE & OELKE
11Neuer Wall U. Alsterarkaden 11
2 Hamburg 36
40/34-47-48
(Traditional menswear)

LUDWIG BECK
Marienplatz 11
Munich
89/23-6910
(Upscale department store)

MEY & EDLICH
Theatinerstrasse 7
Munich
89/290-0590
(Upscale department store)

PFEIFEN TESCH
Colonnaden 10
20354 Hamburg
40/34-25-84
(Pipes)

STABEN
Rathansmarkt 5
Hamburg
40/37-73-53
(Traditional menswear)

GREAT BRITAIN

AGNÈS B.
35–36 Floral Street
London
171/379-1992
(Clothes and accessories)

ANDERSON & SHEPPARD
30 Savile Row
London
171/734-1420
(Hand-tailored sportswear)

ASPREY LTD.
165-169 New Bond Street
London
171/493-6767
(Accessories)

BROWNS
23-27 South Molton Street
London
171/491-7833
(Designer clothing)

BUDD
1A & 3 Piccadilly Arcade
London
171/493-0139
(Custom-tailored shirts and formal accessories)

BURBERRY'S
18–22 Haymarket
165 Regent Street
London
171/930-3343
(Outerwear, clothing, and accessories)

G.J. CLEVERLEY & CO. LTD.
12 Royal Arcade
28 Old Bond Street
London
171/493-0443
(Custom-fitted shoes)

CONNOLLY LTD.
32 Grosvenor Crescent Mews
London
171/235-3883
(Leather goods)

CORDINGS
19 Piccadilly
London
171/734-0830
(Classic outerwear)

CUTLER & GROSS
16 Knightsbridge Green
London
171/581-2250
(Fashion eyewear)

DICKINS AND JONES
224-244 Regent Street
London
171/734-7070
(Fashion-based department store)

FLANNELS
4 St. Ann's Place
Manchester
161/832-5536
(Designer clothing)

THE GAP
31 Long Acre
London
171/379-0779
(Clothing and accessories)

HACKETT GENTLEMAN'S CLOTHIERS
138 Sloane Street
London
171/730-3331
(Classic menswear)

HARRODS
Knightsbridge
London
171/730-1234
(Upscale department store)

HARVEY NICHOLS
109–125 Knightsbridge
London
171/235-5000
(Upscale department store)

HERBERT JOHNSON
30 New Bond Street
London
171/408-1174
(Hats)

H. HUNTSMAN & SONS
11 Savile Row
London
171/734-7441
(Custom-tailored menswear)

JIGSAW MENSWEAR
9-10 Floral Street
London
171/240-5651
(Fashionable menswear)

JONES
15 Floral Street
London
171/240-8313
(Clothing and accessories)

JOSEPH
77–79 Fulham Road
London
171/823-9500
(Designer clothing)

LIBERTY PLC.
210–222 Regent Street
London
171/734-1234
(Clothing and accessories)

THE LIBRARY
268 Brompton Road
London
171/589-6569
(Assorted designer menswear and books)

JOHN LOBB LTD.
9 St. James Street
London
171/930-3664
(Custom-fitted shoes)

LONGMIRE
12 Bury Street
London
171/839-5398
(Cufflinks)

MARKS AND SPENCER PLC
458 Oxford Street
London
171/935-4422
(Department store)

MUJI
26 Great Marlborough Street
London
171/494-1197 for stores
(Natural-fiber clothing)

NEXT PLC.
160 Regent Street
London
171/434-2515
(Clothing and accessories)

PATRICK COX SHOES
8 Symons Street
London
171/730-6504
(Shoes)

PAUL SMITH
40–44 Floral Street
London
171/379-7133
(Fashionable menswear)

HENRY POOLE & COMPANY
15 Savile Row
London
171/734-5985
(Classic tailored menswear)

SWAINE ADENEY BRIGG & SONS
10 Old Bond Street
London
171/409-7277
(Umbrellas)

TED BAKER
1 Langley Court
London
171/497-8862
(Stylish shirts)

TURNBULL & ASSER
71-72 Jermyn Street
London
171/930-0502
(Ready-made and custom-made dress shirts, ties)

REPUBLIC OF IRELAND

BROWN THOMAS
88-95 Grafton Street
Dublin
1/679-5666
(Ireland's premier department store showcasing designer names)

ITALY

ARMERIA CENTRALE
via Pellicceria 30R
Florence
55/210-162
(Hunting and outdoor clothes)

CASA DELLO SPORT
via Tosinghi 8-10R
Florence
55/215-696
(Athletic wear)

CREDI CHIARINI ROYAL
via Roma 18/20/22R
Florence
55/284-478
(Menswear and sportswear)

ERMENEGILDO ZEGNA
Via P. Verri 3
Milan
2/7600-6437
(Designer clothing and accessories)

GIORGIO ARMANI
Via Sant'Andrea 9
Milan
2/7602-2757
(Designer clothes)

H. NEUBER
Galleria Tornabuoni
via Tournabuoni
Florence
55/215-763
(Traditional menswear and sportswear)

LA RINASCENTE
Piazza Duomo
Milan
2/7200-2210
(Department store)

LUISA VIA ROMA
via Roma 19-21R
Florence
55/217-826
(Designer menswear)

MAS
Piazza Vittorio Emanuele
Rome
6/446-9010
(Discount shopping, bargain cashmere)

OLIVER
via Vaccereccia 15R
Florence
55/239-6327
(Designer menswear and sportswear)

PRINCIPE
Piazza Strozzi 1
Florence
55/292-764
(Traditional menswear)

TIE YOUR TIE
via della Spada 8R
Florence
55/211-015
(Expertly crafted ties, shirts, shoes)

UGOLINI
via Tornabuoni 20-22
Florence
55/216-664
(Gloves, shoes, and cashmere sweaters and ties)

ZORAN
Corso Matteoti 1A
Milan
2/760-7958
(Simple, luxurious clothes)

JAPAN

BEAMS
2F Noir Haratuku Boulevard
3-24-7 Jingumae
Shibuya, Tokyo
3/3470-3948
(Fashionable and custom-made menswear)

ISETAN
3-14-1 Shinjuku
Shinjuku-ku, Tokyo
3/3352-1111
(Specialty store)

LLOYDS
5-18-4 Minami
Aoyama, Tokyo
3/3409-9335
(Hand-made shoes and leather goods)

OYSTER
2-18 Minamiaoyama 3 Chome
Minato, Tokyo
3/3478-1918
(Classic menswear)

SHIPS
1-11-1 Jinnan
Shibuya, Tokyo
3/3496-0487
(Fine menswear)

TAKASHIMAYA
2-4-1 Nihonbashi
Chuo-ku, Tokyo
3/3211-4111
(Designer clothing)

UNITED ARROWS
6-13-6 Chome
Shibuya, Tokyo
3/3797-9791
(Classic menswear)

SWEDEN

PEAK PERFORMANCE
Jakobsberggatan 6
Stockholm
8/611-3400
(Outdoor clothes)

resources

14 **BOXER SHORTS**—Brooks Brothers

16 **RAZOR AND PEWTER SHAVING DISH**—Paul Smith (Private Collection); **COCONUT SHAVING SOAP AND BADGER BRISTLE SHAVING BRUSH**—The Art of Shaving

17 **GLYCERIN SOAP**—Mettler, Ad Hoc

18 **OLD SPICE**—Available at all drugstores

19 **BASEBALL MITT**—From the private collection of Bradley Friedman; **CITRUS BOXES**—Origins, Bergdorf Goodman, New York

20 **BLUE PLAID SHIRT AND BOW TIE**—Paul Stuart; **COTTON KHAKI JACKET AND PANTS**—Bergdorf Goodman; **LEATHER WING-TIP SHOES**—J. M. Weston; **ATTACHÉ CASE**—Bill Auberg; **BURNISHED JAVA LEATHER BELT**—Trafalgar; **ORANGE COTTON SHIRT**—Tommy Hilfiger; **GOLF SHOES**—Hush Puppies; **HAT**—J. Crew; **VINTAGE GOLF CLUB**—Private Collection

21 **KHAKI JACKET**—Bergdorf Goodman; **WHITE COTTON T**—Old Navy; **DARK RINSE JEANS**—Levi's 501; **CANVAS AND LEATHER SHOULDER BAG**—Holland & Holland; **SILVER "AIRMAX" SNEAKERS"**—Nike

23 **MONEY CLIP**—Ad Hoc and The Museum of Modern Art

24 **POCKET KNIFE**—Swiss Army;

LEATHER MOTORCYCLE JACKET—The Perfecto, Canal Jeans; **BANDANNA**—Canal Jeans; **10" ADJUSTABLE WRENCH**—General Tech, H. Brickman & Sons

25 **NAVY SUIT, WHITE SHIRT, TIE, EYEGLASSES, BELT, POCKET SQUARE**—Polo by Ralph Lauren; **SHOES**—Brooks Brothers

31 **EMBOSSED LEATHER BELT**—Riga by Trafalgar; **NAVY WOOL JACKET AND TROUSERS**—Paul Stuart; **COTTON DRESS SHIRT**—Joseph Abboud; **LEATHER CAP-TOE SHOES**—Cole-Haan; **SOCKS**—Brooks Brothers; **SILK KNIT TIE**—Hugo Boss; **NAVY SUIT**—(center) Donna Karan; **WHITE COTTON POINT SHIRT**—Joseph Abboud; **BLUE SILK TIE AND BLACK SOCKS**—Brooks Brothers; **WATCH**—Universal Genève; **BLACK LEATHER BELT**—DKNY; **DOUBLE BUCKLE BLACK SHOES**—John Lobb

32 **NAVY SUIT OUTFIT**—(left) listed for p. 31; **NAVY PINSTRIPE SUIT, SHIRT, TIE**—Polo by Ralph Lauren; **BLACK WING-TIP SHOES**—Edward Green/Paul Stuart

34 **NAVY SACK SUIT, BELT**—Brooks Brothers; **BLUE OXFORD CLOTH BUTTON-DOWN, RED SILK KNIT TIE, LINEN POCKET SQUARE**—Paul Stuart; **SHOES**—J. M. Weston; **WATCH**—Holland & Holland; **WOOL CREPE SUIT**—Emporio Armani; **WHITE COTTON BAND-COLLAR SHIRT AND BLACK SOCKS**—Dockers; **GLASSES**—Morganthal Frederics; **MONK STRAP SHOES**—J. M. Weston; **BELT**—Brooks Brothers

35 **NAVY PINSTRIPE SUIT, WHITE LINEN HANDKERCHIEF, CORDOVAN LEATHER CAP-TOE SHOES**—Paul Stuart; **WHITE SPREAD-COLLAR SHIRT**—Paul Stuart "Stuart's Choice"; **SILK PRINT TIE**—Brooks Brothers;

ANTIQUE WATCH—Time Will Tell; **SOCKS**—Holland & Holland; **GLASSES**—Oliver Peoples; **PLAID CASHMERE SUIT AND VEST, CASHMERE KNIT TIE**—Polo by Ralph Lauren; **WHITE COTTON DRESS SHIRT**—Ralph Lauren Purple Label; **ANTIQUE SILVER AND ENAMEL "HORSE & ROOSTER" CUFF LINKS**—Tender Buttons; **WATCH**—Hermès; **SUEDE WING-TIP SHOES**—Paul Stuart; **SOCKS**—Today's Man

36 **WOODEN SUIT HANGER**—Hold Everything

37 **PERSONAL GYM**—Gym Source

38–39 **NAILHEAD WOOL JACKET AND WHITE COTTON HANDKERCHIEF**—Paul Stuart; **RED-AND-BLUE PRINT TIE**—Ermenegildo Zegna; **PURPLE PLAID COTTON SHIRT**—Thomas Pink; **NAVY CHALK-STRIPE WOOL THREE-BUTTON JACKET**—Joseph Abboud; **PINK COTTON SHIRT WITH WHITE COLLAR AND FUCHSIA STRIPED SILK TIE**—Brooks Brothers; **MINI HOUNDSTOOTH PLAID WOOL JACKET, STRIPED WHITE COTTON SHIRT, GOLD SILK PATTERNED TIE**—Paul Stuart; **NAVY PINSTRIPE WOOL JACKET**—Brooks Brothers; **BLUE-AND-WHITE COTTON STRIPED SHIRT, GREEN STRIPED SILK TIE**—Paul Stuart; **GLEN PLAID WOOL JACKET**—Paul Stuart Classic; **BLUE-AND-WHITE STRIPED COTTON SHIRT, NAVY-AND-LIGHT-BLUE PLAID SILK TIE**—Paul Stuart; **BROWN HERRINGBONE WOOL AND MOHAIR JACKET**—Ermenegildo Zegna "Soft"; **BLUE-AND-WHITE STRIPED SHIRT, CRIMSON STRIPED SILK TIE**—Paul Stuart

41 **COTTON VISCOSE SHIRT**—Ermenegildo Zegna; **NAVY WOOL CREPE SUIT**—Emporio Armani; **NAVY SILK KNIT TIE**—Paul Stuart; **BLACK LOAFERS**—Gucci; **WATCH**—Eddie Bauer;

SOFT GARMENT BAG—Innovation Luggage

43 **OLIVE SUEDED MOLESKIN HACKING JACKET, BLUE-AND-WHITE PLAID COTTON SHIRT, SILK BIRD-PRINT TIE, SILK PRINT POCKET SQUARE**—Holland & Holland; **CAVALRY TWILL JACKET, TATTERSALL SHIRT, SILK "AMMO" PRINT TIE**—Holland & Holland

44 **BLACK WOOL THREE-BUTTON JACKET AND PANTS**—Banana Republic; **GRAY-AND-WHITE STRIPED COTTON SHIRT, TIE**—Ermenegildo Zegna; **BLACK LEATHER BELT**—Riga by Trafalgar; **WATCH**—Hublot; **CHARCOAL GRAY SOCKS**—Brooks Brothers; **BLACK LEATHER SHOES**—Polo by Ralph Lauren

46 **GRAY SEERSUCKER SUIT**—Luciano Barbera at Bergdorf Goodman; **WHITE PIQUÉ COTTON SHIRT**—Banana Republic; **BEIGE SUEDE SHOES**—To Boot New York at Bergdorf Goodman; **SUNGLASSES**—Ray•Ban

47 **THREE-PIECE LINEN SUIT, FLAX LINEN SHIRT, SILK TIE**—Joseph Abboud; **WING-TIP BUCK SHOES**—Timberland; **EYEGLASSES**—Morganthal Frederics; **FOUR-BUTTON JACKET AND CUFFED TROUSERS**—Ermenegildo Zegna; **PLAID COTTON SHIRT**—Polo by Ralph Lauren; **SUNGLASSES**—Calvin Klein; **JACK PURCELL SNEAKERS**—Converse; **EMBOSSED LEATHER BELT**—Brooks Brothers; **STAINLESS STEEL WATCH**—Swiss Army; **COTTON KHAKI JACKET AND PANTS OUTFIT WITH ATTACHÉ CASE**—listed for p. 20

48 **GRAY TROPICAL WOOL THREE-BUTTON SUIT, BLACK SOCKS**—Brooks Brothers; **PINK OXFORD CLOTH SHIRT, SILK KNIT TIE, WHITE LINEN HANDKERCHIEF**—Paul Stuart; **BLACK LEATHER CAP-TOE SHOES**—Cole-Haan;

POLISHED CALF BELT—Trafalgar; **BRUSHED SILVER WATCH**—Timex

49 **CHARCOAL WOOL MILITARY JACKET, BLACK STRETCH KHAKIS**—DKNY; **CHARCOAL GRAY FRENCH CUFF COTTON SHIRT**—New Republic; **CORDOVAN LACE-UP LEATHER BOOTS**—Kenneth Cole; **BLACK SILK KNIT TIE**—Paul Stuart; **BLACK LEATHER BELT**—Banana Republic; **WOOL AND CASHMERE CHARCOAL GRAY DOUBLE-BREASTED JACKET AND PANTS**—Calvin Klein Collection; **BLACK CASHMERE TURTLENECK SWEATER**—Polo by Ralph Lauren; **BLACK LEATHER BELT**—Trafalgar; **WATCH**—Swiss Army; **LEATHER BOOTS**—Gucci

50 **CLASSIC NAVY WOOL DOUBLE-BREASTED JACKET**—Ralph Lauren

51 **BLAZER**—Polo by Ralph Lauren; **SHIRT**—Armani; **TROUSERS**—Polo by Ralph Lauren; **SHOES**—Polo by Ralph Lauren

53 **SPORT COAT**—Paul Stuart; **WHITE SHIRT**—Dockers; **WOOL PLAID TIE**—Paul Stuart; **EYEGLASSES**—Christian Roth/Optical Affairs

54 **GRAY WOOL SUIT JACKET**—Boss, Hugo Boss; **WHITE COTTON DRESS SHIRT, BLACK SILK TIE**—Boss, Hugo Boss

55 **SUEDE BLAZER**—Ermenegildo Zegna; **CASHMERE TURTLENECK, PLAID CASHMERE SUIT PANTS**—Polo by Ralph Lauren; **LEATHER GLOVES**—LaCrasia; **VINTAGE LONGINES WATCH**—Time Will Tell; **PENNY LOAFERS**—Prada; **LINEN JACKET, CHECKED COTTON SHIRT, SILK ELEPHANT-PRINT TIE**—Hermès; **CUFFED KHAKI TROUSERS**—Hugo Boss; **LEATHER BELT**—Trafalgar; **VINTAGE CARTIER WATCH**—Time Will Tell; **TORTOISE RIM SUNGLASSES**—Morganthal Frederics; **CARAMEL SUEDE DRIVING MOCCASINS**—

J. P. Tod's

56–7 (From left) **TWEED PANTS, DARK GREEN TROUSERS**—Holland & Holland; **GRAY FLANNEL TROUSERS**—Polo by Ralph Lauren; **DARK GREEN CORDUROY TROUSERS**—Holland & Holland; **TAN GABARDINE PANTS**—Brooks Brothers

58 **CHARCOAL GRAY WOOL FLANNEL TROUSERS**—Personal collection of Jeff Stone

59 **BEIGE KHAKIS**—Bill's Khakis

61 **LIZARD WALLET**—T. Anthony; **MEN'S WALLET**—Ghurka; **BLACK COIN PURSE** with gold clasp—T. Anthony; **COIN PURSE WITH ZIPPER**—Ad Hoc

62 **WHITE BAND-COLLAR SHIRT**—Paul Stuart; **GOLD AND SILVER COLLAR BARS**—Paul Stewart

63 **SHIRT COLLARS**—Bergdorf Goodman Men

64 **COTTON SHIRTS** (from top)—Polo; Vestimenta; Alan Flusser; Brooks Brothers

65 **HANGING SHIRTS**—Equipment at Bergdorf Goodman; **FOLDED SHIRTS**—The Gap

66 **COTTON SHIRTS** (from top)—Gordian Knot; Sulka; Garrick Anderson; Hackett; Ferrell Reed; **SILK TIE**—Sulka

67 **SHIRT AND TIE**—Giorgio Armani

68 **COTTON SHIRTS** (from left)—Charvet; Nautica; Ermenegildo Zegna; Ermenegildo Zegna; Ermenegildo Zegna; Giorgio Armani

69 **COTTON SHIRT**—Paul Stuart; **SILK TIE**—Gene Meyer

70 **BLUE SHIRTS** (from left)—Ermenegildo Zegna; Ermenegildo Zegna; Brooks Brothers; Joseph Abboud

71 **WOOL CREPE SUIT**—Hermès; **STRIPED COTTON SHIRT**—Polo by Ralph Lauren; **SILK APPLE PRINT TIE**—Thomas Pink; **LEATHER BELT**—J. M. Weston;

LEATHER SHOES—Kenneth Cole; **DRESS SOCKS**—Brooks Brothers

72 **TYPEWRITER KEY CUFF LINKS**—Paul Smith; **GOLD CUFF LINKS**—Tiffany & Co; **14-KARAT REVERSE-PAINTED CRYSTAL GOLF CUFF LINKS**—Tender Buttons; **SILK KNOT CUFF LINKS**—Paul Stuart

73 **CUFFS**—Bergdorf Goodman Men

74–5 **WATCHES** (from left)—Swiss Army; Rolex; Timex; Van Cleef & Arpels

76 **WHITE OXFORD SHIRT**—Dockers; (Ties from left to right) **BRONZE WOOL KNIT TIE**—Paul Stuart; **WOOL PLAID TIE**—Paul Stuart; **SILK CLUB TIE**—Polo by Ralph Lauren; **PHEASANT PRINT HERRINGBONE TIE**—Paul Stuart; **PLAID SILK SEERSUCKER TIE, SILK FLORAL TIE, SCOTTY DOG TIE**—Brooks Brothers

77 **BLACK SILK KNIT TIE**—Polo by Ralph Lauren

78 **SILK BOW TIE**—Bill Robinson

79 **SILK TIES** (from left)—Gucci; Hackett; Tino Cosmo; Sulka

80 **CHARCOAL GRAY WINDOWPANE WOOL JACKET WITH MATCHING VEST, COTTON PINK DRESS SHIRT, BLACK-AND-WHITE CHECKED SILK TIE, GOLD TIE PIN, CHECKED POCKET SQUARE**—all by Alan Flusser

81 **DIGITAL STILL CAMERA, DIGITAL COLOR PRINTER**—Sony; (in Polaroid) **GRAY NAILHEAD WOOL DOUBLE-BREASTED JACKET**—Perry Ellis; **COTTON SHIRT WITH WHITE COLLAR**—Paul Stuart; **RED BALLOON PRINT SILK TIE**—Pink (Jermyn & London)

82 **EYEGLASSES**—Oliver Peoples

83 **ETCHED SILVER CASE**—Oliver Peoples; **TORTOISE CASE**—Alain Mikli from Oliver Peoples; **BLUE LEATHER CASE**—Alain Mikli; **WOODEN CASE**—Robert Marc;

SILVER CASE—Martine Sitbon from Private Eyes; **BROWN ALLIGATOR CASE**—Private Eyes; **ANTIQUE CASE**—Selima Optique; **GOLD WIRE-FRAME GLASSES**—Selima Optique

84–5 **GLEN PLAID JACKET**—Ermenegildo Zegna; **BLUE-AND-WHITE STRIPED SHIRT**—Paul Stuart; **SILK REP TIE**—Brooks Brothers; **SILK PRINT POCKET SQUARE**—Hermès; **TWEED JACKET**—Joseph Abboud; **COTTON PLAID BUTTON-DOWN**—The Gap; **BURGUNDY "DEER" PRINT TIE**—Holland & Holland

86 **PLAID SUIT OUTFIT** (on left)—listed for p. 35; **CASHMERE PLAID VEST**—Polo by Ralph Lauren; **COTTON BUTTON-DOWN, PAISLEY TIE**—Paul Stuart; **OLIVE CORDUROY PANTS**—Ermenegildo Zegna; **BROWN BUCKLED SHOES**—Paul Stuart; **LEATHER BELT**—Trafalgar

87 **TAN GLEN PLAID LAMBSWOOL JACKET**—Polo by Ralph Lauren; **WHITE COTTON SHIRT**—Joseph Abboud; **CHARCOAL LAMBSWOOL V-NECK SWEATER**—Boss, Hugo Boss; **COTTON PLEATED KHAKIS**—Holland & Holland; **BROWN LEATHER WING-TIP SHOES**—J. M. Weston; **HERRINGBONE SOCKS**—Brooks Brothers; **WATCH**—Timex; **SUEDE BLAZER AND TURTLENECK OUTFIT**—listed for p. 55

88 (Top left) **WHITE COTTON BUTTON-DOWN SHIRT**—Dockers; **GREEN COTTON/POLYESTER SWEATER VEST**—Dockers Golf; (Top right) **WHITE BAND-COLLAR COTTON SHIRT**—Dockers; **BLACK VEST**—Joseph Abboud; (Bottom left) **BROWN HERRINGBONE VEST**—Polo; **RUST MOLESKIN SHIRT**—Holland & Holland; **INDIGO-BLUE TIE WITH YELLOW DUCKS AND PHEASANT PRINT**—Holland & Holland; (Bottom right) **POLARTEC FLEECE VEST**—Patagonia; **KHAKI COTTON

SHIRT—Dockers; **SILK SCOTTIE TIE**—Paul Stuart

89 (From top left, clockwise)—**TWEED VEST**—Joseph Abboud; **LEATHER VEST**—Levi Strauss & Co.; **RIBBED SLEEVELESS CARDIGAN**—TSE; **TAN SUEDE VEST**—J. Peterman Co.

90 **BLACK CASHMERE CARDIGAN**—N. Peal; **GRAY FLANNELS**—Falke; **WHITE SHIRT**—Polo by Ralph Lauren; **BLACK SILK TIE**—Donna Karan Men; **SOCKS**—Barneys New York; **WATCH**—Sector; **BELT**—Trafalgar; **SHOES**—J. M. Weston

91 **BLUE CHECK SHIRT**—Holland & Holland; **CHARCOAL GRAY CASHMERE POLO**—Banana Republic

92 **SOCKS**—(from left) Cole-Haan; Gold Toe; Cole-Haan

93 **BELTS**—Joseph Abboud (braided); Polo by Ralph Lauren

94 **LOAFER**—Brooks Brothers; **BROWN SUEDE SHOE**—Johnston & Murphy

95 **BLACK LEATHER CAP-TOE DRESS SHOE**—Johnston & Murphy; **CEDAR SHOE TREE**—Hold Everything

96 **BROWN LEATHER WING TIP**—Cole-Haan

97 **BROWN LEATHER TASSELED LOAFERS**—Brooks Brothers

98 **REVERSIBLE RAINCOAT**—Paul Stuart

99 **GRAY HERRINGBONE WOOL TOPCOAT**—Boss, Hugo Boss

100 **HARD CASE LEATHER SUITCASE**—Peal & Co. Ltd for Brooks Brothers; **SOFT LEATHER BRIEFCASE**—Bill Auberg

101 **LEATHER BACKPACK**—Ghurka

102 **CAMEL CASHMERE POLO COAT**—Alan Flusser; **NAVY PIN-STRIPED SUIT, WHITE DRESS SHIRT**—Joseph Abboud; **PATTERNED SILK TIE**—Hermès; **SILK POCKET SQUARE, SOCKS**—Brooks Brothers;

LEATHER BELT—J. M. Weston; **CORDOVAN CAP-TOE SHOES, CUFF KNOTS**—Paul Stuart; **BLACK LEATHER EXPANDABLE BRIEFCASE**—T. Anthony

103 **CAMEL CASHMERE POLO COAT**—Alan Flusser; **WOOL POLO SWEATER**—J. Crew; **WOOL GABARDINE PANTS**—Gucci; **BLACK PATENT LEATHER BELT**—DKNY; **BROWN LEATHER SIDE-ZIP BOOTS**—Dolce & Gabanna; **COTTON SOCKS**—The Gap; **COPPER-RIMMED SUNGLASSES**—Swiss Army; **WATCH**—Holland & Holland; **BROWN LEATHER GLOVES**—LaCrasia

104–5 (Clockwise from top center) **VINTAGE COWBOY HAT**—Stetson; **RACCOON TRAPPER'S CAP**—Worth & Worth; **POLARTEC FLEECE CAP**—Nautica; **VINTAGE BASEBALL CAP**—Private collection of Glenna Gross; **TWEED HOUNDSTOOTH DRIVING CAP**—Holland & Holland; **NAVY GOLF CAP**—J. Crew; **PANAMA HAT** (center)—Worth & Worth

111 **WHITE TERRY ROBE**—Pratesi

112–13 **GRAY SWEATSHIRT**—Champion; **WORN BLUE JEANS**—The Gap; **BROWN LEATHER MOCCASINS**—Timberland

115 **JEANS**—Levi Strauss & Co.

116 **YELLOW COTTON "GO" T, NAVY POLYESTER "VELOCITY VEST"**—Patagonia; **WHITE COTTON BUTTON-FLY JEANS**—Levi's; **SUNGLASSES**—Ray•Ban; **BROWN SUEDE SANDALS**—Birkenstock; **TAN REINDEER LEATHER BLAZER**—Baldessamini, Hugo Boss; **TURTLENECK**—Donna Karan; **BLACK BUTTON-FLY JEANS**—Levi's; **BROWN LEATHER LOAFERS**—Cole-Haan; **STEEL-FRAMED SUNGLASSES**—Bottega Veneta

117 **BLUE LINEN JACKET**—Bergdorf Goodman; **GOLF SHIRT**—Bobby

Jones; **WHITE COTTON 501 JEANS**—Levi Strauss & Co.; **WHITE SUEDE SHOES**—Cole-Haan; **NAVY VELVET DOUBLE-BREASTED JACKET**—Dolce & Gabanna; **STRIPED COTTON SHIRT WITH WHITE SPREAD COLLAR**—Ralph Lauren Purple Label; **PRINT SILK TIE**—Polo by Ralph Lauren; **BRACES**—Paul Stuart; **DENIM JEANS**—The Gap

118 **WHITE COTTON T-SHIRT**—The Gap

119 **ALL COTTON T-SHIRTS**—Barneys New York

120 **RIVER SANDALS**—Teva

121 **SUPERFINE WOOL BUTTON-FRONT SHIRTS**—TSE

122 **SUNGLASSES** (from top left, clockwise)—Ray•Ban at Bausch & Lomb; Ray•Ban wraparounds; Wayfarer; Army-Navy; Aviators at Bausch & Lomb

124 **VINTAGE HAWAIIAN SHIRT**—What Comes Around Goes Around

125 **BLUE-AND-WHITE CHECKED COTTON SHIRT**—Joseph Abboud; **RELAXED PLAIN FRONT KHAKI SHORTS**—The Gap; **BLACK CANVAS BELT**—Stüssy; **BLACK POLYURETHANE SANDALS**—Birkis by Birkenstock; **TAN LINEN JACKET WITH MATCHING TROUSERS, AQUA-BLUE COTTON PIQUÉ POLO**—Bergdorf Goodman; **BRAIDED BROWN LEATHER BELT**—Trafalgar; **GREEN-TINTED SUNGLASSES, LEATHER LOAFERS**—Bottega Veneta; **WATCH**—Swiss Army; **VINTAGE HAWAIIAN SHIRT**—What Goes Around Comes Around; **CREAM LINEN PANTS**—Joseph Abboud; **BROWN LEATHER SANDALS**—Kenneth Cole

126 **DRIFTWOOD COLORED CAMP SHIRT, SURF TRUNKS**—Patagonia; **FLIP FLOPS**—Private collection of Leah Esposito; **BLACK SYNTHETIC RUBBER-CORE TEMP SHORTS, RED**

NYLON AND POLYESTER RIVER SHORTS—Patagonia;

128 **LEATHER RIDING GLOVES**—Good Hands

129 **FLANNEL SHIRT**—Dockers; **CASHMERE TURTLENECK**—Paul Stuart

130 **BLACK TURTLENECK**—J. Crew

131 **GRAY CASHMERE V-NECK SWEATER**—Paul Stuart

132 (Left) **FLAT-FRONT KHAKIS**—Dockers Authentics; **ZIP-FRONT SHORT-SLEEVE STRIPED COTTON SHIRT**—Dockers Authentics; **PLAID WOOL AND POLYESTER JACKET**—Dockers; **ARGYLE SOCKS, BLACK CALF SQUARE-TOE LACE-UP LUG-SOLE SHOES, BLACK CALF BELT**—Dockers; **NAVY WOOL JACKET**—Nordstrom; **WHITE COTTON T-SHIRT**—Levi Strauss & Co.; **BLUE-WHITE-AND-GRAY DENIM BUTTON-DOWN SHIRT**—Levi Strauss & Co.; **555 RED-TAB JEANS**—Levi Strauss & Co.; **BLACK COTTON-BLEND SOCKS**—Dockers; **BLACK CALF CAP-TOE CASUAL SHOE**—Bacco Bucci; **BLACK CALF BELT**—Banana Republic; **WHITE COTTON SHIRT**—Joseph Abboud; **CHARCOAL EXTRA-FINE LAMBSWOOL V-NECK SWEATER**—Boss, Hugo Boss; **TAN GLEN PLAID LAMBSWOOL JACKET**—Polo by Ralph Lauren; **COTTON PLEATED KHAKIS**—Holland & Holland; **BROWN LEATHER WING-TIP SHOES**—J. M. Weston; **HERRINGBONE SOCKS**—Brooks Brothers; **WATCH**—Timex

133 **HACKING JACKET**—Polo by Ralph Lauren; **WOOL TURTLENECK**—Paul Stuart; **LEATHER GLOVES**—Good Hands

134 **CANISTER**—Personal pipe tobacco mixture by Lane Limited; **YELLOW-AND-GRAY ASHTRAY**—Private collection of Jeff Stone; **PIPE WITH BRUYERE-FINISH** (left)—Dunhill; **PIPE** (right)—

Private collection of Jeff Stone; **PIPE TOOLS AND LEATHER TOBACCO POUCH**—Dunhill (private collection)

136 **SILK-AND-CASHMERE REVERSIBLE SCARF**—Salvatore Ferragamo

137 **IVORY CABLE-KNIT SWEATER**—DKNY

138 **BLANKET**—Pendleton at Paula Rubenstein

139 **FLANNEL SHIRT**—Timberland; **WOOL SHIRT**—Pendleton; **VINTAGE TIE**—Sixth Avenue Antique Market, New York, New York

140 **BLUE RIPSTOP NYLON SUPER PLUMA JACKET**—Patagonia

141 **BLACK CORDUROY JACKET**—Polo by Ralph Lauren; **BROWN FLANNEL SHIRT**—Banana Republic; **DARK GREEN KHAKIS**—Ermenegildo Zegna; **BROWN SUEDE SHOES**—Kenneth Cole; **VINTAGE GLYCINE WATCH**—Time Will Tell; **WOOL PLAID SHIRT**—Pendleton; **BLACK TEKWARE AURORA VEST**—The North Face; **TAN CORDUROY PANTS**—Slates; **LEATHER AND NYLON MID BOOTS**—Timberland; **BROWN SHEEPSKIN SHEARLING JACKET**—Donna Karan; **BROWN CASHMERE TURTLENECK SWEATER**—TSE; **BROWN COTTON PIQUÉ PANTS**—Joseph Abboud; **BROWN LEATHER ANKLE BOOTS**—Dolce & Gabbana

142–3 (Top row, from left) **BROWN SUEDE DRIVING SHOES**—J. P. Tod's; **BROWN LEATHER BOAT SHOES**—Timberland; **WHITE SUEDE BUCKS**—Brooks Brothers; (Bottom row, from left) **BROWN LEATHER WESTERN BOOTS**—Private collection of Jeff Stone; **SUEDE CHUKKA BOOTS**—Joan & David; **WORK BOOTS**—Timberland

144 (Clockwise from top left) **BLACK-AND-WHITE COTTON T-SHIRTS**—The Gap; **BLACK**

CHECKED RIVER SHORTS—Patagonia; **TRAVEL KIT AND ACCESSORIES**—Personal collection of Jeff Stone; **BLACK LEATHER LOAFERS**—Cole-Haan; **LEATHER DUFFEL BAG**—Ghurka; **BLACK V-NECK CASHMERE SWEATER**—Paul Stuart; **501 JEANS**—Levi Strauss & Co.; **OLIVE GREEN TIE CASE**—Bottega Veneta; **DARK GRAY SILK TIE**—Alan Flusser; **BLACK SILK KNIT TIE**—Barneys; **LEATHER DOPP KIT**—Ghurka; **CROSS-TRAINER ATHLETIC SHOE**—Nike

145 **THREE-BUTTON JACKET**—DKNY; **BUTTON-DOWN SHIRT**—J. Crew; **LINEN SUIT PANTS**—Joseph Abboud; **BROWN LOAFERS**—Gucci; **BRAIDED LEATHER BELT**—Dockers; **TANK WATCH**—Cartier; **BROWN LEATHER BACKPACK**—Coach; **SPORT COAT**—Brooks Brothers; **MERINO WOOL TURTLENECK**—Paul Stuart; **SUEDE VEST**—Brooks Brothers; **CORDUROY PANTS**—Dockers; **LEATHER WEEKEND BAG**—Ghurka; **JODHPUR BOOTS**—J. M. Weston

147 **TRENCH COAT**—Burberry's of London; **BROWN SUEDE TRENCH COAT**—Ralph Lauren Purple Label; **GRAY CASHMERE TURTLENECK SWEATER, WOOL-AND-CASHMERE GRAY CHALK STRIPE PANTS**—Ralph Lauren Purple Label; **BROWN LEATHER GLOVES**—LaCrasia; **BROWN LEATHER BOOTS**—Dolce & Gabbana

148 **NAVY WOOL CARNABY JACKET**—Boss, Hugo Boss; **BLUE JEANS**—Levi Strauss & Co.; **BLACK LEATHER COMBAT BOOTS**—DKNY; **GRAY KNIT HAT**—Nautica; **BLUE COTTON SOCKS**—The Gap; **NAVY WOOL PEA COAT, BLACK VELVET PANTS**—Hugo Boss; **NAVY COTTON SHIRT**—Donna Karan; **BLACK LOW BOOTS**—Prada; **SILK TIE**—Brooks Brothers; **LEATHER GLOVES**—Hermès;

EMBOSSED LEATHER BELT—Trafalgar; **WATCH**—Swiss Army; **NAVY SOCKS**—Today's Man

149 **GREEN WOOL-AND-NYLON REVERSIBLE COAT**—Hugo Boss; **WOOL PLAID SHIRT**—Pendleton; **CORDUROY PANTS**—Dockers; **LEATHER AND NYLON MID BOOTS**—Timberland; **HANDMADE BROWN LEATHER BELT**—Sean Whelan; **REVERSIBLE WOOL-AND-NYLON JACKET, WOOL TWEED THREE-BUTTON JACKET, CHARCOAL WOOL TURTLENECK**—Hugo Boss; **MOSS GREEN CORDUROY TROUSERS**—Dockers; **BROWN LACE-UP BOOTS**—Hugo Boss

154 **TANKTOP, RUNNING SHORTS, "AIR" RUNNING SHOES, LYCRA RUNNING PANTS**—Nike

155 **BLUE FLEECE ZIP-FRONT SHIRT, ORANGE NYLON JACKET, REFLECTIVE JOGGING PANTS**—Nike; **YELLOW G-SHOCK SPORTWATCH**—Casio

156 **GREEN COTTON GOLF JERSEY**—LaCoste; **CAMEL-HAIR CHARCOAL SWEATER VEST**—Bobby Jones; **BROWN CORDUROYS**—Slates; **BLACK-AND-TAN SUEDE GOLF SHOES**—Hush Puppies

157 **CHECKED SILK GOLF CAP, JACKET, GREEN ALPACA BUTTON-DOWN CARDIGAN, COTTON GOLF SHIRT, KHAKI PANTS, ARGYLE SOCKS**—Paul Stuart; **LEATHER GOLF SHOES**—Polo by Ralph Lauren; **WHITE ACRYLIC HAT, WHITE COTTON GOLF SHIRT, BLACK V-NECK PULLOVER, CHARCOAL SHADOW PLAID GOLF PANTS, ATHLETIC SOCKS, WHITE AIRMAX 2 LEATHER GOLF SHOES**—Nike

159 **WHITE COTTON POLO SHIRT**—Lacoste

161 **METALLIC POLYESTER-AND-DOWN JACKET**—Ga Neve Giorgio Armani

162 **CAPILENE SHIRT AND PANTS**—

Patagonia; **TEKWARE BLACK SHIRT**—The North Face; **BLACK NYLON TALUS PANTS**—Patagonia; **TAN POLYESTER CARDIGAN**—Patagonia; **BUNTING FINGERLESS GLOVES**—Patagonia

163 **RED POLYESTER JACKET**—Nike; **STRIPED GOLF SHIRT**—Nike; **PURPLE POLYESTER-CORE SKIN SHIRT**—Patagonia; **KHAKI SHORTS, BLACK SYNTHETIC RUBBER CORE TEMP SHORTS**—Patagonia

164 **YELLOW-AND-BLACK GORE-TEX HELISUIT**—The North Face

165 **BLACK POLYESTER SHIRT**—Timberland Performance; **LODEN WOOL SKI JACKET, PANTS, SHIRT**—Prada; **SUNGLASSES**—Ray•Ban "Predator"; **BLACK ANKLE BOOTS**—DKNY; **VINTAGE GLYCINE WATCH**—Time Will Tell; **PLAID WOOL BUTTON-DOWN SHIRT**—Pendleton; **BEIGE CORDUROY TROUSERS**—Slates; **KNIT SILK TIE**—Hugo Boss; **CHARCOAL SUEDE BELT**—Matsuda; **COTTON CREW SOCKS**—The Gap; **SHOES**—DKNY

166 **TWEED JACKET**—Polo by Ralph Lauren (private collection of Jeff Stone); **FISHING FLY**—Orvis

167 **BROWN LEATHER HUNTING VEST**—Orvis; **GREEN KHAKI EASY-ENTRY-MESH FISHING VEST**—Orvis; **FISHING ROD**—Private collection of Jeff Stone

168 **NORFOLK JACKET**—Holland & Holland; **OLIVE BUSH JACKET, BROWN SUEDE-AND-KHAKI COTTON VEST, BEIGE AND GREEN PLAID LINEN BUTTON-DOWN SHIRT, KHAKI COTTON PANTS**—Holland & Holland

169 **OLIVE BUSH JACKET, BROWN SUEDE-AND-KHAKI COTTON VEST, BEIGE-AND-GREEN PLAID LINEN BUTTON-DOWN SHIRT, KHAKI COTTON PANTS**—Holland & Holland; **BROWN CROCODILE BELT**—

Trafalgar/Ghurka; **BROWN SUEDE CHUKKA BOOTS**—Bottega Veneta; **BLACK LEATHER FLASK, CANVAS FLASK**—Holland & Holland; (bottom right) **KHAKI PATCH-POCKET SHIRT**—Dockers; **SILK PLAID TIE**—Ermenegildo Zegna; **NORFOLK JACKET**—J. Peterman Co.

175 **GOLD-PLATED LIGHTER**—Dunhill; **CHROME LIGHTER**—Zippo

176 **WOOL HOUNDSTOOTH BLAZER**—Ermenegildo Zegna; **WHITE DRESS SHIRT**—Ralph Lauren Purple Label; **CHARCOAL WOOL TROUSERS**—The Gap; **SILK GIRAFFE-PRINT TIE**—Hermès; **CUFF KNOTS**—Paul Stuart; **BROWN LOW BOOTS**—Dolce & Gabbana; **SUNGLASSES**—Ray•Ban; **SOCKS**—Today's Man; **LEATHER BELT**—Brooks Brothers; **BLACK CASHMERE POLO SWEATER**—Malo; **OLIVE TEXTURED CORDUROY PANTS**—Joseph Abboud; **POLISHED CALF PENNY LOAFERS**—Prada; **SOCKS**—Today's Man; **SUNGLASSES**—Ray•Ban; **EMBOSSED LEATHER BELT**—Trafalgar; **VINTAGE WRISTWATCH**—International Watch Co.

177 **BLACK WOOL AND LEATHER COLLAR JACKET, GLEN PLAID WOOL PANTS**—John Bartlett; **BLACK CASHMERE TURTLENECK**—Polo by Ralph Lauren; **BLACK LEATHER DRIVING MOCCASINS**—J. P. Tod's; **ANTIQUE ROLEX WATCH**—Time Will Tell

179 **WHITE TUXEDO SHIRT**—Polo by Ralph Lauren; **BLACK TUXEDO PANTS**—Ermenegildo Zegna; **SATIN BOW TIE AND CUMMERBUND, WHITE SILK POCKET SQUARE, BLACK CALF EVENING PUMPS**—Paul Stuart

180 **SHAWL-COLLARED TUXEDO JACKET AND TUXEDO PANTS**—Brooks Brothers; **RED ZIP-FRONT VEST**—Issey Miyake;

WHITE BAND-COLLARED SHIRT—Donna Karan; **PATENT LOAFERS**—Belgian Shoes; **VINTAGE ROLEX "PRINCE" WATCH**—Time Will Tell; **WIRE-RIMMED SPECTACLES**—Morganthal Frederics

181 **NOTCH LAPEL TUXEDO JACKET AND PANTS**—Gucci; **BLACK SILK SHIRT, LEATHER BOOTS**—Gucci; **BLACK SILK CUMMERBUND**—Brooks Brothers; **BLACK SQUARE CUFF LINKS WITH SILVER EDGES**—Paul Stuart; **WOOL TUXEDO JACKET WITH PEAKED LAPELS AND TUXEDO PANTS, WHITE COTTON TUXEDO SHIRT**—Paul Stuart; **BLACK-AND-WHITE SILK VEST**—Joseph Abboud; **OVAL SILVER-AND-BLACK CUFF LINKS**—Paul Stuart; **POCKET WATCH AND CHAIN**—Time Will Tell; **BLACK CALF EVENING PUMPS, BOW TIE**—Paul Stuart; **WOVEN SILK BLACK EVENING HOSE**—Brooks Brothers

182 (Clockwise from top left) **TUXEDO SHIRT WITH TUCKED BIB**—Paul Stuart; **PLEAT-FRONT TUXEDO SHIRT WITH WING COLLAR**—Brooks Brothers; **PLEAT-FRONT TUXEDO SHIRT WITH WING COLLAR**—Polo by Ralph Lauren; **COTTON TUXEDO SHIRT WITH BAND COLLAR**—Donna Karan; **PLEAT-FRONT TUXEDO SHIRT**—Brooks Brothers; **SILK BOW TIE**—Barneys New York; **GOLD SHIRT STUDS**—Tiffany; **SILVER-AND-GOLD CUFF LINKS**—Hermès; **TUXEDO SHIRT WITH PIQUÉ BIB AND WING COLLAR, 14-KARAT GOLD CUFF LINKS**—Paul Stuart

184 (Top left) **LAVENDER CUFF KNOTS**—Paul Stuart; **18-KARAT GOLD AND BLUE ENAMEL CUFF LINKS**—Tender Buttons; **RED CUFF KNOTS**—Paul Stuart; **18-KARAT GOLD FOX FACES CUFF LINKS WITH RUBY EYES, SILVER-AND-ENAMEL PLAYING-CARD CUFF LINKS, 14-KARAT**

GOLD STUDS, 14-KARAT GOLD LAPIS-AND-EMERALD CUFF LINKS—Tender Buttons; (Top right) **SILK GRAPHIC BLUE-AND-BLACK BRACES**—Paul Stuart; **WATCH-PRINT SILK BRACES**—Riga by Trafalgar; **LIME-GREEN SILK BRACES**—New Republic; **BEAR-AND-BULL SILK BRACES**—Calvin Curtis by Trafalgar; **CHECKED GOLD-AND-BLACK SILK BRACES**—Brooks Brothers; **SILK WOVEN "CIRCLE" BRACES IN GREEN AND NAVY**—Paul Stuart

185 (Bottom left) **VINTAGE POCKET WATCH AND CHAIN, VINTAGE ROLEX "PRINCE" WATCH, CARTIER WRISTWATCH**—Time Will Tell; **VINTAGE WRISTWATCH**—Mathey Tissot; (Bottom right) **BLACK-AND-WHITE SILK CUMMERBUND**—Joseph Abboud; **WINE PAISLEY BOW TIE**—Paul Stuart; **BLACK-AND-WHITE PLAID SILK BOW TIE**—Paul Stuart; **GOLD SILK BOW TIE**—Brooks Brothers; **RED CUMMERBUND**—Paul Stuart

186 **CREAM-COLORED SUMMER-WEIGHT WOOL TUXEDO JACKET, BLACK TUXEDO PANTS**—Paul Stuart; **WHITE COTTON PIQUÉ WING-COLLAR SHIRT, BLACK SILK BOW TIE, PAISLEY SILK CUMMERBUND**—Paul Stuart; **GOLD "X" STUDS AND CUFF LINKS**—Paul Stuart; **BLACK PATENT EVENING PUMPS**—Brooks Brothers; **WIDE GROSGRAIN PEAK LAPEL TUXEDO JACKET, HORIZONTAL STRIPED COTTON TUXEDO SHIRT**—Alan Flusser; **BOW TIE, POCKET SQUARE, PATTERNED BRACES, SHIRT STUDS**—Alan Flusser; **COTTON FLAT KHAKI PANTS**—Banana Republic; **CUFF LINKS**—Brooks Brothers; **PATENT LOAFERS WITH BOW**—Belgian Shoes; **EYEGLASSES**—Morganthal Frederics

187 **WOOL PLAID EVENING DOUBLE-BREASTED JACKET**—Paul Stuart; **WHITE COTTON PLEATED**

WING-COLLAR SHIRT, BURGUNDY SILK BOW TIE—Paul Stuart; **VELVET CREST SLIPPERS**—Belgian Loafers; **WOOL TUXEDO PANTS**—Paul Stuart; **SQUARE GOLD STUDS AND CUFF LINKS WITH BLACK TRIM**—Brooks Brothers; **BLACK SATIN CUMMERBUND**—Paul Stuart; **NAVY VELVET DOUBLE-BREASTED SMOKING JACKET WITH NOTCH LAPEL**—Dolce & Gabbana; **WHITE COTTON PLEATED TUXEDO SHIRT WITH FRENCH CUFFS**—Paul Stuart; **BLACK SATIN BOW TIE**—Barneys New York; **BLACK-AND-GOLD ROUND CUFF LINKS**—Brooks Brothers; **WOOL TUXEDO PANTS**—Donna Karan New York Couture; **BLACK LEATHER EVENING PUMPS, BLACK SATIN CUMMERBUND**—Paul Stuart

188–9 (From left to right) **BLACK GROSGRAIN LOAFER**—J. P. Tod's; **BLACK PATENT LEATHER SLIPPER WITH SMALL BOW**—Belgian Shoes; **BLACK PONY-SKIN LOAFER**—Donna Karan; **BLACK CALF EVENING PUMP**—Paul Stuart; **BLACK CAP-TOE SHOE**—Cole-Haan; **VELVET CRESTED LOAFER**—Belgian Shoes; **BLACK BUCKLE BOOT**—Gucci;

190 **MIDNIGHT-BLUE CASHMERE TOPCOAT WITH VELVET COLLAR**—Alan Flusser; **WHITE SILK PAISLEY SCARF WITH FRINGE**—Paul Stuart

191 **SUEDE GLOVES**—Ralph Lauren Collection

192 **HANDMADE HUMIDOR**—Davidoff; **BLACK CERAMIC MATCH HOLDER**—Personal collection of Jeff Stone; **MATCHES**—Porto Ramos Pinto; **CRYSTAL CIGAR ASHTRAY AND CIGAR**—Dunhill; **CIGAR GUILLOTINE**—Dunhill

193 **BLUE-AND-GOLD PATTERNED SMOKING JACKET**—Sulka

quotes

2 Mark Twain, from *The Comedian's Quote Book: Quick Takes from the Great Comics,* (Merritt Sterling Publishing Company, 1993).

6 Australian Aboriginal saying.

12 Djuna Barnes, *Nightwood* (New Directions, 1937).

15 Michael Douglas as Gordon Gekko in the film *Wall Street* (20th Century Fox, 1987).

17 Raymond Chandler, *Farewell, My Lovely* (1940; Vintage Crime, 1988).

18 John Cheever, "Reunion," *The Stories of John Cheever* (Alfred A. Knopf, 1978).

19 Robert Duvall as Lt. Col. Kilgore in the film *Apocalypse Now* (Omni Zoetrope/United Artists, 1979)

22 Charles Dickens, *Great Expectations* (1907; Alfred A. Knopf, 1992).

28 John Le Carré, *The Tailor of Panama* (Alfred A. Knopf, 1996).

33 Madonna, from *The Columbia Dictionary of Quotations,* Robert Andrews, ed. (Columbia University Press, 1993).

36 Andy Warhol, from *Uncle John's Second Bathroom Reader,* The Bathroom Readers' Institute (St. Martin's Press, 1989).

42 Ernest Hemingway, "Fathers and Sons," *The Nick Adams Stories* (1927; Charles Scribner's Sons, 1972).

45 Harvey Keitel and Lawrence Tierney in Quentin Tarantino's film *Reservoir Dogs* (Miramax, 1992).

47 William Styron, *Sophie's Choice* (Random House, 1976).

49 Elizabeth Kaye, "Agent Elvis,"

George magazine, August, 1997.

57 T. S. Eliot, "The Love Song of J. Alfred Prufrock," *The Waste Land and Other Poems* (1934; Harcourt, Brace & World, 1962).

64 Procol Harum, "A Whiter Shade of Pale," *A Whiter Shade of Pale* (RCA, 1967).

69 Homer Simpson, from the TV series *The Simpsons.*

71 George Bernard Shaw, *Caesar and Cleopatra* (1899; Penguin, 1964).

74–5 Issey Miyake, from *Issey Miyake,* Rudolph Handy (Graphic Society/Little, Brown & Co., 1988).

77 Wright Morris, from *A Bill of Rites, A Bill of Wrongs, A Bill of Goods* (1967; University of Nebraska Press, 1981).

78 Clark Gable in the film *The Hucksters* (MGM, 1947)

81 e.e. cummings, from *21st Century Dictionary of Quotations,* Princeton Language Institute (Dell Publishing, 1993).

97 George Bernard Shaw, *Pygmalion* (1913; Penguin, 1955).

108 Ian Fleming, "From Russia with Love," *A James Bond Quintet* (1957; Jonathan Cape, 1992).

111 Nancy Kwan as Suzie Wong in the film *The World of Suzie Wong* (Paramount, 1960).

121 Oscar Wilde, from *Oscar Wilde,* Richard Ellmann (Vintage Books, 1987).

124 Edward Hoagland, *The Tugman's Passage* (Lyons Press, 1995).

130 Humphrey Bogart as Sam Spade in the film *Casablanca* (Warner, 1942).

138 Jack Kerouac, *The Dharma Bums* (1958; Viking Press, 1986).

145 Paul Theroux, *The Old Patagonian Express* (Harper & Row, 1979).

152 Richard Ford, "Hunting with My Wife," *Esquire Sportsman* magazine (Fall/Winter, 1993).

159 John McEnroe, "He's the Man," *Esquire* magazine (January, 1988).

163 P. J. O'Rourke, *Holidays in Hell*

(1988; Vintage Departures, 1992)

168 Evelyn Waugh, *Brideshead Revisited* (1937; Everyman's Library, 1994).

172 Umberto Eco, *Foucault's Pendulum* (Harcourt Brace Jovanovich, 1988).

175 Ian Fleming, "From Russia with Love," *A James Bond Quintet* (1957; Jonathan Cape, 1992).

177 Humphrey Bogart, from *The Harper Book of Quotations,* Robert I. Fitzhenry, ed. (HarperPerennial, 1993).

179 Dean Martin, from *Frank Sinatra and the Lost Art of Livin',* Bill Zehme (HarperCollins, 1997).

180–1 Michael Kinsley, *The New York Times Magazine* (December 8, 1997).

184 P. J. O'Rourke, *Modern Manners* (The Atlantic Monthly Press, 1989).

189 Frank Sinatra, from *Frank Sinatra and the Lost Art of Livin',* Bill Zehme (HarperCollins, 1997).

190 Maryon Pearson, from *The Harper Book of Quotations,* Robert I. Fitzhenry, ed. (HarperPerennial, 1993).

192 Frank Sinatra, from *Frank Sinatra and the Lost Art of Livin',* Bill Zehme (HarperCollins, 1997).

193 Ernest Hemingway, *The Sun Also Rises* (1934; Charles Scribner's Sons, 1985).

224 Jean-Dominique Bauby, *The Diving Bell and the Butterfly* (Alfred A. Knopf, 1997).

ACKNOWLEDGMENTS

A grateful acknowledgment to John E. Leslie who many of you may know from AOL as the UPTOWN GUY. John shared his invaluable information on the concerns and interests men have about modern day dressing. John can be reached at UPTWNGUY@AOL.COM

And special thanks to: Joseph Abboud; Agnès B.; Giorgio Armani; Paul Boccardi; Barneys New York; David Bashaw; Geoffrey Beene; Bill Blass; Paul Bogaards; Claire Bradley-Ong; Gabrielle Brooks; Amy Capen; Tony Chirico; Jill Cohen; Cole-Haan; Tom Ford; Bradley Friedman; Jane Friedman; Stefan Friedman; Deborah Fugit at Neiman Marcus, Stanley Marcus; David, Glenna, and Carolyn Gross; Diego Hadis; Peter Lyons Hall at Nordstrom; Kevin Hanek; Katherine Hourigan; Andy Hughes; Carol Janeway; Pat Johnson; Donna Karan; Elina Kazan at Macy's Herald Square; Calvin Klein; Nicholas Latimer; Ralph Lauren; Carl Lennertz; William Loverd; Anne McCormick; Dwyer McIntosh; Nancy McNamara at Giorgio Armani; Colby McWilliams; Margaret Muldoon at Cerrutti; Derrill Osborn; Joshua Palau at Chroma Copy; Prada; Mona Riley at Paul Stuart; Mel Semensky; Sonny Mehta; Dayna Steinberg at Ermenegildo Zegna; Morgan Stone; Dylan Stone; Shelley Wanger; Helen Watt; Amy Zenn; Damon Zucca. —

HOMAGE

A special thanks to Alan Flusser, whose *Clothes and the Man* is a wonderful inspiration on men's dressing. Alan gives his time and advice on men's clothes unselfishly—their place in our culture and their historical underpinnings. His research on fine men's stores around the world is invaluable and for real (or imagined) visits, *Style and the Man* is a must-have in your library. The fact that Mr. Flusser also produces wonderful suits is the dimple in the knot.

INVALUABLE RESOURCES

• Farid Chenoune, *A History of Men's Fashion* (Flammarion, 1993).
• Alan Flusser, *Clothes and the Man* (Villard Books, 1985)
• Alan Flusser, *Style and the Man* (Harper-Collins, 1996)
• Woody Hochswender, Kim Johnson Gross, *Men in Style: The Golden Age of Fashion from Esquire* (Rizzoli, 1993).
• Riccardo Villarosa and Giuliano Angeli, *The Elegant Man* (Random House, 1990).
• Bill Zehme, *Frank Sinatra and the Lost Art of Livin'* (Harper-Collins, 1997).

CHIC SIMPLE STAFF

PARTNERS Kim & Jeff
PRESIDENT Steve Diener
SENIOR VICE PRESIDENT Jim Davis
ASSOCIATE EDITOR Carolina Kim
PRODUCTION ASSOCIATE Andrea Weinreb
EDITORIAL PRODUCTION Borden Elniff
ASSOCIATE EDITOR Gillian Oppenheim
OFFICE MANAGER Joyce Fisher
INTERN Susan Levy

COMMUNICATIONS

In our earlier books, we asked for your feedback and you responded from all over—Ecuador to Malaysia, Hong Kong to Edinburgh, Seattle to Miami—and every day we receive more. So thanks, and please keep on writing, faxing, and e-mailing your comments, tips, suggestions of items, topics, stores, and various insights that occur to you. Since a lot of the questions we get are about what else is in the Chic Simple book series, we created a catalog. If you would like to receive one for FREE, please send us twenty eight gold collar bars in a brown leather case, or just your address to:

CHIC SIMPLE
84 WOOSTER STREET
NEW YORK, NY 10012
Fax: **(212) 343-9678**
e-mail address: **info@chicsimple.com**
web site address: **http://www.chicsimple.com**
Stay in touch because . . .
"The more you know, the less you need."

A NOTE ON THE TYPE

The text of this book was set in New Baskerville and Futura. The ITC version of **NEW BASKERVILLE** is called Baskerville, which itself is a facsimile reproduction of types cast from molds made by John Baskerville (1706–1775) from his designs. Baskerville's original face was one of the forerunners of the type style known to printers as the "modern face"—a "modern" of the period A.D. 1800. **FUTURA** was produced in 1928 by Paul Renner (1878–1956), former director of the Munich School of Design, for the Bauer Type Foundry. Futura is simple in design and wonderfully restful to read. It has been widely used in advertising because of its even, modern appearance in mass and its harmony with a great variety of other modern types. Additional display faces: **GOTHIC (AGFA)**.

SEPARATION AND FILM PREPARATION BY

PROFESSIONAL GRAPHICS
Rockford, Illinois

PRINTED AND BOUND BY

BUTLER & TANNER, LTD.
Frome, England

HARDWARE

Apple Macintosh Power PC 8100, Quadra 800 personal computers; MicroNet DAT Drive; SuperMatch 21" Color Monitor; Radius PrecisionColor Display/20; Radius 24X series Video Board; Hewlett-Packard LaserJet 4; Supra Fax Modem; Iomega Zip Drives.

SOFTWARE

Quark XPress 3.31; Adobe Photoshop 3.0.5; Microsoft Word 6.0; FileMaker Pro 2.0; Adobe Illustrator 6.0.1

MUSICWARE

Fred Astaire (*Steppin' Out: Astaire Sings*); Beck (*Odelay*); David Bowie (*Earthling*); James Brown (*The Godfather of Soul*); Jeff Buckley (*Live at Sin-é*); DJ Krush (*Milight*); Bob Dylan (*Time Out of Mind*); *The End of Violence* (Motion Picture Soundtrack); Anson Funderburgh & Sam Myers (*That's What They Want*); Marvin Gaye (*Anthology*); Lida Husik (*Fly Stereophonic*); *Jackie Brown* (Motion Picture Soundtrack); June of 44 (*Four Great Points*); k.d. lang (*Drag*); Peggy Lee (*Collectors Series*); Loop Guru (*Amitra*); Madonna (*The Immaculate Collection*); Bob Marley (*Dreams of Freedom*); Joni Mitchell (*Court and Spark*); Moby (*I Like to Score*); Passengers (*Original Soundtracks 1*); Pink Floyd (*The Division Bell*); Portishead (*Portishead*); Giacomo Puccini (*Turandot*); Radiohead (*OK, Computer*); Ruby Braff George Barnes Quartet (*Salutes Rodgers & Hart*); Save Ferris (*It Means Everything*); *Seven Years in Tibet* (Motion Picture Soundtrack); Sexus (*Universal*); Sonny Rollins Quartet (*Tenor Madness*); Spacehog (*Resident Alien*); *Stealing Beauty* (Motion Picture Soundtrack); *The Tango Lesson* (Motion Picture Soundtrack); Jacky Terrasson & Cassandra Wilson (*Rendezvous*); Amon Tobin (*Bricolage*); Tricky (*Pre-Millenium Tension*); U2 (*Pop*); Various Artists (*Disco in the House*); Various Artists (*The Last Temptation of Elvis*); Various Artists (*Ranking & Skanking*); Various Artists (*Return of the DJ, v.2*); Dinah Washington (*The Complete Dinah Washington on Mercury, v.3*); Cassandra Wilson (*Blue Light 'til Dawn*)

"…I see in the clothing a symbol of continuing life. And proof that I still want to be myself. If I must drool, I may as well drool on cashmere."

Jean-Dominique Bauby, **The Diving Bell and the Butterfly**

INTERNATIONAL CHECKLIST
- ❏ Addresses for correspondence
- ❏ Auto registration
- ❏ Cash, including some of the currency of the country to which you are traveling
- ❏ Credit cards
- ❏ Emergency contacts
- ❏ Extra prescription glasses and contacts
- ❏ Health certificates
- ❏ Insurance papers
- ❏ International driver's license
- ❏ Lightweight tote bag for purchases
- ❏ Medical information
- ❏ Passport
- ❏ Phrase book or dictionary
- ❏ Prescriptions and medications
- ❏ Sunglasses
- ❏ Tickets and travel documents
- ❏ Travel itinerary
- ❏ Traveler's checks and personal checks
- ❏ Visa

THE TEN ESSENTIALS
The Mountaineers, founded in 1906, is a nonprofit outdoor activity and conservation club, based in Seattle, Washington. They established a list of Ten Essentials that should always be taken on any outing, whether for an hour ramble or an expedition.
- ❏ Compass
- ❏ Extra clothing
- ❏ Extra food
- ❏ Firestarter, candle
- ❏ First aid
- ❏ Flashlight with an extra bulb and batteries
- ❏ Map
- ❏ Matches and waterproof container
- ❏ Pocketknife
- ❏ Sunglasses

INFANTS & TODDLERS
- ❏ Baby pillow
- ❏ Bibs
- ❏ Blankets
- ❏ Bottles; nipples, caps
- ❏ Burping towel
- ❏ Disposable bags
- ❏ Disposable diapers
- ❏ Eating utensils
- ❏ Formula/milk
- ❏ Jacket/coat
- ❏ Juices
- ❏ Lotions/ointments
- ❏ Lovey
- ❏ Medication
- ❏ Music tapes
- ❏ Pacifier
- ❏ Paper towels
- ❏ Port-a-crib
- ❏ Tape player
- ❏ Teething biscuits
- ❏ Thermometer
- ❏ Toys
- ❏ Training cup
- ❏ Vitamins
- ❏ Washcloths/wipes
- ❏ Waterproof changing sheet

YOUNG CHILDREN
- ❏ Address book with important phone numbers
- ❏ Books/magazines
- ❏ Crayons/pencils
- ❏ Electronic games
- ❏ Games
- ❏ Gum (for airline travel)
- ❏ Identification
- ❏ Juice packs
- ❏ Medicine
- ❏ Money
- ❏ Name tags with destination—for child and luggage
- ❏ Paper
- ❏ Snack food
- ❏ Spare batteries
- ❏ Toys/cards

CHECKLIST FOR PETS
- ❏ Blanket
- ❏ First-aid kit
- ❏ Flea collar
- ❏ Food
- ❏ Grooming tools
- ❏ Leash and muzzle
- ❏ Name and address tag
- ❏ Pet carrier
- ❏ Pet toys
- ❏ Plastic bowls
- ❏ Proof of immunizations
- ❏ Veterinarian certificate of good health
- ❏ Water

ACTIVEWEAR WARDROBES
Golf
- ❏ Cotton argyle socks
- ❏ Golf clubs
- ❏ Knit cap
- ❏ Performance golf sweater
- ❏ Roomy, full-cut corduroy trousers
- ❏ Silk golf cap
- ❏ Sleeveless sweater vest
- ❏ Soft spiked golf shoes
Gym Workout
- ❏ Athletic supporters
- ❏ Headband
- ❏ Membership card
- ❏ Padlock for locker
- ❏ Plastic bag for wet things
- ❏ Shirts
- ❏ Shorts
- ❏ Sneakers
- ❏ Socks
- ❏ Stretch-wrap bandages
- ❏ Towels
- ❏ Warm-up suit
- ❏ Water
- ❏ Wristbands
Tennis
- ❏ Racquet
- ❏ Short-sleeved polo shirt
- ❏ Tennis shoes
- ❏ Tennis shorts
- ❏ Visor
- ❏ White athletic socks

THE BEACH
- ❏ Bathing suit
- ❏ Beach blanket
- ❏ Flip-flops
- ❏ Folding chair
- ❏ Food and beverages
- ❏ Hat with visor
- ❏ Ice pack
- ❏ Lip balm
- ❏ Music
- ❏ Nose plugs
- ❏ Pail and shovel
- ❏ Plastic bag for wet things
- ❏ Reading material
- ❏ Sunblock
- ❏ Sunglasses
- ❏ Towels
- ❏ Umbrella

142 BOOKS
Some books speak at a certain time in a man's life; they are mileposts or guides and help you realize someone else has gone the same way. This is a collection put together to reflect that—the titles chosen are favorites, sometimes the authors' best known, sometimes not—but all of them are worth the journey.
- ❏ Ashbery, John: *Self-Portrait in a Convex Mirror*
- ❏ Baldwin, James: *Giovanni's Room*
- ❏ Banks, Russell: *Continental Drift*
- ❏ Barnes, Djuna: *Nightwood*
- ❏ Bedford, Sybille: *A Legacy*
- ❏ Bellow, Saul: *The Adventures of Augie March*
- ❏ Bowen, Elizabeth: *The House in Paris*
- ❏ Bowles, Paul: *The Sheltering Sky*
- ❏ Bradbury, Ray: *Dandelion Wine*
- ❏ Broch, Hermann: *The Sleepwalkers*
- ❏ Brodkey, Harold: *First Love and Other Sorrows*
- ❏ Burns, John Horne: *The Gallery*